As an Episcopal priest serving various churches over the past twenty-five years and a trained spiritual director in the Ignatian tradition, I have witnessed the yearning so many Christians have for a deeper prayer life. Resources that are both accessible to the average person yet deep and comprehensive enough to be meaningful are rare. Now, in Celia Wolf-Devine's excellent book, we have a unique resource that Christians can use to enter more deeply into this rich and fruitful life of prayer. Our lives, and our church, are richer for it.

The Rev. Mark R. Moore, B.A., M.Div., M.Ed., J.D.

There are many books on prayer, but this one stands out for its warm encouragement and for its reflection on how prayer relates to desire. Drawing on her training as a professional philosopher and many years of seeking God in prayer, Celia Wolf-Devine talks about prayer in a way that is accessible and engaging and very practical. She makes it easier to see how prayer fulfills desire and how prayer changes us in ways that we rarely expect but always make us more human and more ourselves. In my ministry as a priest, I know many young adults who are looking for guidance about prayer that is both solidly rooted in Christian tradition and tailored to the circumstances of contemporary culture. This could be the book for them. *Nicholas E. Lombardo, OP*

There are many books on prayer. But Celia Wolf-Devine's is unique — and uniquely necessary. Not only is it filled with sound practical advice about all aspects of the life of prayer; but it is also written by a gifted philosopher, uniquely capable of recognizing the role of mind as well as heart in the life of the spirit. The whole person prays. And it is the whole person — mind, heart, intellect and will — to whom Prof. Wolf-Devine speaks in this inspiring book.

Ronald K. Tacelli, SJ, Boston College

As an instructor on prayer for the Oakland, CA diocese's School for Pastoral Ministry and Serra Catechetical Institute, I highly recommend Celia Wolf-Devine's book as a practical guide on prayer, suitable for the classroom. The book is full of insightful descriptions of the process of spiritual growth that will help a teacher illustrate what occurs when we allow God's grace to penetrate our psyches. For instance Celia describes spiritual wounds as healing, like physical wounds, "from the bottom up." Her discussion of the difficulties we all encounter in prayer, and her suggestions on how to counteract them, display a depth of understanding that can only come from one who has honestly faced herself in an ongoing conversation with God. Useful analogies such as comparing God's judgment to "a light flooding into a dark place" give the reader easily remembered images of how to distinguish between correction from God and demonically inspired self-condemnation. This book will have a great appeal to anyone who wants to grow more deeply in an intimate but honest relationship with the Being we are called to love above all others.

Edith Black

THE HEART TRANSFORMED: PRAYER OF DESIRE

Visit our web site at
www.albahouse.org
(for orders www.stpauls.us)

or call 1-800-343-2522 (ALBA)
and request current catalog

THE HEART TRANSFORMED:
PRAYER OF DESIRE

"Whoever drinks of the water that I shall give him
will never thirst;
the water that I shall give him
will become in him
a spring of water welling up to eternal life."
(John 4:14)

One human heart fully transformed is not a small thing.

CELIA WOLF-DEVINE

ST PAULS

Celia Wolf-Devine has permission to use the painting which I own, an image of the Sacred Heart by my friend Claire Brown. I have lost touch with Claire and have been unable to locate her, but I know that she would be delighted to have her work used for this purpose. My only condition is that the artist be appropriately credited, however and wherever the painting is used.

Elizabeth King

Library of Congress Cataloging-in-Publication Data

Wolf-Devine, Celia, 1942-.
  The heart transformed: prayer of desire / by Celia Wolf-Devine.
      p. cm.
   ISBN 978-0-8189-1287-0
  1. Prayer—Christianity. 2. Spiritual life—Christianity.   I. Title.
   BV210.3W63   2009
   248.3'2—dc22

                        2008041346

Produced and designed in the United States of America by the
Fathers and Brothers of the Society of St. Paul,
2187 Victory Boulevard, Staten Island, New York 10314-6603
as part of their communications apostolate.

ISBN 10: 0-8189-1287-1
ISBN 13: 978-0-8189-1287-0

Printing Information:

Current Printing - first digit   1   2   3   4   5   6   7   8   9   10

Year of Current Printing - first year shown

2009   2010   2011   2012   2013   2014   2015   2016   2017   2018

TABLE OF CONTENTS

INTRODUCTION

That we are living in stressful and unsettled times, that many of the networks of family and community that previously sustained us are disintegrating, that the ship seems to be adrift with no one at the helm, that anxiety and anger in our society are reaching dangerous levels — all these things have been noted by social observers with increasing alarm. Enormous numbers of people feel overtaxed, spread too thin, and as though they are constantly running on empty and having to go faster and faster just to stay in the same place. Leisure time has been almost completely squeezed out of many people's lives. Job insecurity and worries about terrorism have caused a pervasive background anxiety. The well-intentioned person is pressured from every direction by fervent advocates of various causes who seem to be running around in the dark, bumping into each other, threatening us with disaster if we do not heed them, and reproaching us for our complicity in or indifference to vast and apparently unmanageable social and ecological problems. When subjected to these sorts of cross-pressures, it is easy to just try to shut the world out entirely and live for ourselves and a few friends or family, but there remains a persistent malaise and sense that we should *do* something.

In the Psalms, the believer is likened to a tree planted by streams of water, still full of sap and green, bearing fruit even in times of drought (Ps 1:3).[1] How we long to find this sort of nourishment and strength ourselves! Elijah, at an important point in

---

[1] Unless otherwise indicated, all Scripture citations are to the Revised Standard Version.

his mission, was in the wilderness and ravens brought him food. The Lord commanded him to get up and eat three times, saying that otherwise the journey would prove too much for him (1 K 17:4, 6). We, too, need to be alone with God and allow Him to nourish us so that we will have the strength to carry on.

Although prayer is needed throughout our lives, it is, I think, especially important in the middle of life's journey. When we are young we have a certain resilience and animal energy — an ability to bounce back, to be fresh and hopeful. But as we get older the animal energy begins to diminish, and without God I think it is not possible to avoid a certain sourness or cynicism. We've seen so much incompetence, indifference, malice, and just general human perversity. Instead of trying to stimulate our flagging appetites and go on as before, we need to turn to God and put our lives on a new foundation. For God is an inexhaustible source of life and joy and fullness, and if you learn to be receptive to these gifts you will have the inner strength to move forward and face the trials of life. This does not mean you won't experience suffering, but only that your sufferings will not overcome you and that through it all you will be "still full of sap and green" at your center.

And prayer is itself a kind of work; it changes things. It changes us as well. Public worship is an important part of Christian life. But so too is private prayer, because in private prayer God is able to meet us where we are, guide us into the particular vocation to which we are called and do the long, slow work of transforming us more and more into the image of Christ. There are Christians who believe in "instant holiness." But although God's power is such that He *could* transform us instantly, this is not His ordinary way of working. Expecting instant holiness is likely to lead people to be hypocritical and try to fake the behaviors they take to be characteristic of holy people, with disastrous results for themselves and others.

Private prayer can enable us to find that deep well to draw on that springs from the heart of Christ. The more we learn to depend on Him alone, the more strength we will have. He will be our guide and our anchor in the storms of life. This book, then, is an invitation to prayer.

In what follows, I will share a method of prayer that the Lord has been leading me into over a period of many years. I do not intend to tell readers in great detail about my own prayer experiences. Books recounting other peoples' experiences of God can be helpful sometimes, but it is a bit like reading someone else's love letters. Nor do I propound a general theory about prayer — how many stages one goes through and in what order, and so on. In fact, I am suspicious of all such theories. They tend to lead people to constantly monitor their experiences to see which stage they have reached. This throws our focus off from God to ourselves, and can therefore short circuit the process of prayer. Besides, since prayer involves allowing God to work in us, it seems pretentious to claim to know how God will work in all people, since each of us has different talents and weaknesses, and begins prayer from a different starting point. There are, of course, certain common patterns discernible in the lives and writings of various saints, mystics, and ordinary believers. But the point of prayer as I understand it is to enter more into the walk with God that He has planned for us; He is the spiritual director and it is to Him that we must look. He alone knows how to untangle the knots we have gotten tied into, heal our wounds, and direct us in the right way. People do, of course, sometimes go to another Christian for spiritual direction, and that is all right. But the role of a spiritual director should be to help you discern the direction in which God is leading you (see section on spiritual direction in Chapter Five).

To imitate the practices of saints and hope thereby to attain the same sort of holiness they attained is to confuse cause and effect. Their holiness resulted from the action of the Holy Spirit in their hearts ("Holy Spirit, sanctifier of the faithful"); their experiences and spiritual practices are a function of the ways in which the Spirit led *them*. But these may not be the ways in which He is currently trying to lead *us*. In His role as physician of our souls, Jesus naturally tailors the remedies He prescribes to the individual He is working with. We can, of course, learn from the saints, but uncritically following the regimen some saint followed is like taking someone else's prescription drug. Maybe if you are very similar to that person in character it will be useful, but there is a danger that you may get it wrong. An arrogant, headstrong person who can never admit to being wrong may adopt devotions that emphasize God's affirmation and comfort, while one whose besetting sin is beating on himself all the time for his sins, may gravitate to spiritual exercises that encourage visualizing oneself as a vile worm or a leper and to live in constant fear of hellfire.

I remember how several times, inspired by spiritual writers I had looked at, I tried to do the Jesus prayer, but with very meager results. (The long form of the prayer, to be repeated constantly, is "Jesus Christ, son of God, have mercy on me a sinner." Shorter forms are just "Jesus, mercy," or simply "Jesus.") But years later when I felt guided by the Lord to repeat His name as a prayer, this practice became very fruitful for me. The examples set by various saints, then, should inspire us to turn to God and let His Spirit move us also. If you point something out to a dog or a cat, the animal will not understand the gesture, but will attend to your finger rather than what you are pointing to. A saint is like a finger pointing toward God.

Although there has been a burgeoning interest in mysticism recently, much of what is out there has slipped its Christian moorings. Americans who are spiritually searching and want to learn to meditate have come to believe that they need to look toward Eastern religions for techniques. This book is intended to fill a gap — to provide a Christian way to grow into a deepening experience of God. You don't have to already be a committed Christian to find it useful, but you need to be willing to seriously give Christianity a try. The path starts from precisely where you find yourself at this moment.

I call what I do "prayer" because I understand myself to be directing my attention toward God and seeking to enter into a relationship with Him, but there is a meditative element as well. I reflect slowly and deeply on certain words or images, and try to be quiet and receptive. What I will offer, then, is not a theory, but a method or way of praying. A method is essentially practical. It is more like a carpentry manual than a book on architecture, with the essential difference that the house can only be built by God, and the habits we must acquire if the work is to go forward are things like receptivity, trust, thankfulness and praise. As St. Paul says, we are being built into a spiritual building — a dwelling place for the Holy Spirit (1 Cor 3:16; Eph 2:22). Christians who emphasize the importance of being "born again" are right to say we must invite Jesus to come into our hearts, but they all too often talk as though this was something one does at one point in time, and then we just shed our old selves and become totally new. People who come up to you and ask "are you saved?" are usually operating with this sort of picture of Christian life. But while there are certainly turning points in our lives, faith is not just an on/off thing. Turning to Christ and putting your trust in Him is only the beginning of a lifelong relationship; conversion of heart (often called "*metanoia*") is something that is meant to grow deeper each day; and prayer is the lifeblood of this sort of living faith.

There is an intellectual content to Christianity, and it is important to have a good background understanding of some of the central doctrines of the faith; love of God and knowledge of God are connected. I have included the Apostles' Creed and the Nicene Creed in the Appendix. There is also quite a bit of solid, mainstream Christian theology built into the prayers suggested in Chapter Two and the annotations to them in the Appendix. This, I think, is an advantage of this method of prayer by contrast with those forms of prayer or meditation that involve the repetition of a single word. The words of the prayers make clear who we are addressing and what we are asking from God. By the same token, they declare our openness to receive what we are asking for. Jesus asks blind Bartimaeus, "What would you have me do for you?" (Lk 18:41). In using the prayers provided in Chapter Two, you are asking God for the fullness of Christian faith and life, and over time you will grow into a deeper understanding of what that involves.

The focus in this book is on the sort of conversion of heart that occurs in prayer, which is why I have entitled it *The Heart Transformed: Prayer of Desire*. The "heart," however, should not be understood as merely our feelings or emotions. There are connections between emotions and the heart, but the heart is much more than just feelings. A more Biblical understanding of the heart is that it is the center or core of the person. In Ezekiel, God promises to give His people a new spirit or a new heart, replacing their hearts of stone with hearts of flesh so that they will now obey His statutes and ordinances; they will be God's people and He will be their God (Ezk 11:19). In Psalm 90, Moses prays for "a heart of wisdom." Jesus says that what comes out of the mouth proceeds from the heart (Mt 15:18), and tells the paralytic, "Take heart my son, your sins are forgiven" (Mt 9:2; see also Mt 9:22). He also proclaims: "If any one thirst, let him come to me and drink. He who believes in me, as the scripture has said, 'Out of his heart shall flow rivers of living water'" (Jn 8:37-38). And throughout the New Testament, the term "heart" is used in an extraordinarily rich and complex way to include all sorts of things other than emotions.[2]

People often think of the head and the heart as opposed to each other, since our emotions and our reason often come into conflict. But both faculties have their root in the core or center of the person. So if we have a more Biblical understanding of the heart, then in giving God our hearts we give Him everything, because everything springs from our center and is interconnected. The phrase, "cleanse the thoughts of our hearts," in the opening prayer (see Chapter Two) resonates very strongly with this way of

---

[2] Any adequate discussion of the Biblical notion of the "heart" would be a book in itself. But a few examples indicating the broad way in which the term is used may be useful. People are described as "questioning in their hearts" (Lk 5:22), or "pondering" in their hearts (Lk 2:19). The pure in heart are praised (Mt 5:8). The heart is said to have purposes (1 Cor 4:5). People hold other people in their hearts, and are encouraged to love one another from their hearts (1 P 1:22), to forgive from their hearts, to be obedient from their hearts (Rm 6:17), or to do the will of God from the heart (Eph 6:6). "The good man out of the good treasure of his heart produces good, and the evil man out of his evil treasure produces evil; for out of the abundance of the heart his mouth speaks" (Lk 6:45).

understanding the heart. The key thing, then, is to give the center over to God and then everything else will fall into its proper place. The more completely you give your heart to God, the clearer your mind will become.

Many expressions people commonly use without thinking about it reflect something like the Biblical understanding of the heart. We praise people for being "kind hearted," "warm hearted," "tender hearted," "open hearted," or "having a heart as big as all outdoors." "Getting to the heart of the matter" means getting to what is really important – to the center. We speak of "the heart of the city," or deep in the "heart of the jungle," again, meaning the center. Giving "from the heart" is praised by contrast with doing so mechanically, from duty, or in order to look good to others. Doing or saying something "with all your heart" indicates sincerity. If some word or action is "heartfelt" it is deeper or richer than just the word of the lips. Something is "heartening" if it is encouraging and inspires us with courage and hope. Negatively, we speak of people as "hard hearted," "cold hearted," or "heart-less." Weak or cowardly people are described as "faint hearted." When a person is sad we speak of them as "down hearted," or "disheartened." People brought low by some dreadful loss are sometimes said to be "broken-hearted," and those unlucky in love to be afflicted with "heartache." "My heart sank within me" is an expression indicating a sort of horror, discouragement or deep sadness. "Losing heart" means becoming downcast and feeling unable to go on.

Central to the sort of conversion of heart that we seek is the re-ordering of our desires, and ultimately only God can effect this. We must allow Him to do this — to draw us to Himself by increasing our desire for Him. Thus the subtitle, "Prayer of Desire." For religion to be something that makes us more whole and vibrantly alive, as Christianity is supposed to do, it must engage the passionate side of our nature and satisfy the deepest longings of our hearts. Otherwise, it becomes dry and legalistic and can easily become a vehicle of the will to dominate others. It is significant in this regard that Jesus cites as the first and greatest commandment,

"You shall love the Lord your God with all your heart, with all your soul, with all your mind and with all your strength" (Mk 12:30). It is not just our duty to love God. It is our joy.

The heart is, I believe, the root of a particular sort of desire, called "eros." Unfortunately in our culture the terms "eros" and "erotic" tend to be used almost exclusively for sexual desire (and worse yet for pictures, films, and literature bordering on the pornographic), but this is a mistake. Eros is something much broader and deeper that pervades our nature on a number of levels – a painful awareness of our incompleteness and a longing for wholeness through union with another who completes and fulfills us. Mystics in many traditions have recourse to sexual metaphors to describe the soul's union with God, and lovers often employ religious imagery in their poems. It is because eros pervades our nature on many different interconnected levels, that the way we exercise our sexuality is religiously important. It is *not* because God is a prude, or sex obsessed. Even our desire for material things can take on a kind of erotic tone: "Oh, if only I had that beautiful dress, or that marvelous car, then I would be a new person; everything would be all right; I would be satisfied!" But when we obtain the thing or person desired, the longing begins to attach itself to something else, like a mirage that keeps receding as we approach it. What we desire seems always to hover just out of reach, drawing us on but forever eluding us. This, of course, is the phenomenon so well described by St. Augustine — the kind of restless desire or longing that cannot find rest in any earthly thing. "Thou hast made us for Thyself and our hearts are restless until they rest in Thee."[3]

Desires take root in us if we let them (and even sometimes when we don't want them to). We often find ourselves unable to control them, and feel dissatisfied and pulled apart. Attempting to exert our will to control our desires may enable us at least not to act on bad desires, but leaves us still beset by feelings of inner conflict. Only God can put our restless hearts in the right order.

---

[3] *Confessions*, book 1, section 1.

We must ask Him to increase our desire for Him, for as He comes into our souls, bad things are driven out before Him. The joy and delight of His presence puts all our earthly desires in a new perspective, and what once seemed very attractive may not seem so wonderful any more. This does not mean that we will cease to delight in earthly beauty of various sorts, or become sour and dry and excessively ascetic, but merely that our desire for earthly things will not have the sort of desperate, fevered quality that it takes on when we look to them for what they cannot give.

Trying to force, or repress, or do battle with our desires is likely just to wear us out. If you find you have desires that are horrible or frightening to you (and most of us do), don't panic. Just quietly turn your mind to something else. We are drawn toward and entangled by those things on which we focus our attention, so we need to pray constantly that God will magnetize our being to Him so that we remain turned toward Him. Eros or desire is like the compass needle of our souls, and when we pray God redirects and purifies our desires so that our compass needle points to Him, the True North. Our desire for God is God's work in us; the very fact that we desire Him, thus, indicates that He is already present. It is the deepest response of our being to God whose touch has awakened that desire, and as such gives us a certain sort of joy.[4]

The pierced heart is popularly used as a symbol for love; Valentines have pictures of hearts with arrows through them, and Cupid is pictured as shooting arrows into the hearts of lovers, thereby inflaming them with love for the beloved. The parallel here with Jesus's heart being pierced with a lance as He hung on the cross is a profound one. Sustained reflection upon, and devotion to the Sacred Heart of Jesus has nourished and sustained many of the greatest saints and mystics, and is one of the central

---

[4] C.S. Lewis says something similar. He describes Joy as "an unsatisfied desire which is itself more desirable than any other satisfaction." He says that it might be called "a particular kind of unhappiness or grief. But then it is a kind we want. I doubt whether anyone who has tasted it would ever, if both were in his power, exchange it for all the pleasures in the world. But then Joy is never in our power and pleasure often is." (*Surprised by Joy.* New York: Harcourt Brace & World, Inc., 1955, pp. 17-18).

components of the method of prayer outlined in this book. "Jesus meek and humble of heart, make our hearts like to yours." For if the heart is the center or core of the person, and if we accept the Christian doctrine of the Incarnation – namely that God became man in Christ — then it follows that it is in the heart of Jesus Christ that humanity and divinity touch and intermingle most intimately and perfectly. Hence asking Him to dwell in our hearts and make them like His own is a wonderful and powerful prayer. Some Protestants may think that "devotion to the Sacred Heart of Jesus" sounds forbiddingly Catholic. It shouldn't. Most of the verses of the Sacred Heart Litany are taken from Scripture, and you can think of praying it (or whatever parts of it you feel comfortable with) as a way of opening your heart to the transforming power of His love.

What I think is most distinctive about the type of prayer described here, is its radical emphasis on receptivity and surrender on the one hand, and the way in which it integrates the erotic side of our nature into our prayer life on the other. All too often religious people regard desire as the enemy and think they need to wage war on it — particularly in a Puritan-influenced culture such as the United States where there seems to be an assumption that pleasure and sin are co-extensive. Chocolate desserts are "decadent" or "sinfully delicious," and behaving in sinful ways is thought to be a way to grab all the gusto — to really enjoy life. This is of course totally silly. Many of the worst sins are not even pleasant — envy or despair, for example. And there are lots of perfectly innocent physical pleasures. But this way of thinking has a strong hold on the American mind. Hence the suggestion that we ought to desire God and find delight in Him has a vaguely obscene or irreverent sound to many people. The Psalmist, however, says, "Take delight in the Lord and He will give you the desires of your heart" (Ps 37:4).

Although this may seem strange, I think the method of prayer offered here, focusing as it does on the heart, also accords a larger and more positive role to the mind than many other methods. It is the whole person who prays; all our faculties should come into play in prayer. The mind is not an enemy any more than desire is. Perhaps it is the influence of Eastern (and especially Buddhist) forms of meditation that has caused people to try to stamp out their desires — even the mind's desire to understand. (The Buddha taught that so long as we desire anything, we cannot attain *Nirvana*.) Granted, our minds can never completely understand God, but that does not mean we should not seek to grow in our understanding of Him. The Buddhist ideal of *Nirvana* and the Christian understanding of the afterlife with God are deeply different. An old *Sacred Harp* hymn describes Heaven thus: "Then shall I see, and hear and know all I desired and wished below; and every power find sweet employ, in that eternal world of joy."[5] The prayers provide nourishment for the mind that treasures and reflects upon their meaning. The mind should be mainly passive and receptive rather than active and analytical, but it is nonetheless involved in prayer.

Using the same set prayers regularly does not preclude spontaneity and flexibility. Over time you will develop your own way of working within the basic framework (but be open to the possibility that this may change over time). Also, people have different personal styles, and it is important to respect these sorts of differences and not pass judgment on each other in a matter so intensely personal as our walk with God in prayer. Even if all you did was repeat the prayers slowly and reflectively from beginning to end each day, you would find that you felt drawn to dwell on some more than others. You can do more extended meditations on particular verses employing visualization or images — your own or some of those suggested in Chapter Two or in the annotations to the prayers found in the Appendix. You can use some of the short prayers suggested at the end of Chapter Two in between the set prayers, or improvise your own prayers and conversation with God as the Spirit moves you. Using the same pattern regularly makes it easier for your conversation with God each day to build on what

---

[5]   *The Sacred Harp*. 1991 Revision. Sacred Harp Publishing Company, Inc., p. 48. (Hereinafter "*The Sacred Harp*") All quotations used with permission of the publisher.

went on the day before rather than having to start from scratch every day. For the repetition of a particular phrase can bring back to mind a particular insight or feeling that you experienced the day before so that it can develop more deeply today.

This book differs from much of the already existing literature on prayer in that it is written by a married person. Most of the spiritual classics were written by people who were members of religious congregations. Being celibates writing predominantly for other celibates, the problems they faced were in some ways different from those of people not vowed to poverty, chastity and obedience, so some of their ways of resolving them are not easily available to us — at least not without considerable adaptation. And our situation is culturally so very different from theirs, that the healing of our wounds may require if not wholly different remedies from those employed in the past, at least a different order of application of the remedies and some changes in emphasis; spiritual formation must operate on the already existing structures of our personalities. The emphasis since Vatican II in the Catholic Church has been on the universal call to holiness, and prayer must be a part of living out this call. Lay people are called to holiness just as much as priests and religious.

Too many people tend to think that experiences of God are confined only to monks and nuns living in other centuries, or that religious faith is no longer possible in the 21st Century. This isn't true. Religious faith is, if anything, more vibrantly alive and widespread than it was when Nietzsche proclaimed the death of God in the late Nineteenth Century, although it may be that the center of gravity of Christianity is shifting more toward the Southern Hemisphere, with its most spectacular growth being in Africa, Latin America and Asia. God hasn't changed. Jesus Christ hasn't changed. And human nature at its most basic level hasn't changed either. Therefore there is no reason why we should not be able to experience God now; Christians have done so throughout history, are doing so now, and will continue to do so. Perhaps you will not experience ecstatic states in prayer like

St. Teresa of Avila, or be blessed with the sort of constant sense of God's presence that Brother Lawrence enjoyed, but don't rule out the possibility in advance. Give your whole self to God and let Him do as He wills with you.

The method of prayer presented here is a rather eclectic one, largely coming out of my own experience but with some obvious influences of various spiritual writers. Brother Lawrence's little book *The Practice of the Presence of God* has been particularly influential on me. I also did Transcendental Meditation for several years at one point, so I have some familiarity with *mantra* meditation. I have never done contemplative prayer in the Ignatian tradition in any serious way, since I am not good at visualization or the sort of concentration that this method seems to call for. (This is not to say that this style of meditation may not be extremely valuable for a lot of people, as it has been for some people I know.) Contemplative prayer is the cultivation of a kind of active passivity — allowing God's Spirit to move in us and fill us, to hold us and still us. And since prayer is more something God does in us than something we do, it happens in us but not by our own effort. Thus I find I can pray often in spite of distracting noises in a way that I never could do before when I was trying to concentrate. As St. Paul says, the Spirit prays in us, with us, for us, and "intercedes for the saints according to the will of God" (Rm 2:7).[6] I realize that the charismatic and the contemplative forms of prayer are sometimes seen as in tension with each other. But I am often moved to pray quietly in tongues as a form of praise, find it very strengthening and uplifting, and see no reason to be dogmatic one way or the other. Some people pray in tongues and others do not, but you should let it flow if it comes naturally and don't worry if it doesn't. (I am only talking here about the ordinary gift of tongues as a personal prayer language and not the gifts of prophecy or interpretation of tongues

---

[6] By "saints" here he means other members of the Christian community. We can and should, of course, pray for non-believers also, but have a special duty to pray for other Christians.

as they are practiced in public prayer meetings — practices about which I have no settled opinion.)

The prayers and meditations recommended in Chapter Two and the Appendix bear the imprint of a number of different Christian groups with which I have come in contact over the years. I am now a Roman Catholic.[7] But I was raised in a relatively high church Episcopal church, attended a broadly Protestant summer camp, have worshiped with Quakers (hence my love of silence), attended an evangelical house church for a short while, been involved for several years with a group that combined New Age and Christian elements,[8] and had quite a bit of experience with churches that are in communion with the Roman Catholic Church but employ the form of the liturgy used by the Eastern Orthodox Churches, and thus acquired a deep love for the beautiful music and prayers of the Orthodox tradition. I sang in a Gregorian chant choir at an Anglican church for several years, and am also an enthusiastic participant in the current revival of shape note singing from the old *Sacred Harp* hymnal.[9]

I am particularly grateful to Fr. John Langlois, OP for his help in steering me in the right direction at the beginning of this project, and to Rev. Mark Moore for his helpful suggestions on the Appendix. I also want to express my thanks to my husband Phil Devine for his encouragement and support, his help on some theological points, his willingness to talk out ideas with me, and his suggestions for how to make some points more clearly. Finally, my heartfelt thanks to all those whose prayers have sustained me on the way.

---

[7] My conversion story, "From New Age Christianity to the Catholic Church," appears in a book entitled *The New Catholics* edited by Dan O'Neill and published by Crossroads in 1987.

[8] The group used to be called the Holy Order of MANS. They have since made some major changes and joined the Orthodox Church. My experience with them is described in my conversion story (see footnote 7).

[9] Information about this type of singing may be obtained at www.Fasola.org

PREVIEW

In Chapter One, I first say some things about why I think private prayer is especially important in light of the current fragmentation of our society and the tendency of many churches to lose sight of the transcendence of God. I then discuss some of the common barriers to prayer, and some helpful attitudes we should cultivate as we approach prayer. In Chapter Two, I briefly state some of the key ideas or guiding principles of this method of prayer, just to give readers some idea of how it differs from other types of prayer that they may have done before. I then provide the actual prayers I use, together with a number of practical suggestions about ways of using them, and ways of understanding or imaging what is going on in prayer. I also provide a few short prayers I have found useful that you may wish to intersperse with the set prayers. This material forms the core of a packet of notes on prayer that I have been circulating for a number of years to a variety of different people who have found them helpful and have encouraged me to expand on them.

Chapter Three discusses some common obstacles that you may encounter along the way and suggests ways of dealing with them. In Chapter Four, I look more closely at what occurs during prayer, discussing some different types of prayer, and suggesting some ways you might integrate prayer more with your daily life. Chapter Five is entitled "Christian Life," and discusses a few topics of importance for nurturing the new life that has been planted in us so that it will prove fruitful, focusing on those that are especially relevant to our prayer life.

The Appendix contains the Apostles' Creed, the Nicene Creed, some popular short prayers, and annotations to the prayers I use, which should be especially helpful for readers who are not already familiar with Christian Scriptures, prayers or hymns. They go through the prayers suggested in Chapter Two line by line, offering suggestions for further reflection and meditation.

Biblical Abbreviations

OLD TESTAMENT

Genesis	Gn	Nehemiah	Ne	Baruch	Ba
Exodus	Ex	Tobit	Tb	Ezekiel	Ezk
Leviticus	Lv	Judith	Jdt	Daniel	Dn
Numbers	Nb	Esther	Est	Hosea	Ho
Deuteronomy	Dt	1 Maccabees	1 M	Joel	Jl
Joshua	Jos	2 Maccabees	2 M	Amos	Am
Judges	Jg	Job	Jb	Obadiah	Ob
Ruth	Rt	Psalms	Ps	Jonah	Jon
1 Samuel	1 S	Proverbs	Pr	Micah	Mi
2 Samuel	2 S	Ecclesiastes	Ec	Nahum	Na
1 Kings	1 K	Song of Songs	Sg	Habakkuk	Hab
2 Kings	2 K	Wisdom	Ws	Zephaniah	Zp
1 Chronicles	1 Ch	Sirach	Si	Haggai	Hg
2 Chronicles	2 Ch	Isaiah	Is	Malachi	Ml
Ezra	Ezr	Jeremiah	Jr	Zechariah	Zc
		Lamentations	Lm		

NEW TESTAMENT

Matthew	Mt	Ephesians	Eph	Hebrews	Heb
Mark	Mk	Philippians	Ph	James	Jm
Luke	Lk	Colossians	Col	1 Peter	1 P
John	Jn	1 Thessalonians	1 Th	2 Peter	2 P
Acts	Ac	2 Thessalonians	2 Th	1 John	1 Jn
Romans	Rm	1 Timothy	1 Tm	2 John	2 Jn
1 Corinthians	1 Cor	2 Timothy	2 Tm	3 John	3 Jn
2 Corinthians	2 Cor	Titus	Tt	Jude	Jude
Galatians	Gal	Philemon	Phm	Revelation	Rv

THE HEART TRANSFORMED: PRAYER OF DESIRE

CHAPTER ONE

STANDING IN THE NEED OF PRAYER

PART I: OUR HUNGER FOR THE LIVING GOD

Christians understand God to be both immanent in the world (present at each point in it) and transcendent. Through revelation and through the Incarnation (the Word became flesh and dwelt among us — Jn 1:14), God breaks into history from a place beyond the natural order of things. Unfortunately, people tend sometimes to go from one extreme to the other. In our cultural memory an emphasis on transcendence has been associated in people's minds with a harsh and authoritarian type of spirituality, and therefore there has been a movement in the churches toward emphasizing God's immanence and neglecting His transcendence. Some real good has come out of greater focus on the presence of God in our neighbors. Many churches provide worshipers with genuine fellowship, engage fruitfully in works of mercy (visiting the sick and prisoners, feeding the hungry, clothing the naked, etc.), support and sustain families, educate children and engage in some constructive sorts of political action. But if we wall out God's transcendence, we truncate Christian faith.

Encountering God in private prayer is, thus, particularly urgent at this time, because in it we can encounter the living

God who saves and heals us — who meets us where we are. So, without belittling the good they are doing, we need to look at how contemporary trends in many churches are depriving members of something they very badly need. Articulating the problems will, I think, be helpful to believers (or would-be believers) who come away from church feeling vaguely dissatisfied and worrying whether perhaps there is something wrong with them because they are not full of joy and thankfulness and burning to go out and pour themselves out for others.

At the deepest level, I believe, the problem is forgetfulness of the transcendence of God. Yes, Christ is present in our neighbors, but He is also (as the Nicene Creed tells us) seated at the right hand of the Father and will come in glory to judge the living and the dead. If God is to nourish and form us anew, then it must be the true God and not one cut to our own measure. The loss of transcendence manifests itself in a number of ways: a decreased sense of reverence for God; less emphasis on personal devotion to Jesus Christ; silence about the hope of Heaven; an impoverished and distorted understanding of the sort of joy that Christians hope to find and manifest to others; judging the success of our efforts in too worldly and utilitarian terms; and a tendency to equate the church primarily with some particular group of believers or perhaps with the clergy. It is as though something three-dimensional has been flattened out to fit into two dimensions.

One of the signs of God's presence is a sense of awe, majesty and glory, which move us to bow in worship. This does not mean that God is not also intimate to us — intimate in a way no one else can be — but that this does not make Him our buddy or our "co-pilot" (as the bumper sticker puts it). The extraordinary juxtaposition of glory, awe, and transcendence on the one hand and intimacy on the other lies close to the heart of prayer, and we must not flatten out the spiritual dimension by letting go of either one. We must allow Him every intimacy with us, while still reverencing Him as God.

The crucial element of personal devotion to Jesus has tended to be neglected or else cultivated in a way that de-emphasizes His divinity. "Thee will I cherish, Thee will I honor, Thou my soul's glory, joy and crown." (In what follows, I will often cite hymns, both because they have been important to my own religious life, and because I believe that the songs we are made to sing in church often leave a far deeper impression on us than the sermons we hear.) These words from the ever popular "Fairest Lord Jesus"[10] convey something of the spirit of devotion appropriate to Jesus. But in a church I attended, the tune had been recycled to become a song oriented almost entirely to the pursuit of social justice. Believers are, it seems, being asked to do more and more with less and less. But it is only by staying close to Jesus, and entering into an ever deepening relationship with Him, that we can have the strength to go out and act in the world as He calls us to. There are no quick fixes. Our brokenness and neediness are very deep, and we can't just come to church for an hour a week and then rush out and give, give, give all week.

Traditional hymns of many Christian communities are full of images testifying to peoples' intimate devotion to Jesus. "Visit us with thy salvation, enter every trembling heart" (*1940 Hymnal*, # 479)[11]; "in the arms of my dear Savior, oh there are ten thousand charms" (*The Sacred Harp*, p. 312); "where meek souls will receive him still, the dear Christ enters in" (verse from "O Little Town of Bethlehem"). Christ is eminently worthy of worship and devotion, and the more we are in right relation to Him, the more naturally these will come and the more we will find ourselves nourished and strengthened in worship.

---

[10] #346 in *The Hymnal of the Protestant Episcopal Church of the USA* (New York: The Church Pension Fund, 1943). (Hereinafter "*1940 Hymnal*".) All quotations used with permission of the publisher.

[11] These verses have been eliminated in some contemporary versions of this hymn. In part I think that elimination of these sorts of verses is part of a general cynicism and embarrassment about the ideals of romanticism or romantic love. Flowery, passionate, and earnest love songs are quite out of fashion and even sometimes laughed at. Why, I wonder, do we feel so uncomfortable about this?

4   THE HEART TRANSFORMED: PRAYER OF DESIRE

"Holy, holy, holy; all the saints adore thee, casting down their golden crowns around the glassy sea." "Earth's redeemer plead for me, where the songs of all the sinless sweep across the crystal sea." "And when earthly things are past, bring our ransomed souls at last, where they need no star to guide, where no clouds thy glory hide." These hymns from the *1940 Hymnal* (#266, 347, 12) were important to me as a child, instilling in me a sense of longing for Heaven. Or from the broader Protestant tradition, there is the song ending "When in thy likeness I then shall awake, I shall be satisfied then,"[12] or "There may I find a settled rest, while others go and come, no more a stranger nor a guest, but like a child at home." "When shall I see my Father's face, and in His bosom rest?"[13] "Oh, when shall I see Jesus and reign with Him above, and from the flowing fountain drink everlasting love? Oh had I wings, I would fly away and be at rest, and I'd praise God in His bright abode" (*The Sacred Harp*, p. 106).

Silence about the Christian hope of Heaven, then, is another way in which the sense of transcendence has gotten lost. Obviously human concepts are wholly inadequate to describe the afterlife with God, and the image of people sitting around on clouds playing harps, saints with halos floating over their heads, and angels with wings, has become more the subject matter for cartoons than anything else. Still, at the heart of Christianity is the breaking in of the transcendent into human history — God giving Himself to us in Christ ("Emmanuel," meaning God with us) — in order to reconcile us with Himself and draw us into communion with Him. It is that communion for which the human heart hungers — not sitting around on clouds playing harps. And if one has a full-blooded understanding of God's transcendence, the fact that we cannot locate Heaven at some particular spot in space and time should not trouble us.

---

[12] From the singing of Joel Cohen and the Boston Camerata. The song is called "I shall be satisfied" and it is on their CD entitled *The American Vocalist*.

[13] These two folk hymns are from the singing of Jean Ritchie on a record entitled *Sweet Rivers*.

Another unfortunate result of the flattening out of the Christian world-view, has been a loss of the proper understanding of joy, and a tendency to confuse it with a kind of forced cheerfulness. Joy is the natural fruit of a deepening relationship with God, as when Jesus tells the disciples, "I have food to eat that you know not of... my food is to do the will of Him who sent me" (Jn 4:34). Joy is a kind of soft glow given off when our inner lamp is burning with God's love, and it can be present even when we are experiencing sorrow or trials. It can express itself in exuberant ways sometimes; the psalms speak of the joyful shout of those praising God, and David danced before the ark of God. But there is no reason why it should always express itself in this way. We often come to God feeling broken, needy and even desperate. This may not be at the surface of our consciousness, but it often lurks just below consciousness and comes to the surface when we let ourselves relax and be open.[14] "Praise the Lord anyway" used to be a common saying among charismatics, and there is something to this of course (brooding endlessly about our troubles is something we need to let go of). But the addition of the word "anyway" introduces the necessary element of awareness that it can be difficult to do this sometimes. The cross and the resurrection are intimately connected in Christianity, and a spirituality that doesn't acknowledge the reality of the cross makes religion look like a pleasant and rather childlike fantasy we indulge in on Sundays, but unrelated to our everyday lives. People in the throes of conversion or undergoing deep trials are especially likely to be driven away by forced cheerfulness, which is very unfortunate since they are particularly in need of God.

Christians, and especially those in positions of leadership,

---

[14] Liturgy is not my focus in this book, but if I am right here, it would have implications for liturgical music. Specifically, the opening hymn should be one that praises God, but also expresses our longing for the peace and wholeness that can be found only in Him. It should allow and even encourage the worshiper to bring his or her burdens to the Lord and let Him be present in those painful spots. The closing hymn, then, might more appropriately express the joy that can flow out of our experience of Christ in Scripture, prayer, song and sacrament.

thus need to be careful not to make those who are sorrowing (or perhaps just feeling overwhelmed and beset) feel judged, or to suggest that there is something defective about their faith if they are not exuding happiness, joy, and love to everyone around them all the time. Doing so makes them feel obliged to stuff down painful emotions instead of bringing them to the Lord to be healed, or worse yet to fake constant cheerfulness, which does not really cheer either them or others. True joy does not grate on the feelings of those bowed down by care or sorrow, but forced cheerfulness often does.

One source of this sort of forgetfulness of the importance of the cross in Christian life may be that people feel a need to dissociate themselves from certain negative stereotypes of Christians as people who are gloomy, guilt-ridden, and world denying. There have certainly been Christians who have erred in these directions, although sometimes they may appear to have these faults mainly to people who themselves err in the opposite direction. The Christian path, if followed faithfully may involve sorrow, an awareness of one's own guilt, and a realization of the transience of the physical world, but excessive gloom, brooding over one's guilt, and hatred of the body or the physical world are deformations of Christianity. In any case, spending one's energies trying to prove to the world that we Christians really aren't all the awful things they think we are is a mistake, since it gives others far too much power over us.

Another reason why Christians may feel a need to present themselves as glowingly happy all the time (or as one guru put it "happy, healthy and holy") may be the emphasis that the psychotherapeutic community places upon being normal and adjusted. Psychotherapy has taken the place of religion in the lives of enormous numbers of Americans, with therapists being viewed in the way ministers and priests traditionally have been as physicians of the soul. And while there is much good in the various types of psychotherapy, and much that is not in direct conflict at least with Christianity, there is a sense in which they are in competition with it. For there is a distinctive Christian conceptual framework and vocabulary that we must not lose hold of if we are to remain Christian — concepts such as sin, repentance, conversion, grace, redemption, being born again, new life in the Holy Spirit, bearing our share of the sufferings of Christ, trusting in God's mercy and His providence, the importance of prayer, intercession for each other, being a member of the body of Christ, performing works of mercy and charity, thirst for holiness and for the vision of God, etc. Secular therapeutic movements tend to focus more on positive thinking, self-esteem, and learning to take control of one's own life. Not that we should dwell on negative things, hate ourselves, or allow our lives to get totally out of control, but to the extent that the goods they focus on are to be attained by our own efforts and the creative power of our own minds (the New Age movement, especially, emphasizes the power of mind to create reality), they tend in a very different direction from Christianity.

If MY radiant wholeness and happiness is the end I have in view, we are dealing with something quite different from the Christian's desire that GOD be glorified. Those engaged in the former quest tend to make others feel that they are being looked down upon — "I've got my act together, what's wrong with you?" But the saint is joyful because of his or her deepening experience of the glory of God and His love for us. When we encounter someone who projects *this* sort of joy it does not make us feel condemned, but engenders in us a hope that we too may find peace and healing in God's love. St. Augustine's distinction between the City of Man built on self-love and the City of God which is founded on love of God is, I think, another way of putting this same point.

The flattening out of the transcendent dimension of Christianity often leads us to measure our success too much in worldly terms, and a kind of utilitarian way of thinking creeps in. The vast dimensions of world hunger, oppression, violence, misery, and hatred (to say nothing of our own apparently intractable faults and sins) discourage us and make our small efforts seem a mere drop in the bucket. We should not neglect the practical dimension, and certainly political action can also be entirely appropriate. But we should not forget that there is a whole other dimension of reality that we cannot see. For, as God told Samuel when He instructed him not to anoint as king Jesse's older son who looked so very impressive and kingly, but rather the shepherd boy David, "I do not see as man sees" (1 S 16:7). Small things (in the world's eyes) may be major triumphs for God, and our prayers do far more than we know. One image I have heard is that we are looking at the tangled threads on the back of a tapestry, but do not know just what the picture being formed on the other side is. We must, then, avoid measuring everything in purely worldly and quantitative terms, and have faith that God can bring good out of whatever He permits to happen.

Finally, keeping the transcendence of God firmly in view enables us to get some necessary distance from what theologians call the "visible Church."[15] It is inevitable that outsiders will judge Christianity in part by the behavior of Christians, which is of course one reason why we must beg Him to transform us so that He can be manifest in us. But just because individuals, or groups of individuals (even in their "churchly" capacities), fail to be faithful to their Christian calling (sometimes in ways that deeply wound or even scandalize us) this does not alter the fact of God's love and mercy. Baptism makes the Christian a member of the body of Christ (along with all other Christians living and deceased) — or as the *Book of Common Prayer* puts it, we are "very members incorporate in the mystical body of Christ." It is not a matter of joining some sort of club with *those* people. Thus we should try not to let the failings of individual Christians blind us to the broader reality of the body of Christ.

Keeping in mind that God transcends the visible Church will also help protect us from another common deformation of Christianity in which spiritual life gets crowded out by (or worse

---

[15] The "visible Church" is hard to define, but generally what it means is the Church as a historically and socially visible entity (by contrast with the "invisible Church" which includes all the people God knows are His).

yet viewed as subordinate to or instrumental to) Church politics, in such a way that our passion and zeal gets displaced onto particular political agendas instead of being directed toward God (this can be a problem even when the particular goals we are pursuing are good ones).[16] We cannot, of course, wholly avoid the human level and the various sorts of liturgical and institutional decisions that are part of the daily life of the Church. But we should open ourselves to God in prayer over a sustained period of time and allow Him to direct us toward those works that *He* wants us to undertake. Frantic activism usually indicates that we have lost sight of the fact that things do not all depend on *us* and that there is a God who watches over His own.

Prayer is essentially a practice. There is no substitute for just sitting down and doing it. There are two reasons for this. First, prayer is a way of entering into relationship with God. Simply knowing things *about* prayer doesn't accomplish this. And second, in order to enter into relationship with God we need to develop certain habits that facilitate God's work in us — habits such as openness, trust, persistence, docility, thankfulness, and humility. And regular prayer is a way of cultivating such habits. We become the sort of people we are by what we do and not just through what we know. When I worked in the Harvard Philosophy Library I noticed that the books most frequently stolen were books on ethics, and a colleague of mine reported with horror that her students had cheated on their Social Justice final exam.

You may have tried to pray regularly before and become frustrated and quit. Don't let that deter you from trying again. Sometimes timing is important. We have to come to a point where we fully realize our need for God and our powerlessness to help ourselves before we can have the sort of desperation and tenacity needed to pray wholeheartedly and stick with it. So long as we think that our lives are perfectly under control and that we

---

[16] The spectacle of Christians allowing their political agendas to move into center stage and motivate them to expend their energies bashing each other, is one that seriously hampers attempts to evangelize the un-churched.

know how to go about securing our own happiness and that of those we love, we are far less likely to undertake serious prayer. We need to realize that doing everything our own way has not and will not lead to our happiness, and sometimes it seems this lesson must be learned by trying to do everything our own way and making a mess of things (often more than once). Eventually, like the prodigal son, we come to our senses, and are willing to return home to our Father and acknowledge we've done wrong, that we need help badly, and that He knows the way better than we do. The proper sort of desperation should lead us to keep seeking, knocking, and asking — emulating the widow who kept pestering the unjust judge until he heard her plea. You have to make time for prayer and be jealous for that time. People are often quite "religious" about their exercise regimen or about watching their favorite TV show, and devotees of Eastern religions commit significant blocks of time to meditation daily. Christians too should be willing to commit time to prayer on a regular basis. One way to do this might be to go to bed half an hour earlier and get up half an hour earlier to make time for prayer.

PART II: GETTING STARTED: WHAT IS HOLDING YOU BACK?

Even when we realize our need for a closer relationship with God in prayer, it is not always easy to get started. If you are one of the many people who say "I know I should spend more time in prayer, but..." you should reflect a bit about what is holding you back. Some of the obstacles are right on the surface, and others are more deeply buried. Some common barriers are addressed below, but the list is not meant to be exhaustive.

I'm too busy

One common reason people give for not praying regularly is that they are SO busy and stressed out that they cannot possibly add one more thing to their daily schedule. There are sometimes signs on the highway saying "speed enforced by aircraft." I suppose this means that somehow our speed is being clocked by them and that police will be dispatched to arrest us if we speed, but there is another way of reading it that describes well how we often feel — as though we are being relentlessly driven and harried and never allowed to rest. Prayer is, of course, what we are most in need of when we feel this way, but knowing this intellectually is often not enough to motivate us to change our behavior. There are several things that can be helpful here.

First, don't think of prayer as another thing you have to *do*. It provides an opportunity to disengage yourself from the rat race, to be freed from the pressure of time and experience something of the leisureliness and eternity of God. Prayer focusing on receptivity, surrender and praise provides rest and healing for our minds and hearts. It is like finding an oasis in the desert. Archbishop Fulton Sheen, I am told, used to spend an hour each day in prayer in front of the Blessed Sacrament, but when he was especially busy he would spend longer.

Second, prayer enables us to see things in the right perspective (*i.e.*, seeing ourselves and our lives more from God's perspective, and less from our own or that of the world), and it may turn out that a lot of the things we thought we absolutely *had* to do are of no value at all. And there can be times in our lives when what God wants most from us *is* prayer — prayer through which He can heal us of our wounds and sins, or nourish and form us in a special way for some work we are to do for Him. As the psalmist says, "Unless the Lord build the house, in vain do the builders labor... in vain is your rising earlier and going later to rest eating the bread of anxious toil; for He gives to His beloved in sleep" (Ps 127:2).

And at the deepest level, prayer is itself a sort of work. God can accomplish a great deal through us when we let Him. We are like corks attached to a net and floating on the surface of the water. When one cork pulls downward it also exerts a downward pull on the whole net, especially those closest to it. But when we allow God to buoy us up, those connected with us are also up-lifted, sometimes in hidden ways that bear fruit only much later. He uses our hearts to reinforce what He is doing in the hearts of others, especially those we hold in our hearts and bring to Him in prayer (but sometimes also people we have not even met).

Only special people (e.g. saints and mystics) can experience God

Many people think of prayer mainly as intercession. When they or people they love are sick or in some special need, they pray for them. But the idea of regular prayer as a way of entering into an ongoing relationship with God seems presumptuous and perhaps frightening. We need to realize that this sort of prayer has been an important part of the Christian tradition from the very start. Different people experience God in different ways, and some people may be more sensitive in certain dimensions than others, but a recent survey found that 75% of Christians surveyed said they had at some time experienced a sense of God's presence. The Negro spiritual "Every time I feel the spirit mov-ing in my heart I will pray," testifies to the deep consolation God has poured out to the little people (*"anawim"*); people who were illiterate and oppressed.

Endless examples of folk hymns and devotional music of all sorts could be cited bearing witness to the many wonderful ways in which Christians have experienced God. Indeed, if Chris-tianity is true, it would be strange if people did not experience God's presence sometimes, for Jesus has promised that He will be with us and dwell in us even to the end of the world.

Men, I think, sometimes associate prayer with pious little old ladies clutching their rosaries, and worry that there is some-thing unmanly about prayer. Our frontier past has generated and reinforced patterns of thinking in which men are expected to be rough and tough and mean and go out hunting (and fighting In-dians) while women are supposed to exert a civilizing influence on them, providing a kind of haven in a heartless world where religion occupies an important place (thus becoming associated with the softer feminine virtues). Men, then, have been socialized to be self-reliant and handle things themselves, and may find it difficult to acknowledge their need for God. Those men who feel this sort of discomfort with prayer may be helped by contemplating a man like St. Paul who, although fully yielded to Christ, was an inspiring model of both physical and moral courage. For, it is clear from his epistles, that his deep prayer life was the foundation for his strength. Yet he tells the Thessalonians "We were gentle among you like a nurse taking care of her children" (1 Th 2:7). No one is wholly masculine or wholly feminine. What is important is that there is need for masculine virtues as well as feminine ones in the Christian life.

People who claim to experience God are often fanatics or crazy

Although contemplative prayer has always been widely practiced by ordinary Christians, most of the time people do not talk about it much, and those who do go around publicly claiming that God has spoken to them or revealed something to them are often rather unbalanced. They claim the Virgin Mary has told them that receiving communion by hand is a worse sin than abortion or that they have been appointed as God's instrument to chastise sinners, and so on. This type of thing gives religious experience something of a bad name. Since there is nothing more delicate, intimate, and central to who we are than our own personal walk with God, it is not surprising that people don't go around blabbing about it to everyone. And the desire to dissociate oneself from unpleasant fanatics and kooks provides a further motivation for ordinary believers to keep their personal relationship with God private, and thus the association between having religious experiences and being unbalanced gets reinforced. Nonetheless, the path so many Christians have walked remains open to those who sincerely seek God.

Feelings of embarrassment

Embarrassment is less well defined than guilt, and involves a primal, self-protective impulse — an acute sense of vulnerability and a fear of being open to the gaze of others. Being seen naked is a kind of paradigm case of vulnerability, and thus serves as a kind of metaphor for it. One can feel embarrassed in cases where there is no question of moral wrongdoing. Any situation in which you feel that your vulnerability is open to the gaze of others occasions embarrassment. For example, an adolescent who has a passionate crush on someone is characteristically terrified of these feelings being revealed, either to the loved person (who, after all, may reject, despise, manipulate, or even worse, laugh at the person's feelings), or to peers who might make fun of him or her. This fear may be particularly strong for boys, who dread being exposed as weak or dependent in any way, but this sort of dread is not at all unreasonable given how cruel others can be. If those whose judgment or even malice they fear are people they perceives as alien or different from themselves, this can make the embarrassment more intense, since they are unsure how the others will judge them. They would thus be more willing to make themselves vulnerable without embarrassment to another person or small group of people whom they know well and whose responses are therefore more predictable.

Embarrassment does not presuppose the moral categories of sin or guilt. Many American women, for example, feel acutely embarrassed about other people seeing their houses when they are messy. Since so many of us work, our houses are usually not up to the standards of order and cleanliness that we internalized as children (at least those of us who had stay-at-home mothers with the time to keep their houses spotless). I recently went to my neighbor's back door to borrow baking soda, and she threw up her hands and began to pace around the kitchen in an agitated manner, pleading, "Don't look at the house; don't look at the house!" My neighbor on the other side has never once permitted me to enter her house because it is messy and she has a deeply seated neurosis having to do with her mother about allowing any woman to see it. My grandmother told me that I must always wear clean underwear, because if I didn't and then got in an accident it would be so embarrassing for the doctor to see it! In such cases, what is going on has almost no real moral content. Having a messy house or dirty underwear is not a sin by any stretch of the imagination. But we feel so agonizingly vulnerable and exposed when someone else enters into our intimate, private space! We want everything in us to be clean, orderly, beautiful, and admirable, but instead realize that we are misshapen, warped, wounded, chaotic, and conflicted inside, and that there is much in us that would not be admired if it were brought out into the light.

Although we often feel embarrassment without being conscious of any particular sins (in the sense of a deliberately chosen wrong action), the fact that we experience it does, I think, presuppose the fact that we live in a fallen world. Adam and Eve before the Fall would not have experienced embarrassment. It was only after the Fall that Adam said to God, "I was afraid because I was naked, and I hid myself." God replies, "Who told you that you were naked? Have you eaten of the tree of which I commanded you not to eat?" (Gn 3:10-11). It is in a world marred by our own brokenness and that of others (who are likely to behave maliciously when they detect vulnerability in us) that we experience embarrassment. Since, however, the Garden of Eden is gone for good, we fear to reveal our vulnerability, given that God is experienced as a powerful being who stands in judgment of us and who is in a deep way mysterious or other. "My ways are not your ways; my thoughts are not your thoughts... For as the heavens are higher than the earth, so are my ways higher than your ways and my thoughts than your thoughts" (Is 55:8). We cannot help but feel some anxiety about opening up to God.

The thing to do if feelings of embarrassment are an obstacle to prayer, is to think about how you would feel about a friend's house, and to remember that God has befriended us in Jesus Christ. If I am someone's friend, I naturally want to go into her house and visit with her there regardless of how messy it is. In just the same way, Jesus wants to come in and be with us out of friendship. And, just as the doctor is obviously concerned with the urgent business of saving the patient's life and not about his or her underwear, so also Jesus enters in order to heal and save us, and not to condemn us.

Feelings of guilt over our own sinfulness

Any normal, morally sensitive person is sometimes plagued with feelings of guilt, and it is natural to be afraid to let God's light into our hearts for fear of what it may reveal. After the miraculous catch of fish, Peter exclaimed to Jesus, "Depart from me, for I am a sinful man" (Lk 5:8). We have a terrible fear of condemnation and know in our hearts that we are vulnerable; we have all sinned and fallen short of the sort of holiness we believe God wants of us. "Be perfect even as your Heavenly Father is perfect" (Mt 5:48) is one of those verses that sends morally scrupulous people into agonies of self-reproach, and this can be so painful that they flee Him. This, of course, is entirely irrational. It is like fleeing the doctor when we are sick (not that we don't do that also, of course).

It is true that God's light does reveal our sins to us. But there is a cleanness to His truth. It is like looking at things in the clear light of day for the first time and being able to call them by their proper names. We can expend enormous amounts of energy sometimes trying to hide things from ourselves (as Freud realized), and allowing the light of God to come into the dark places is very freeing. For at least now we know there is someone who can look at us as we really are and not shrink from us. The Spirit is sharper than a two-edged sword, searching heart and mind. But there is a background sense that His love sustains us; we are not rejected and cut off from Him even when we are seeing clearly for the first time some awful thing we have done. Jesus realizes that we need Him especially badly when we are beating on ourselves. The harsh condemning edge that triggers despair comes from the Evil One not Jesus. Satan is called, in Scripture, "the accuser of the brethren" (Rv 12:10). The idea that it is a special mark of being pious and holy to be constantly flagellating oneself for one's faults and sins, then, is wrong.

Fear that God will ask you to give up something you are attached to

Sometimes, of course, this intuition may be correct. God *may* ask you to give up something you are attached to. But don't let this deter you from praying.

First, of all, you may have incorrect ideas about what God will ask of you. I have a friend who is convinced that if he became a serious Christian he would have to starve himself, wear hair shirts, and generally engage in all sorts of harsh ascetic practices. I'm not saying no one is called to such practices, but you may not be. In fact, I think there are people whose besetting sin is self-hatred and being excessively hard on themselves, and going out for a really good dinner, buying a nice comfortable arm chair, listening to beautiful music, or enjoying a warm bath might be things that God would want them to do. I'm not recommending unbridled indulgence of all your appetites, and there are certainly appropriate times for fasting, but you have to let God show you the areas in which you most need to curb your self will. There are even people in whom a bitter resentful disposition and a settled habit of complaining have become so entrenched, that what would most please God would be going about their daily life, including those parts generally regarded as pleasant, without complaint.

Second, even if there is some pattern in your life that you know God will want you to change (and in fact He does want you to change it), it may take time. You may not be able to change all at once, and you certainly won't be able to change something deeply ingrained without God's grace. Christian life is an ongoing process, and the advantage of the method of prayer outlined here is that it allows God to work gradually to transform your heart and thus to change your desires. As you grow into desiring

God more and finding joy in Him, some of the things that you did desire will seem less attractive to you. You may see suddenly and clearly the nature of some bad pattern you were entangled with, and feel a kind of spontaneous revulsion from it. Or other pleasures may just pale by comparison with the satisfaction of your deepest desires. Characteristically, when God takes something away from you He gives something else of greater value.

Unthinking internalization of secular,
materialistic view of the world

The belief that only what can be perceived by the senses, or measured and quantified by the methods of science is real, is, when you think about it, simply a prejudice — in the literal sense of a pre-judgment. The Nicene Creed affirms that God is the creator of all things, visible and invisible, thus implying clearly that there are invisible realities. And if one looks at the religious history of humankind, the belief that there are some sort of invisible beings (gods, demons, the spirits of our ancestors, ghosts, angels, etc.) who can act on us is virtually universal, at least until very recently. The secularization of Western culture that developed in the wake of the scientific revolution has always been only skin deep and mainly confined to intellectual elites, and its influence even in these circles is beginning to wane. Even in the most secular of times, enormous numbers of people have continued to do things like consulting psychics or astrologers, using Ouija boards or throwing the *I Ching* to help them make decisions, or trying to get in contact with angels or "spirit guides." (My point is not to endorse these practices, but only to point out that the majority of people have never been secular materialists.) What is required as a starting point for prayer, in any case, is not a gullible embrace of all sorts of weird, supernatural forces, but merely the intellectual humility to acknowledge that there is a lot we do not understand, and no good reason to exclude the possibility of a being not perceptible to our senses in the way ordinary physical objects are, or capable of being measured by the sorts of instruments scientists have devised to investigate them.

Likewise, the assumptions that I fully know my own nature and capacities, and that my skin forms some kind of sharp border between me and the world need to be brought into question. Science has discovered how deeply things we do not see affect us — e.g., sound waves, x-rays, magnetism. Even on a mundane level, the feelings people around us are projecting — heart-rending grief, anxiety, anger, lust, etc. sometimes seem to penetrate us whether we will or not. We feel their pull on us, often even under misleading external appearances — as when we feel a sense of anger or menace lurking under someone's smiling exterior. Some people may be more sensitive to such things, but everyone has the capacity to discern them to some degree. Beginning to pray seriously does not require us to have a theory about just what capacities human beings have for perceiving spiritual beings. We need merely to acknowledge that there is no good reason to dogmatically deny the possibility that we may have such capacities.

Under the surface, here, lurks a very deep philosophical and theological question — namely, the extent to which we have any sort of "natural" capacity to perceive God, and the extent to which grace is required for us to do so. For our purposes here, it is not necessary to resolve this issue, and two brief comments must suffice. First, since God gave us the nature we have, all our capacities are from Him, and one can't distinguish grace from nature by mere inspection. Second, He manifests Himself to us only when He wills to do so, so in this sense every perception of God is a manifestation of His grace toward us.

Our souls in some ways resemble a dark room with various broken, rusty, or just undiscovered things in it that serve we know not what purposes. When God's light comes in, things are healed and drawn into life and relation, and we discover things we didn't realize were there. Whether God creates them as we pray or whether they were there already is something we cannot know. It is hidden in the mystery of God's creative love. But suffice it to say that it is only in relation with God that we truly and fully become ourselves.

Problems about what language to use

These problems are of two sorts. One that used to trouble me a lot is the sort of flowery and pious language sometimes used in popular devotions and prayers. The answer to this problem is a simple one. You should use whatever language feels natural to you, and avoid anything that feels false or strained. Maybe at some time in the future you will find such language coming naturally to your lips, but if it doesn't, don't let it put you off. Just as children who have no experience of romantic love find the language lovers use in romantic movies "icky" or "squishy," and are made uncomfortable by it, so also the poetic and passionate prose of some saint may well leave us cold. But perhaps just as the child, when grown, will understand what was going on and be moved use this sort of language to someone he or she loves, so also as your relationship with Christ deepens you may find yourself naturally moved to speak in some such flowery or poetic ways yourself. On the other hand you may never feel comfortable with it because it is just not your style to express yourself in this way, and God wants us to be who we are and not some sort of pasteboard image of what we think saintly people should be like.

A second problem with language is the way it is currently being politicized. This makes us nervous and self-conscious about what pronouns we are using. Should we pray to God as "Father" or refer to God as "He"?[17] Is the Holy Spirit masculine or feminine? If we pray the psalms should we adapt the language to be gender-neutral? Feelings about these issues run very high. Since we cannot speak comfortably without using pronouns, we can easily allow worry about which ones to use to paralyze us and prevent us from beginning to pray. A few thoughts may be helpful here:

---

[17] For an in depth discussion of naming the Supreme Being, you might take a look at the last section of a book my husband and I edited, entitled *Sex and Gender: A Spectrum of Views* (Belmont CA: Wadsworth/Thomson, 2003).

First, it is as though people are standing in front of the door arguing over labels instead of going through the door to discover what God is really like. The least real experience of God's presence will make worries about pronouns seem trivial and irrelevant. St. John of the Cross had the experience of nursing at the breast of God, and there is something maternal about the Sacred Heart of Jesus, but this only shows that God transcends gender, not that we need to rewrite our prayers to address God as "Our Mother in Heaven."

Second, being ideological about our pronouns leads us into trying to control or limit how God may reveal Himself to us. This can shade into constructing for ourselves the sort of God we want to worship, which quickly slides into idolatry.

Third, although it is not the case that we should *never* change religious language, it is important to keep in mind that Christianity is an extremely deep and complex religion that operates on a number of interconnected levels (intellectual, affective, imaginative, symbolic, etc.), and small changes in one area may have large unexpected effects elsewhere, perhaps compromising the truth, power and coherence of the whole. Therefore a certain linguistic conservatism is justified. In this spirit, I continue to use "He" to refer to God. But since God has no body, He is obviously not male in the way humans and animals are.

Bad experiences with Christians, especially those in positions of authority

Sometimes if you have been deeply hurt and/or scandalized in the past by someone who claimed to speak in the name of God, or if there is some such person currently in your immediate environment, you may find that when you try to direct your attention toward God, this person's face keeps coming into your mind instead. The face that angers and haunts you may be that of a parent, a pastor, a priest, a nun, a teacher, or simply a friend to whom you opened yourself and who subsequently betrayed your trust in some way — perhaps by being harshly judgmental and rejecting. This problem is especially acute in the case of priests, since Catholics hold that the sacrament of Holy Orders configures a priest to Christ (*some* even hold that it configures the priest to God the Father, but this is incorrect),[18] and the custom of calling priests "Father" can stir up the deep, murky and conflicted feelings that people often feel toward their own fathers. If you have encountered priests who regard themselves as constantly speaking with God's authority (and they *do* exist), their faults and weaknesses are especially likely to get in the way of your relationship to God. Priests, however, do not represent or stand in the place of Christ in their every action or word, but *only* when performing or administering the sacraments. The *Catechism of the Catholic Church* notes that:

> This presence of Christ in the minister is not to be understood as if the latter were preserved from all human weaknesses, the spirit of domination, error, even sin. The power of the Holy Spirit does not guarantee all acts of ministers in the same way. While this guarantee extends to the sacraments, so that even the minister's sin cannot impede the fruit of grace, in many other acts the minister leaves human traces that are not always signs of fidelity to the Gospel, and consequently can harm the apostolic fruitfulness of the Church.[19]

Individual priests may, of course, be quite Christlike when not performing their sacramental duties, and I have known some extremely saintly priests. But the sacrament of Holy Orders does not automatically confer instant holiness; priests, too, are struggling and growing and need our prayers as we need theirs.

---

[18] The *Catechism of the Catholic Church* states that Holy Orders gives the priest "the authority to act in the power and place of the person of Christ himself" (p. 387, quoted from Pius XII's encyclical, *Mediator Dei*).

[19] *Catechism of the Catholic Church*, p. 387.

If you find that the face of some person who claimed religious authority and wounded you deeply in the past (or who is behaving badly now) keeps coming into your mind and becoming an obstacle to your prayers, try holding a crucifix, cross, icon of Christ, or a picture of Jesus and looking at it from time to time to help you direct your attention to God through Christ. Remember that Jesus too is grieved when those who profess to be Christians behave in arrogant or destructive ways that wound and scandalize those who are genuinely seeking God. Remember also that there may be extenuating circumstances in this person's life that at least partly excuse his or her behavior. The person may be in considerable inner pain or deep spiritual darkness of some sort, and thus badly in need of prayers. Jesus advises us to "love your enemies, do good to those who hate you, bless those who curse you, pray for those who abuse you" (Lk 6:27; see also Mt 5:44). So if you can bring yourself to do so, say a quick prayer for him or her and then return your focus to Jesus.

Although old wounds and angers are likely to be a more serious barrier to prayer if inflicted by someone who presented himself or herself as a Christian, intense feelings of anger against anyone can obsess you and make prayer difficult. Your mind keeps reverting to the person's offensive behavior, and your emotions get all stirred up. Complete healing of the wounds that cause us to feel angry can only be attained through the grace of God, usually over a period of time (if the wounds were deep). Forgiveness is a complicated thing (and will be discussed below in more detail in Chapter Five) but briefly, you should at least decide that you *want* to forgive and let go of your grievances, and ask God to help you. Remember that we are all sinful, and only God can be trusted never to hurt, condemn, reject, or betray you. He knows what you have suffered. But remember, also, that you are imperfect yourself; it behooves us to be merciful since we ourselves are in need of mercy. Forgiveness frees you to move forward in newness of life.

Sloth/Despair

Sloth, although usually slighted in favor of the "hot" sins like lust and anger, is one of the seven deadly sins — and in some ways the most insidious. When in the grip of sloth, any effort at all seems like too much; the smallest step like a vast, unscalable mountain. It is as though one is extraordinarily heavy and being held and drawn downward by a strong gravitational pull. At its worst it is closely connected with *thanatos* — the "death wish." Perhaps the experience is like that of those who freeze to death — a kind of slow and horrible letting go in which one ceases to struggle any more, gives in, and falls into a sort of sweet and numbing sleep. But remember that there is no neutral ground in the spiritual life and the stakes are high; if you continue to do nothing you will be pulled down. Recognizing that this is what is going on will hopefully galvanize you into the necessary cry for help. The first step is the hardest. Sometimes you just have to decide that you do not want to go that route, and say, "By God, I am not going to go down without a fight." By this very resolution the grip of inertia will be relaxed and you will find yourself freed to take the necessary steps. Realizing that this happens to many people and that it is possible by God's grace to break free of it is helpful. It is not as though you are uniquely beset by the problem. Don't focus on the top of the mountain and on how far you fall short of it. Just concentrate on the next step; keep putting one foot in front of the other.

Sloth is often, though not invariably, connected with despair. You feel that for some unaccountable reason you are beyond help; others may turn and find God, perhaps, but something is holding you down. People raised in religious communities influenced by Calvinism (including Irish Catholics influenced by Jansenism) may connect this with the fear that they may be among the reprobate — those destined to eternal damnation — but for most people the experience is not so heavily theologically laden. Remember, however, that the Devil's main strategy is to persuade you that he has already won, so don't fall for that line.

He is after all the "father of lies" (Jn 8:44). The Devil has *not* already won, and God's grace is available — both to give you the strength to cry out for help and to answer you when you do. Once you are off dead center, a kind of inertia develops that carries you along in the right way.

PART III: PRAYER OF PRESENCE

The first step in prayer is simply to be willing to sit in the presence of God in an attitude of openness and trust. What is it like to be in the presence of God, and why is this something good and desirable in itself? And with what sort of dispositions or attitudes should we approach Him?

Experiencing oneself to be in the presence of God is not the same thing as "seeing" God[20]; still less is it the same thing as having a full grasp of God's nature. At a minimum, it involves the awareness that you are not alone. God's presence is both like and unlike that of other people. It is like it in that you experience God as a personal being who is perceiving you, but it is different in that God's perception of you is not limited to your outer behaviors, but extends to your thoughts, feelings, and most intimate inward being. In fact, God's perception of us is far deeper and more accurate than our own self-knowledge. Not only do we often fail to see our own faults, but God may also see in us good things that we don't know are there, so don't just think of God as a harsh judge searching for your sins.

Not only is God's perception of us different from the way we are perceived by ourselves or by other people, but our ability to perceive or know Him is very different from our ability to perceive or know other human beings. We can perceive other people with our physical senses and have felt many of the sorts

---

[20] This is not to deny that some people may experience some sort of visual image at times. But this sort of visual imaging is not necessary, and can never be adequate to God's nature.

of things that they feel, so we experience a kind of spontaneous, natural empathy. The difference between perceiving other people and perceiving God, however, is a bit less simple or radical than it might appear. Although people's words and body language can help bridge the gap, their inner being is, and always remains, hidden from us. We can sometimes be badly mistaken about what they are feeling on some occasion, and err by projecting onto them something we feel, or think we would feel in their situation. And, not only is our knowledge of other people far less complete than we sometimes suppose, but the incomprehensibility of God is somewhat mitigated by the Incarnation. The earthly life of Jesus Christ provides a kind of body language that expresses God's dispositions toward us, and enables us to experience through empathy (based on the human nature we share with Jesus) something of the fullness of God's love for us. As St. Paul says, we behold the "glory of God in the face of Christ" (2 Cor 4:6). Even so, God remains uniquely mysterious. We "see through a glass darkly" (1 Cor 13:12).

The Glory of the Lord and the "Fear of the Lord"

God can be intimate with us in a way no one else can be. He can treat us with extraordinary tenderness (far beyond what any human being can do), touching us and working in us in extremely delicate ways, but He is also majestic and glorious and we may sense this as a kind of background when we experience His presence particularly strongly. Our natural response to this is awe, and what has sometimes been called "holy fear." One should approach what has been called "the Throne of Grace" (Heb 4:16) with trust in God's mercy certainly, but also with reverence and trepidation. It has been said that the fear of the Lord is the beginning of wisdom (Ps 111:10; see also Jb 28:28 and Ps 19:9), and I think that this is the kind of "fear" that is meant. We shouldn't think of God as lurking somewhere in the shadows, keeping careful count of our sins and poised to strike us at any moment. But a due sense of His power and majesty produces a kind of reverence that should restrain us from lightly doing things displeasing to Him.

Being granted the vision of God's glory is always treated in Scripture as a gift — as something to be longed for. Moses begs the Lord, "I pray thee, show me thy glory" (Ex 33:18), and the psalms are full of references to the "glory of the Lord" and a longing to behold it — to "behold the beauty of the Lord and to worship in His temple" (Ps 27:4). Psalm 29 contains an extraordinary paean to God's glory. Philip says to Jesus "show us the Father and we shall be satisfied" (Jn 14:8). Jesus prays at the last supper, "Father, I desire that they also, whom thou hast given me, may be with me where I am to behold my glory which thou hast given me in thy love for me before the foundation of the world" (Jn 17:24). It might seem on the face of it that there is something egotistical about Jesus wanting us to behold His glory, or God wanting us to praise Him and acknowledge His glory. Why is this? Does God have a big ego that He needs us to praise Him or acknowledge His glory? (I put the objection in extreme terms; it could be put more subtly.) There is something totally wrong-headed about this sort of objection, but it is useful to understand why.

At root "glory" is a religious concept, and all human uses of that term are parasitic upon its religious use. Kings and rulers throughout history in a number of different cultures have tried to associate themselves through their pomp and display with the divine as a way of reinforcing their authority. The association between kingship, majesty, and glory pre-dates monotheistic religion. Gods were thought of as beings who had power over their worshipers, both to help and to harm. Powerful men and women elicited feelings of awe and dependence from those beneath them and so were thought to be godlike.

Looking, then, at the religious use of the term "glory," I think, our tiny glimpses of God's glory here below are a foretaste of Heaven — of what is called in Christian tradition "the beatific vision." There is something that nourishes the soul in even the briefest moment of apprehension of the glory of God. We do not know God fully in this life, but we begin to know Him in such moments when we experience the breaking in of a transcendent being whom the psalmist describes as "robed in majesty" (Ps 93:1). Knowledge of God, love of God, and fear of the Lord are closely intertwined in the Old Testament; the Jews are to bring up their children in the knowledge and fear of the Lord. Moses instructs them to "love the Lord your God with all your heart, and with all your soul, and with all your might" (Dt 6:5), and Jesus cites this (with slight variations in wording) as the "great and first commandment" in Mt 22:37, Mk 12:30, and Lk 10:27. God is glorious and lovable in Himself, apart from anything we may hope to obtain from Him.

Approaching God: Trust and Docility

"Never forget God's judgment; never presume His mercy; always remember His love." A friend of mine has a poster on her wall with these words, and I think that they express admirably the attitude with which we need to approach God in prayer. The ground for our trust is God's love. Docility is the willingness to be led, and is also appropriate because God is not only Love (and ideally we should follow Him out of love) but also Truth, and ultimately we all stand under His judgment.

God loves us and has reconciled us to Himself in Christ Jesus, "making peace through the blood of His cross" (Col 1:20). This truth undergirds Christian faith and our trust in God is ultimately founded on it. The parable about the good shepherd who goes in search of the lost sheep (Mt 18:12-13 and Lk 15:4) and the one about the prodigal son and the beautiful way in which the father goes out to welcome him (Lk 15:13) are good parables to meditate on in order to get a sense of God's love. Or, at an even deeper level, reflect upon the passion of Christ and the pain, humiliation and betrayal He endured in order to save us. The depth of His suffering reveals the depth of His love. Try to anchor yourself in these truths and hold onto them, because it is only against the background of God's love (either directly experienced or believed in by faith) that you can have the courage and strength to face the truth. For God manifests Himself not only as Love but also as Truth. God's glory, of course, radiates in an infinite number of dimensions, only some of which can be apprehended by the human mind — and those only very imperfectly. We apprehend God as Love and as Truth, but also as Light, Goodness, Beauty, Mercy, Compassion, and Peace, to name only a few.

The sense of standing under the judgment of a truth that transcends our own limited perspective is, of course, integrally connected with the "fear of the Lord" discussed above. But although this sounds frightening, it is also very freeing. We are always under pressure to please different people and concerned about their judgments of us. There is a bumper sticker that expresses very well how this can make us feel. It says: "I can only please one person a day. Today is not your day. Tomorrow doesn't look good either." But if there is only one person whose judgment of us counts, one person — namely God — whom we must make every effort to please, this simplifies things considerably.

Of course this doesn't mean that you don't need to worry from a practical point of view about the judgment of those who evaluate you on the job, for example, but only that their judgments should not be allowed to touch you at your deepest level. Nor does it mean you should simply turn a deaf ear to friends and family who point out some particular fault of yours; God may be using them to correct you. But always pray over it, and don't take other people's judgments of you to heart too quickly. Finally, it does not mean that you should feel free to blithely disregard traditional Christian moral teachings, claiming that you are accountable only to God. Scripture and tradition do carry authority for Christians. As those who heard Jesus perceived, He taught with authority and not as the scribes did, and Scripture and tradition hand on to us the teachings of Jesus.

We think of judgment too often as something purely negative. "Judge not that you be not judged" (Mt 7:1; Lk 6:37). But such passages refer to humans judging other humans. When we think of God as judge, things take on a different character. For God's judgment provides us a standard by which to guide our lives — the sort of fixed point that Archimedes needed in order to move the whole Earth. There is a passage in C.S. Lewis's *Perelandra* that conveys something of the experience of finding oneself standing under God's judgment — of being corrected and re-oriented in the light of His truth. A being called an *eldil* appears suddenly (*eldil* are like angels). It appeared as a faint rod or pillar of light. Lewis says:

> It was not at right angles to the floor. But as soon as I have said this, I hasten to add that this way of putting it is a later reconstruction. What one actually felt at the moment was that the column of light was vertical but the floor was not horizontal — the whole room seemed to have heeled over as if it were on board ship. The impression, however produced, was that this creature had reference to some horizontal, to some whole system of directions, based outside the Earth, and that its mere presence imposed that alien system on me and abolished the terrestrial horizontal.[21]

The difference between the *eldil* and God, of course, is that God does not just have another system of spatial coordinates that differs from ours, but rather that His provides the truth or standard against which *all* others are to be judged. In His presence the truth is revealed, and what we had taken to be straight may now seem to have been somehow askew or off-center. And this is not an alien imposition in the way that the imposition of Martian spatial coordinates upon Earth would be. Rather, it reveals the truth of what has been there all along, and we experience it

---

[21] *Perelandra* (New York: Macmillan, 1944), p. 18.

in this way. Although it may cause us to reverse some of our previous judgments (and see something we previously thought was a virtue as a fault, or vice versa), it is continuous with what was there before, clarifies, fills in gaps, and makes sense of things. In the light of truth, we see our earlier blindness and rationalizations for what they were, although we may not in *every* case be sure whether we were in good faith error or rationalizing (God alone knows this).

Trust lies in between despair and presumption. Awareness of our own sinfulness, if we don't keep God's love firmly in mind, can engender despair. But a one-sided emphasis on God's love and mercy that is forgetful of the fact that we stand under God's judgment can lead to presumption. The person who despairs gives up hope of being saved, while the person who is presumptuous treats salvation as something he or she has some sort of claim on. God does not *owe* us *anything*. It is very important to keep this truth firmly before our eyes if we are to be in right relationship to God. God gives what He give *freely*. Nothing we can do can bind Him in any way. Yet Jesus tells us "Fear not, little flock; it is the Father's good pleasure to give you the Kingdom" (Lk 12:32).

CHAPTER TWO

THE BASICS

What I do is a combination of prayer and meditation. Prayer and meditation are related phenomena, and both include an extraordinary variety of practices. This is not the place, however, to launch into an extensive discussion of the various types of prayer and meditation (although I will discuss some different types of prayer in Chapter Four). I call what I do "prayer" because I understand myself to be directing my attention toward God and seeking to enter into a relationship with Him. It involves reaching toward God, an invocation of God (calling out to Him, calling upon His name) and opening myself to Him. As Scripture says, God wants us to "feel after Him and find Him" (Ac 17:27). An agnostic could engage in prayer in this sense, saying, "God, if you are out there, I'd like to get to know you. Please manifest yourself to me somehow." (In fact I know someone who did just this, and is now an Episcopal priest.) A consistent atheist, however, could not pray. But there is a meditative element as well: I reflect slowly and deeply on certain words or images, try to be quiet and receptive, and sometimes fall into a state of deep contemplation or a kind of heightened awareness, or have a sense of being stilled and held in a way that lifts me out of the busy and distracted state of mind that I tend to lapse into so often.

There is a basic set of prayers I do each day, but they provide structure only in a rather loose way, and a lot of improvised prayers can be fitted in as the Spirit moves, as well as periods of silent receptivity, of course. Don't just plod ahead mechanically repeating the words; if you begin to feel a strong sense of God's presence, pause and allow yourself to rest in Him. When doing the set prayers, I use the plural "we" or "us" and envision myself praying with all Christ's Church, and in a special way with and for those I am most closely connected with. When I improvise prayers I use "I" or "my." I often do not finish the set prayers, but they are there to fall back on, and I always get at least part way into the Sacred Heart Litany. If you don't do them all, be sure at least to do the opening prayer, the surrender prayer, and entrust yourself in some way to the Sacred Heart of Jesus each day.

Keeping your eyes closed makes it easier to concentrate, so it is a good idea to memorize the prayers. You can then say them whenever you want to — for example, if you have trouble sleeping at night, or while driving your car. It took me a while to memorize the Litany — I'd just memorize a few key words in each verse to remind myself of the order — e.g., "abyss, praise, King, wisdom and knowledge," etc., and run over them as I walked around or drove the car. However, if you find the idea of memorizing things daunting, you could read the prayers slowly and reflectively. But try to memorize at least some part of them — say, the opening prayer ("Almighty God unto whom all hearts are open...") — so that you can recite it with your eyes closed. Most people have the ability to memorize a lot more than they realize (in our culture we do not cultivate this capacity as much as many cultures do). But don't feel pressured to memorize everything right at the start.

It important to pray very slowly, reflecting on the words. Best to speak them aloud or at least form them with your lips if you can (*i.e.*, if you are not desperately sick, drifting off to sleep, or unable to speak because of a physical problem like cerebral palsy or stroke). Usually I say them very softly, but you might on occasion want to pray some parts of the prayers more loudly. Try to cultivate a sense of unhurriedness and eternity even if you don't have a large amount of time. Words are like ships moving over the top of the water — deep things happen beneath the surface, moving along with them. They open a channel for God to work in us (like God writing on our souls through them). You can spend a lot of time over a few words sometimes. Prayer is more something that God does in us than something we do. This makes it much easier, since it does not depend on us doing something or being perfect. The key thing, I think, is learning to allow the Holy Spirit to move in us — allowing Him to expand and fill us. As the old Negro spiritual puts it: "Every time I feel the Spirit moving in my heart, I will pray."

Sometimes the Holy Spirit is associated with the gift of tongues as a prayer language. I don't think everyone necessarily receives this particular gift, but if you do, you'll know it. How does one recognize the Holy Spirit? I remember early on often having a feeling of expanding and being filled, and of being more alive. I used to feel empty inside — like I was desperately defending an empty citadel, but I've come to feel more inhabited. The Holy Spirit will of course rearrange things in us — just as when we move into a new home we rearrange the furniture — and at levels that we don't even know about. Traditionally the Holy Spirit is described as the "sanctifier of the faithful" and knows what to do if only we let Him. One thing the Holy Spirit seems to bring is a sense of exaltation in praising God. In fact if you want to receive the gift of tongues, it helps to ask God to give you a tongue to praise Him and ask for the Holy Spirit to pray in you and with you. Visualize yourself with the angels and the saints praising God. Start with words of praise and let it move out from there. I remember that passage in one version of the Mass: "in the sight of the angels I will sing Thy praise O Lord."

Having had my on and off periods with the Lord, I found I needed to keep saying I would not rebel or turn back and that I want to be the faithful bride and not like the one whose love goes away early like the dew (with whom God compared Israel in Hosea 6:4). I prayed that He would magnetize my being to Him so that my soul would always be pointed toward Him (like a compass needle to the pole), and that He would increase my desire for Him. That is scary in a way, since we feel greater need and dependence, but that is all to the good.

I do introductory prayers, Holy Spirit invocation, prayer of surrender, and the Litany of the Sacred Heart in that order now, but this is flexible. I do them all in a row in the morning, but you could do, say, the Holy Spirit prayer in the morning and the Litany in the afternoon. But all prayer should start with some sort of invocation of the Holy Spirit. See what works for you. Prayer at dawn feels particularly appropriate to me. "My soul waits for the Lord and in His word I hope, more than the watchman for the dawn. Let the watchman count on daybreak and Israel on the Lord. For with the Lord there is forgiveness and fullness of redemption" (Ps 130:5-7). The infinitesimally gradual but yet inevitable coming of the light is like the subtle and gradual, yet powerful coming of God into our souls. Also I tend to wake up feeling a bit ragged around the edges, with bits of dreams still clinging around me, and emotions close to the surface, and a long, slow prayer period in the morning brings peace and clarity so I am ready for the day.

Even if you are not a morning person, you should do at least some prayer in the morning. You don't *need* to be clear headed and on top of things. In a way it is better to pray before your mind has gotten geared up for the tasks of the day. I knew a man whose wife used to come sit on his bed just as he was waking up and begin talking about plans for the day. He said, "Please, dear, I haven't got my armor on yet." Precisely. We should come to God before we get our armor on while we still feel vulnerable, letting Him draw us gently out of our night fogginess and bring our minds to clarity and focus so that we will be more open to the leading of the Holy Spirit during the day. In prayer we also receive the nourishment and strength to enable us to make it through the day. If you are a person like me who needs a little caffeine to clear your head, have something caffeinated before you pray, but be careful not to overdo it, or your mind will jump around too much during prayer.

I think it is important to be regular, and pray every day, preferably at the same time. All too often we pray only in crisis situations, instead of allowing God to gradually nourish and form us day by day. I get up, have a cup of tea, and pray each morning before I do anything else or let my mind get engaged with the activities of the day. I sip my tea while I read the Scriptures and sometimes during the first few prayers. It is not necessary to keep one's prayer time hermetically sealed off from the rest of one's life, and having something warm and sweet and comforting to sip eases the transition into prayer for me. An hour would be good, but less if you have to. Still I recommend at least half an hour to start. Once the Spirit started to flow, I found myself eager to get up and do it; I'd look at the clock in the night wondering if it was late enough to get up and pray yet.

GENERAL SUGGESTIONS

Physical posture

I sit with fairly straight back on something comfortable where I can lean my head back if I want to, hands resting loosely on my lap with the palms turned up. When you are traveling, the easiest way to set up a prayer space is to sit on the bed with your back against the headboard or the nearest wall, legs straight out ahead of you on the bed, and pillows arranged behind you so that your back feels comfortable. Good, I think, to sit somewhere private with doors closed so you don't feel self-conscious. Allow your body to take whatever position comes naturally to you. You may also feel moved to accompany particular prayers with small physical gestures involving the head, face, or hands. Just don't get up and start moving around. Some people find it valuable to pray while walking (and far be it from me to discourage anybody from praying in any way he or she finds helpful), but a posture in which my body can be fully relaxed works best for the sort of prayer I do, focusing as it does on surrender and receptivity.

Picture of self and God

God is a person, but an inexhaustible one.[22] A source or point from which radiate His love, mercy, power, etc. We are also, it seems, bottomless in that we cannot touch bottom (as it were) although I presume there is a bottom. God only knows where. (Actually, on later reflection, I am inclined to think that we are not entirely finite, and that what is potentially infinite in us is our desire for God.) The essential point is that we are far more than we know, a lot beyond words or thought and known only to God. There is something in us fitted to receive God (just as we desire food and there is something in us fitted to receive it) but we don't know just where or what this something is; God, however, knows how to find it and fill it. He knows what He wants to do in us, what we are able to receive, and when. Some people fear that God's power is such that it would destroy them or blow them away if they let Him in, but in my experience this does not happen; God is quite able to be delicate and gentle with us. Various mystics and saints have on occasion fallen into transports or ecstasies in which the soul does feel totally overpowered, but this is not the same as being blown away or destroyed. St. Teresa of Avila, for example, noted, in her very common sense way, that her spiritual ecstasies seemed to in no way harm her, but on the contrary benefitted her enormously.

The Purpose of Prayer

It has, of course, many goals, but I'm focusing here on the experiential core — on coming into His presence, being open to Him, worshiping Him, and allowing Him to transform our

---

[22] God is often described as "infinite." I prefer the term "inexhaustible" because the term infinite seems too quantitative, connoting a size that cannot be measured, which makes it too spatial a way to talk about God. The issues here are wildly complex and I am not a theologian. But for prayer at least, thinking of God (and especially God as revealed in and through the Sacred Heart of Jesus) as "inexhaustible" is especially helpful, because it leads us to think about God in a way that invites relationship, rather than in a purely external way — out there somewhere in endless space.

hearts. As we continue in this practice, God reveals Himself to us, searches and knows us, forms us more and more into the image of Christ, and guides us in the right way. Christianity teaches that our ultimate goal is union with God (a union of love and knowledge), and prayer, I think, should be a practice through which we gradually grow into that communion which, Christians believe, will be fully consummated in Heaven. The term "union" can sound a bit alarming, as though we are drops of water that get totally absorbed into the sea. A better way to think about union, I think, is that it is a simultaneous giving and receiving. God gives Himself to us in Christ, and we must allow Him to dwell more and more deeply in us. Receiving of God is sort of like being nourished by Him but it is an odd sort of being nourished in that what nourishes us is not something like food or drink that becomes a part of us, but rather a being who is living and who receives or takes us at the same time as He gives Himself to us. Receptivity is thus crucial, for it allows God's Spirit to take root in us. In receiving we give; in giving we receive. Our goal is a gradually deepening surrender to Him, a richer communion with Him and vision of His glory so we can become more perfect worshipers of God. As Brother Lawrence puts it, "the end we ought to propose to ourselves is to become, in this life, the most perfect worshipers of God we can possibly be, as we hope to be through all eternity."[23] After all, if it will be blissful to do it eternally, we should experience at least a foretaste of that doing it now.

Attuning yourself to the presence of God

I think of it a little as though I am in a dark place and hearing someone nearby that I can't see. Have you ever tried this? You strain with all your power to detect who or what is making the noise and what they are doing or what their intentions

---

[23] Brother Lawrence, *The Practice of the Presence of God* (Old Tappan NJ: Spire Books, 1976), p. 25.

are. I remember that I once actually succeeded in picking up the thoughts of a person under these sorts of conditions. Or it is sort of like scanning the energy field surrounding you trying to turn toward or hone in on the source, the being from whom life, attention, power are emanating. I keep my eyes closed generally. Thus although my approach to prayer is largely focused on receptivity, it requires intense concentration, which is one reason why I do it in the morning when I am fresh.

You may find it helpful to keep a crucifix, cross, icon or picture of Jesus near you when you pray. You can open your eyes and glance at it from time to time, or simply hold it. Always remember, however, that you are reaching toward the living God who is beyond all images, and that visual images are merely imaginative aids that can help us to "feel after Him and find Him" (Ac 17:27). Or, perhaps I should say they may help us to let *Him* find *us*. We are able to find Him only because He is seeking to enter into relationship with us.

Role of the Mind

Occult writers think of it as like a little yapping dog that distracts us and that we need to master and train. I think that this is too controlling and power-oriented. It is like a watch dog guarding the house, and we need to soothe and praise it and tell it that it is all right; God is the rightful owner of the house and will only do us good. Then it can relax and let Him in. Our minds are nourished and satisfied in prayer as we grow in knowledge (and concomitantly love) of God.

Role of the Body

I believe that the body is important in prayer. There has been a Greek influence in Christianity that brings with it a tendency to overemphasize the cognitive and volitional side of human beings to the exclusion of emotional and physical. This is not scriptural. There is a lot in the Old Testament and Psalms especially about this: the heart, the kidneys, praising God "with joyful lips" (Ps 63:6), "panting" for God, tasting and seeing that the Lord is good, etc. St. Paul speaks of the Spirit interceding for us with sighs and groans (Rm 8:26). I don't think we should imitate those Martin Luther once described as acting as though they had swallowed the Holy Spirit, feathers and all. But, on the other hand, we are not like those angels you see in paintings sometimes who are only a head with wings. We have bodies, and they too are affected by and respond to God's presence in us. The whole person should be engaged when we pray — heart, soul, mind, body, imagination, emotion, desire (eros), and spirit. The Psalmist says, "Bless the Lord, O my soul; and all that is within me, bless His holy name" (Ps 103:1).

The body should generally respond rather than initiate. However, people who are very inhibited physically may find raising their arms slightly with the palms upward in whatever position comes naturally will help to facilitate an attitude of supplication or praise. Many forms of meditation that have their roots in Eastern religions emphasize attaining mastery of our minds and bodies. But since the goal of Christian prayer and meditation is not self-mastery but surrender, we should not try too much to direct what happens in prayer, but allow God to do what needs to be done.[24]

---

[24] The temptation to slip into various kinds of spiritual technology involving concentration, visualization, breathing techniques, and the deliberate channeling of energies within you to achieve certain results is one you should resist, especially in prayer. A remark by the famous German philosopher, Immanuel Kant, provides a useful analogy here. He scorned the use of common sense in philosophy, saying: "Chisels and hammers may suffice to work a piece of wood, but for etching we require an etcher's needle. Thus common sense and speculative understanding are both useful, but each in its own way." Our clumsy attempts to remake ourselves resemble the chisel; God has the etcher's needle to do the delicate work.

Emotions

If you are upset emotionally, this can interfere with prayer, and sometimes deep and painful emotions will suddenly come up while you are praying. When we relax and let God in, the sorrows and griefs that we have been keeping at bay in order to go on with our daily lives, may come to the surface and even bring tears to our eyes. This is entirely healthy. You need to bring yourself in all your woundedness to the Lord for healing. Denying your emotions and keeping up a cheerful front can make life easier on those around you, but God is the one being with whom you can be completely open — in fact with whom you *must* be completely open. Unlike human beings, He can bear our sorrows without being pulled down by them, and when we allow them to rise to the surface and let go of them, He can heal them. The only thing to do is cling to Him and weep and ask for help. A few times I have cried off and on for nearly an hour before beginning to receive a little consolation. Pains and sadness that you have repressed can block your heart, so it is a sign that healing is taking place when these begin to become conscious in prayer.[25] Letting them flow out opens the way for God's healing love to come in and soothe the troubled waters. But it can take time.

Distractions

Our minds tend to run on about all sorts of things, and this can interfere with prayer or meditation. I keep a pad of paper and a pencil next to me as I pray and if anything occurs to me that I really need to remember to do that day, I just write it down so I

---

[25] I once went to a New Age workshop on "opening the heart chakra." One of their central principles was that old pains that have been repressed block the heart, and that letting them come to the surface is healing. One of the activities during the weekend was having people sit in couples in lines facing each other, sharing with each other the saddest thing that ever happened to them, while people went up and down the line with boxes of Kleenex. It may sound a bit silly, but in fact I was left at the end of the retreat with an amazing feeling of clarity, peace, and openness.

won't forget and so I can put it out of my mind. But this should only be for very important things; writing down too many little things can prevent you from really entering into meditation. You can also use the pad for insights or guidance that come to you while meditating, but again be careful not to keep interrupting your meditation too much. The other thing that helps is to simply ask the Holy Spirit to help you pray; to pray in you, for you, with you, through you, and to intercede for the saints as God wills. Ask God to direct your prayer. Or say "God, please free me from all these distracting thoughts."

One thing that struck me when I began to pray in this way, was that I was less distracted by noises than I had been when I tried to concentrate and do it all myself. Since prayer is predominantly something God does in us and not something we do, we can be more independent of our surroundings than we would be, say, if we were trying to write an important letter or understand a difficult text. But still a quiet place is preferable. Prayer is something that begins to happen in us, sometimes in surprising ways; a life breathed into us that is more than just plodding through words or even doing guided reflections on various themes (valuable though this may be also).

Role of the Imagination in Prayer

Since we do not perceive God with our ordinary physical senses, it is necessary to employ analogies or images drawn from our imaginations in our thinking about God. The fact that our understanding of God and our relationship to Him is structured to some degree at least by the images or analogies through which we understand that relationship should not worry us or make us fear that somehow we are making it all up. We are physical beings whose minds and imaginations are shaped to a large extent by our sense experience. Jesus Himself employed such images, comparing the Kingdom of God to a mustard seed, a pearl, and yeast. And the more extended analogies — the well-known parables about the sower and the seed, or the prodigal son, likewise draw on images familiar to Jesus's hearers. If you look at the way various saints and mystics describe their prayer life, you will notice that they think of themselves in relation to God using a variety of imaginative images. And as you persist in prayer, you may find your own prayer experience suggests new images to you, or feel that God is leading you at a given time to understand what He wants of you in terms of some particular image (as I feel that the images of the spring, the dance, and the flower — given below — were given to me).

I do not deliberately visualize anything at all when employing the images suggested below. Rather they help me understand how I stand in relation to God and structure my response to Him. If you think of God as a harsh judge searching out and keeping careful count of all your sins, you will respond differently to Him than if you think of Him as a lifeguard rescuing you from drowning. If I feel like a drowning swimmer, recognizing that this is what is going on, it helps me realize that the appropriate thing to do is to relax and trust and let Him buoy me up. Thus different images may be helpful at different times. Some days you may feel particularly like an enemy occupied city — beset by temptations and powerless to do anything to help yourself. Another day you may feel like dry, hard, brambly ground longing for the softening dew or rain of the Spirit. Another day you may feel a sense of delight as though you are drinking from a spring of living water. So use whichever of the following you find helpful.

IMAGES I HAVE FOUND HELPFUL

Enemy occupied territory

In some ways we are like enemy occupied territory, or, more accurately, like *partially* enemy occupied territory. The Lord has won the essential victory, but pockets of resistance still need to be taken, and our job in prayer is to do our best to allow Him to do this. So think of Him as a victorious king entering into the city and open the gates to Him so that He can drive out all the enemy forces and bring peace at last to the war torn city. After I finish praying I sometimes pray that He will remain in me, and continue to hold dominion over any part of me that I have succeeded in surrendering to Him even for a moment — that I won't try to take things back.

Drowning swimmer image

When we become fearful we clutch onto God sometimes so hysterically that we are impossible to rescue. We have to relax and let Him lift and carry us. Imagining this concretely in your body can help here.

Sunbathing

If we are to bear fruit for God, we need to allow Him to warm and soften us. Just as plants need the sun to grow, so the new life God implants in us needs the light of His presence and love to grow. Plants naturally turn toward the light. And thinking of ourselves as simply lying in the sun and letting it warm us is a helpful image in that it helps engender an attitude of trust, relaxation, and openness. Occasionally you can experience a sort of warm, golden light.

Prayer of desire/underground river

I recently found a good book on the Holy Spirit in the life of Jesus[26] that compared prayer of desire to a river that sometimes runs underground (when we are busy with other things) and sometimes comes to the surface. The desire for God is itself already God's action in our souls, and we should allow it to

---

[26] Raniero Cantalamessa, *The Holy Spirit in the Life of Jesus* (Collegeville, MN: The Liturgical Press, 1994).

grow; somehow it draws God to fill us (or is perhaps the natural response of our souls to God's approach — surprising how something which so transcends our human nature can also be so natural). The book says, "Desire means something very deep; it is the habitual reaching for God; it is the yearning of the entire being, the longing for God."[27] This sort of prayer of the heart, he says, can go on ceaselessly, even when we are asleep. Desire carries us out of ourselves, and leads to a kind of surrender and death that opens us to a new life and fullness.

Flower opening

Think of how a flower turns toward the sun and gradually opens its petals, giving off whatever sweetness is in it as the petals unfold more and more completely. Just so, our souls must turn toward the light — toward God — so that we may open and bloom and give off a sweet odor to God and those around us.

Drinking from a spring

One of my central images has been drinking from a spring. A spring, of course, is a source of water that wells up from the ground and is therefore pure to drink. It is "living water" by contrast with stagnant water. Remember how Jesus told the Samaritan woman that, had she asked, He would have given her "living water" (Jn 4:10-14). The Litany talks in one of its verses of the "Heart of Jesus of whose fullness we have all received." And in prayer God often fills us — we are gradually stretched so we can hold more of Him. I'm not very ascetic, and my prayer is more oriented toward receptivity and fullness — although this of course does require some sort of emptying of what was there before. But God's coming in drives other things out and we don't have to worry about trying to do it ourselves. Also the spring

---

27 *Op. cit.*, p. 58.

image fits well with passing on what God gives us to others, as the way to clean a spring is to empty out all the water and let it refill (sort of like the feeding of the 5000). Think of your heart as like an empty glass, that God is gradually filling. A spring of water opens within us welling up to eternal life (Jn 4:14). You no longer feel empty but nourished and satisfied. St. Paul speaks of all believers as having been "given to drink of the one Spirit" (1 Cor 12:13).

Nursing at the breast of God

Sometimes the spring image blends with that of thinking of ourselves as nursing at the breast of God, but the nursing image is more primal and oral in nature. This image is quite common in the writings of the mystics — St. Teresa of Avila, Julian of Norwich, St. Francis de Sales, St. John of the Cross, and Brother Lawrence to name only a few — and is usually used while retaining masculine pronouns for referring to God. Although the sucking reflex is one of our strongest instincts, a newborn will squirm and flail around at first and not know how to find the breast and properly keep the nipple in its mouth. The mother has to hold the infant to her breast and carefully keep placing the nipple in its mouth. But after a while the infant begins to nurse more steadily and strongly. So, I think, it is with us and God. Nursing provides a wonderful image or analogy for the sort of active receptivity that happens in prayer. We must let God calm our restless thrashing around, hold us, guide us to His breast (to which we have access through the Sacred Heart of Jesus), and help our hungry souls to drink in the nourishment that He longs to pour out to us.

Prayer as like a dance

When properly done, a dance involves two persons moving as one. I do English country dancing, and the teachers always say that when you are dancing with someone you need to maintain a gentle pressure in your arms and hands — "give a little weight." If you hold your arm too rigidly your partner cannot guide you. The same problem occurs if you let your arm go totally limp. To be led, one also has to be a little off one's own center of gravity rather than having one's feet firmly planted foursquare trying to control everything. The old gospel song speaks of "leaning on the everlasting arms." (This image probably comes more easily to women who have experienced trying to follow the lead of a male dancer.) Ultimately, this sort of off-centeredness turns out to be rightly centered, and our earlier attempts to maintain our own separate center of gravity appear in retrospect to have been the thing that was really not centered (off balance), since we were after all created to live centered in God. I seldom feel just blankness when I pray, but rather a kind of gentle pressure and sense of concentration, following and contact. This didn't happen all at once, however. There is a kind of intricacy and precision to the dance; it is not a matter of mushy feelings. Ideally I wish I could come to the point where I anticipate the movements or desires of my partner before He has to push me in that direction (or for that matter always notice and respond when He does), but once I am engrossed in the business of the day I find this comes hard still.

Spousal Imagery

As a married woman, I am less inclined to think of Jesus as my husband in quite the way that many celibates have (although at some deep level it is indeed true that He is the lover or spouse of my soul). Union with Him in love remains the central thing we all seek, and the marital union provides a useful model or analogy here.[28] And interestingly male mystics as well as female

---

[28] Mystics in the Jewish and Christian traditions have been especially drawn to the Song of Solomon when thinking of the relationship between God and the soul as akin to that of a bridegroom to his bride. If you feel especially drawn to this particular image, you might want to pick up the Song of Solomon (in the Old Testament) and pray slowly those passages that you feel drawn to.

mystics employ the spousal image — St. John of the Cross, for example. In spite of some people's suspicions that experiences of mystical union with God are just displaced sexual feelings on the part of frustrated celibates, the sort of erotic longing for union with God and our earthly sexual desires, although connected, operate on different planes. We should receive and enjoy God's love and allow God to take pleasure in us and our love for Him. Both the union between spouses and the soul's union with God involve a simultaneous giving of oneself to the other and a receiving of the other. One important difference, however, is that our union with God can be much closer than that with another human being. Our relationship with God is unique in that we are dependent on God for our very life and being. Thus our love for Him is also His gift to us.

House or dwelling

We invite God to dwell or live in us, and if He makes His home in us, then we have to allow Him to rearrange the furniture to suit Himself. The house is His, the work He is doing in us is His. Sometimes I imagine myself sort of stepping aside, as though I am detached from myself or sitting beside myself almost, and handing myself over to Him saying, "The house is yours; come dwell in me."

Clay in the hands of the potter

Another image that is extremely common in the mystical literature is to think of yourself as clay in the hands of the potter, or marble in the hands of a sculptor. "Mold as Thou wilt my passive clay; but let me all thy stamp receive" (*The Sacred Harp*, p. 448). As a philosopher, I tend to understand this in terms of Aristotle's categories of form and matter. Marble is made up of matter and form (form is what makes it be the kind of thing it is — marble instead of granite), and it can also be formed by the sculptor into a statue — thus acquiring a higher level form. In a similar way, St. Paul talks about our bearing the image of the first man (Adam) but receiving as Christians the image of Christ which restores in us the divine image we lost through the Fall. In prayer, then, we are gradually being re-formed in the image of Christ, receiving His imprint (as it were) in our soul and bodies. Our very substance ultimately is to be transformed and raised up (the technical term for this is "deification").

Holy Spirit as wind in the sail

Another image is that of wind in a sail, with the Holy Spirit being the wind.[29] Once the wind catches the sail, I find that I often embroider on the prayers I am saying, adding words of hymns, songs, Scripture, or just of my own devising as I feel moved. Hildegard von Bingen, the famous medieval mystic, has a similar image — that of being a "feather on the breath of God." How lightly it floats, kept aloft by the breath and wholly directed by it! Say "yes Jesus," or "I will, help me" as the spirit moves (since I'm not entirely sure what I'm committing myself to, this last one is a bit more scary).

Breath

Breath is intimately associated with life. In Genesis (Gn 2:7) God is described as breathing into Adam's nostrils the "breath of life," and in one of His post-resurrection appearances, Jesus breathes upon the disciples and says "receive the Holy Spirit" (Jn 20:22). Think of the opening prayer "cleanse the thoughts of our hearts by the *inspiration* of thy Holy Spirit." Imagine this filling and expanding you, refining you, infusing your being with

---

[29] Remember that at Pentecost "suddenly a sound came from heaven like the rush of a mighty wind" (Ac 2:2), and Jesus compares those born of the Spirit with the wind that "blows where it wills, and you hear the sound of it, but you do not know whence it comes or whither it goes" (Jn 3:8).

light, lifting you up. Try praying: "Breathe on me breath of God, till I am wholly thine, till all this earthly part of me glows with thy fire divine" (*1940 Hymnal*, #375). Your breathing may speed up (as when the Psalmist speaks of our panting after God) or become quick and light, or slow and deep, or almost stop for a short while. Don't try to control it; just let whatever happens happen.

Garden

Another image, and one rooted in the Scripture passage about the sower who sows the seed on the rock, on the thin soil, etc., is to think of our hearts as like stony, dry, brambly ground. There is a beautiful line in a poem by W.H. Auden: "In the deserts of the heart let the healing fountain start; in the prison of his days, teach the free man how to praise" ("In Memory of W.B. Yeats"). In prayer God plows the soil of our hearts and softens and waters it so we can better receive Him and bear fruit.[30] Several summers ago we experienced a severe drought in Maine. The plants and the very earth itself were desperate for rain. The plants seemed pale, stunted, and droopy. In some places the ground was so hard that water just ran off it, but next to a birch tree by our door the ground was covered with leaves and thus still soft. I poured a five-gallon bucket of water there for the tree, and it was absorbed by the ground so fast it was literally like pouring the water down a hole, or like ink poured on blotting paper. We should be that eager and receptive.

The cares and pleasures of our daily lives can be seen as like the weeds and brambles that choke out the implanted word and make it unfruitful. I don't generally focus on these. Indeed the point of meditation is to try to find a clear space into which the weeds do not extend their tendrils. So focus on receptivity and let God keep the weeds at bay. St. James is working with this sort of model when he tells us to put away the "rank growth of wick-

---

[30] See Heb 6:7 for analogy with ground being watered.

edness," and "receive with meekness the implanted word which is able to save your souls" (Jm 1:21). Mary, in whose womb the Word first took flesh is, of course, a good model of receptivity and generosity, and the analogy with pregnancy is one some people may find helpful. It is an imperfect analogy, however, since at the end of nine months, the infant is fully formed and goes on his or her own independent way, while the person who is receptive to God's life within him or her grows into an ever deepening communion with God, who continues to be present within, raising us to a new and higher level of life.

Yeast

Another scriptural image, and one that conveys an even deeper sense of the sort of transformation that God works in our hearts, is the comparison between the Kingdom of God and the yeast that a woman took and "hid" in three measures of meal until the whole lump was raised (Lk 13:21). Like the image of the seed, this one involves a long slow working of God in us that remains secret and hidden for a period of time. Just as the seed must break open and put down roots before the plant is ready to begin to show itself above the ground, so also (as the bread makers among you know) bread needs a warm, dark and moist place to rise, and this takes time. Chemicals are released as the leaven ferments that produce little bubbles of air, so that the dough becomes lighter and more porous, doubling or sometimes tripling in size before it is ready to put in to bake. And while it is baking you should not keep opening the oven door to peer at it, or it may not rise properly. The very substance of the bread is being transformed in a hidden sort of way. In a similar way our substance, through God's action in us, is gradually permeated by light — rendered less dark and dense and more responsive to the action of the Spirit in us. Hence, saints are often described and represented as radiating a kind of light. Long before I became a Catholic, I had the experience of perceiving this phenomenon when I had the good fortune to see Pope John XXIII going by in an open car blessing the crowds in Rome only a few months before his death. Although his complexion was grey-hued as a result of his cancer, he seemed to me to radiate a kind of light. If one takes seriously the doctrine of "deification" as Catholic Christians do, perhaps the analogy with a nuclear reaction (an analogy which was not available to Jesus) would be a good one.

CULTIVATING A MEDITATIVE STATE OF MIND

The human mind is deeply mysterious, and has many levels. You need to let go of your practical engagement with the world and the sort of push, push, push mentality that tends to go with it in order to open up a quiet place for God to come. God can, and probably does, act on our hearts and souls even while we are rushing around in a distracted state of mind (I think our hearts often know Him better than our minds). But there are, it seems, certain gifts He wants to give us that we can only receive when we open ourselves to receive them. In the Psalms it says, "Open wide your mouth and I will fill it" (Ps 81:11). Someone cannot put a gift into your hand if you keep your fist clenched tight.

Hopefully employing some of the above images and praying the words of the prayers slowly and reflectively will engender a sense of inner quiet and receptivity. But there are also a few techniques that may help. You want to try to simultaneously reach upward toward God and keep a focus on your deepest center; "Further up and further in" was the phrase C.S. Lewis used (*The Last Battle*, last chapter). The mind should remain clear ordinarily (although some mystics have experienced states in which ordinary consciousness is suspended for some period of time), but there should also be a sense of going deeper and letting go. You might try thinking of your mind being held suspended while letting your body drift into sleep or fall away. One image I have used is thinking of myself as going slowly down a ladder into deep water and finally pushing off and trusting to the water to buoy me up. I also think of the passage in Scripture where Jesus tells Peter: "Put out into the deep and let down your nets for a catch" (Lk 5:4). Another involves imagining myself as a heavy object just rounding the crest of a hill — trembling at the brink of the hill and then allowing gravity to take hold of me and slowly gathering momentum as I begin to descend the other side of the hill. Although you may sometimes feel you are at a deeper level of your mind than your ordinary consciousness, your rational mind is not, ordinarily at least, overpowered completely, and you can always recall yourself to a more practical mode of consciousness if the need arises or if something you are experiencing seems suspicious.

If you find that you have fallen into a deep state of meditation so that it feels a little jolting to suddenly open your eyes and get up, take a little more time to come out of your meditation. Keep your eyes closed for a minute or two, beginning to move your body very gradually while breathing slowly and deliberately — first your fingers, then arms, shoulders, head, and then open your eyes slowly.

PRAYER ROUTINE AND THE PRAYERS I USE

Before I start the prayers, I normally read the Scripture readings and prayers for the day which are in the Missal. (The Missal can be obtained from Oregon Catholic Press 1-800-LITURGY or http://www.ocp.org).[31] Also at this time I often bring whatever is most on my mind to the Lord and ask for clarification or help. One of the most valuable prayers in my experience is "show me

---

[31] I recommend these readings because they have been selected for use at worship services, so at least some of them are likely to inspire a prayerful attitude. There is a place for concentrated Bible study, slogging through entire books of the Bible in a systematic way, but before prayer you want readings that will feed into your prayer, and there is a lot in the Bible that wouldn't serve this purpose well.

the truth God even if it hurts." But if you find this a bit frightening, ask God to give you a desire for the truth. Often (although not invariably) in the course of prayer whatever was troubling me comes clear or is resolved. Deep and complicated things will require a more lengthy period of asking daily for clarification or guidance (see the section on guidance in Chapter Four). You might also want to ask the Lord before you start to direct your prayer and make it pleasing to Him.

I always start prayer by making the sign of the cross,[32] done in the style of the Orthodox, with the thumb and first two fingers together and the other two fingers together against the palm. The two fingers stand for the two natures in the person of Christ, while the three fingers stand for the Trinity. As I make the sign of the cross, I say, "Two natures in one person — Jesus Christ true God and true man. Three persons in one God. I pray in the name of the Father, Son and Holy Spirit." It is important to make clear to whom we are directing our prayer.

Opening Prayers

"Oh God, come to my assistance. Lord make haste to help me. Glory be to the Father and to the Son and to the Holy Spirit, as it was in the beginning, is now, and will be forever." (All the monastic hours of prayer begin this way.)

"Almighty God, unto whom all hearts are open, all desires known, and from whom no secrets are hid, cleanse the thoughts of our hearts by the inspiration of Thy Holy Spirit, that we may perfectly love Thee and worthily magnify Thy Holy Name, through Christ our Lord. Amen." (from *Book of Common Prayer*)

During the first part of this I concentrate on letting God search my heart and know me, giving me contrition for my sins, asking Him to make me defenseless before Him. During the

---

[32] This is done by touching first one's forehead, then somewhere in the region of the solar plexus, and then one shoulder after the other. Roman Catholics touch the left shoulder first, while the Eastern Orthodox touch the right one first.

second half, I concentrate on the promise of the gift of the Holy Spirit and try to be receptive.

Holy Spirit Invocation

Oh come Creator, Spirit come, and make within our souls Thy home. Supply Thy grace and heavenly aid to fill the Hearts which Thou hast made.

Oh gift of God most high, Thy name is Comforter whom we acclaim the fount of life and fire of love and sweet anointing from above.

The sevenfold gift of grace is thine, Thou finger of the hand divine. The Father's promise true to teach our earthly tongues Thy heavenly speech.

Thy light to every sense impart, pour forth thy grace in every heart. Our weakened flesh do thou restore to strength and courage evermore.

Oh most blessed light divine, shine within these hearts of thine, and our inmost being fill. Where thou art not man hath nought, nothing good in deed or thought, nothing free from taint of ill.

Heal our wounds, our strength renew, on our dryness pour thy dew; wipe the stains of guilt away.

Bend the stubborn heart and will, melt the frozen, warm the chill, guide the steps that go astray.

On the faithful who adore and confess thee evermore, in thy sevenfold gift descend.

Drive far away our spirit's foe, thine own abiding peace bestow. Where thou dost go before as guide, no evil can our steps betide.

Through thee may we the Father learn, and know the Son and Thee discern, who art of both and thus adore perfectly for evermore. Amen.[33]

---

[33] This version of the Holy Spirit invocation is a combination of verses from two hymns to the Holy Spirit in the *1940 Hymnal* (#108 and 109). I have omitted a few verses so as to avoid overlap and make it flow better. You might want to use some of these verses that I omitted. *Come thou Holy Spirit come; and from Thy celestial home, shed a ray*

Surrender Prayer

"Dear Heavenly Father, please help me now and throughout this day to surrender more to you; to receive you and allow you to dwell more deeply in me than yesterday, and help me to live in you and for you only, Jesus, more today than yesterday."

I started simply with the request that He would help me to surrender more, and the two later phrases are simply ways of spelling out what this means, so you can omit them if you want. I had considered just asking to surrender a *little* more than yesterday, but realized there is no need to limit God. He created us from nothing, and if He chooses to transform us by leaps and bounds we should place no limits on what He may do with, in, or to us. In fact I think a lot of dryness in prayer can be caused by thinking things like "Well, I guess I can't expect Him to always give me the sorts of graces He did yesterday," or "I'm too tired or irritated to pray right today," or "I really shouldn't presume to ask for this or that." We should at least *ask* for His presence, His life in us, and receive it if He gives it. If one does not receive, it should never be for want of asking.

When thinking of surrender, it is important to realize that it is not as though we are all sort of tied up and neatly under our own control so we can magnanimously hand over the keys to the lord of the city. Rather, we are lying in ruins, needing His healing touch in order to even be one integrated person at all. We are not really masters of ourselves, but can only allow Him to work — sort of like going to a chiropractor who adjusts our neck when we are able to let it go limp. God realigns our hearts and wills when we let Him. At the deepest level, our surrender to God is His gift to us, so we should not think of it as something we need to *try* to *do*. Trying gets in the way of letting Him act in us. It is ultimately in surrender that we find true joy.

---

of light divine. Come thou Father of the poor; come thou source of all our store. Come within our bosoms shine. Thou of comforters the best; thou the soul's most welcome guest; sweet refreshment here below. In our labors rest most sweet; grateful coolness in the heat; solace in the midst of woe.

Litany of the Sacred Heart of Jesus

Lord have mercy, Christ have mercy, Lord have mercy.
Christ hear us. Christ graciously hear us.
God the Father of Heaven have mercy on us.
God the Son, redeemer of the world, have mercy on us,
God the Holy Spirit, sanctifier of the faithful, have mercy on us.
Holy Trinity One God, have mercy on us.
Heart of Jesus Son of the eternal Father, have mercy on us.
Heart of Jesus formed by the Holy Spirit in the womb of
*   the virgin mother, have mercy on us.*
Heart of Jesus substantially united to the Word of God,
*   have mercy on us.*
Heart of Jesus of infinite majesty, have mercy on us.
Heart of Jesus sacred temple of God, have mercy on us.
Heart of Jesus tabernacle of the Most High, have mercy on us.
Heart of Jesus house of God and gate of Heaven, have mercy on us.
Heart of Jesus burning furnace of charity, have mercy on us.
Heart of Jesus abode of justice and love, have mercy on us.
Heart of Jesus full of goodness and love, have mercy on us.
Heart of Jesus abyss of all virtues, have mercy on us.
Heart of Jesus most worthy of all praise, have mercy on us.
Heart of Jesus King and center of all hearts, have mercy on us.
Heart of Jesus in whom are all the treasures of wisdom and knowledge,
*   have mercy on us.*
Heart of Jesus in whom dwells all the fullness of divinity,
*   have mercy on us.*
Heart of Jesus in whom the Father is well pleased, have mercy on us.
Heart of Jesus of whose fullness we have all received,
*   have mercy on us.*
Heart of Jesus desire of the everlasting hills, have mercy on us.
Heart of Jesus patient and most merciful, have mercy on us.
Heart of Jesus enriching all who invoke you, have mercy on us.
Heart of Jesus fountain of life and holiness, have mercy on us.
Heart of Jesus propitiation for our sins, have mercy on us.
Heart of Jesus loaded down with opprobrium, have mercy on us.

Heart of Jesus bruised for our offenses, have mercy on us.
Heart of Jesus obedient to death, have mercy on us.
Heart of Jesus pierced with a lance, have mercy on us.
Heart of Jesus source of all consolation, have mercy on us.
Heart of Jesus our life and resurrection, have mercy on us.
Heart of Jesus our peace and reconciliation, have mercy on us.
Heart of Jesus victim for our sins, have mercy on us.
Heart of Jesus salvation of those who hope in you, have mercy on us.
Heart of Jesus hope of those who die in you, have mercy on us.
Heart of Jesus delight of all the saints, have mercy on us.
Lamb of God, you take away the sins of the world, spare us O Lord.
Lamb of God, you take away the sins of the world,
    graciously hear us O Lord.
Lamb of God, you take away the sins of the world, have mercy on us.

Jesus meek and humble of heart, make our hearts like to yours.

Almighty and eternal God, look upon the heart of your most beloved Son and on the praises and satisfaction that He offers you in the name of sinners, and to those who implore your mercy, of your great goodness grant forgiveness. Through the same Christ our Lord. Amen.

A few thoughts on the meaning of the Sacred Heart: American religion tends to be overly emotional, so we think of the heart too much just in terms of feelings. The heart is the center or core of the person and includes far more than feeling or emotion. The heart of Jesus is both divine and human. As human, Jesus is able to connect with us in our humanity, but as divine, He can incorporate us into Himself. In the Catholic Mass there is a prayer about coming to share in His divinity who humbled Himself to share in our humanity. It's like that. I thought once of the Litany as like looking at the heart of Christ from different perspectives — through different lenses or colored glass, but now I see myself more often as enclosed in it, and it (the Sacred Heart) is a vast cathedral with various windows that I can contemplate for as long or as short a time as I feel moved, or like many notes or chords in a piece of music that ultimately are all sounding at once although we can't focus on them all at one time (or even one really fully). It may help to try to visualize Jesus and direct your attention generally toward His heart. We must try to hold Him in our hearts, as He holds us in His.

Some days I will focus on one part of the Litany,[34] and other days other things will strike me. That's why invocation of the Holy Spirit to guide prayer helps. You may feel moved to make up additional verses of your own.[35] In some way His heart becomes planted in ours and beats with ours — His life in us. We are a ground in which new life — that of Christ — takes root. Ultimately the aim is intimacy of heart with Him. Sometimes the juxtaposition of His divinity and His intimacy with us is so intense that it almost breaks us. But if He chooses to give us this gift who are we to refuse it? I think of the passage about how "It is the same God who has said 'Let there be light' who has shone in our hearts to give the knowledge of the glory of God in the face of Christ" (2 Cor 4:6). Or of the seed that falls to the ground and dies and thus bears much fruit. New life swells in us as in the seed. A certain amount of awe and trepidation about approaching Him, and letting Him take the initiative is appropriate. Although we can't reach out and touch Him exactly, He can always reach out and touch us, and knows the way into the deepest part of our hearts. The more we let Him come there the more His feet will wear a path and the easier it will be the next time.

---

[34] If you find that you keep returning to a particular verse, that may indicate something about what God is calling you to.

[35] For example, "Heart of Jesus, my refuge, my treasure, my love."

A FEW USEFUL SHORT PRAYERS YOU MAY WANT TO USE

The prayers above provide an underlying structure for your prayer time. But within that structure there is room to enter into your own personal dialogue with God as the Spirit moves. Obviously no one else can write a script for this. But a few short prayers that I have found helpful are given below. Their purpose is to clear the way for prayer, put us in right relationship to God, and dispose us rightly to receive what God chooses to give us.

"Jesus." Just the name of Jesus repeated slowly with the intention of invoking Him is a very good background prayer to use while using the various images suggested above.

My soul waits for the Lord and in His word I hope, more than the watchman for the dawn; more than the watchman for the dawn.

Come Lord Jesus.

Remove the things that separate me from you.

Direct my prayer Lord.

Open my ears to hear you, my heart to receive you, and my lips to praise you.

Jesus, thank you for your Love. (Useful if you are feeling a bit unsure of His love.)

Jesus, please. (He knows what you want better than you do.)

Lord, conform my heart and mind and will to yours.

Lord, I will be what you will make me.

Sacred Heart of Jesus, I entrust myself to you.

Jesus I love you. (Note that this is not just a report of your feelings. It expresses your intention to love Him. Tell Him you want to love Him, and ask Him to increase your love for Him.)

Jesus I love you; help me!

Jesus, fight for me and deliver me. (For when you feel afraid and powerless and beset by evil things.)

Yes or *I will with the help of Your grace.* (Again, this is open-ended in the sense that you are expressing a willingness to allow His will to guide you.)

I will be yours forever, with the help of your grace (without limit and without end).

I will receive whatever you choose to give me and give you what you ask of me, with the help of your grace.

Make me to be love as you are love.

Make me your own.

Thank you for the gift of faith. Form me more deeply in that faith. (Don't worry if you feel you do not have much faith at this point. The fact that you feel moved to try praying is an indication that you already have at least that tiny mustard seed of faith required.)

Help us, save us, have mercy on us, for you are good and a lover of mankind. (When feeling helpless and desperate.)

Holy God, holy mighty one, holy immortal one, have mercy on us. (When for a moment you catch a glimpse of His glory.) This prayer is usually repeated three times by the Eastern Orthodox and often followed by *Most Holy Trinity have mercy on us; Lord cleanse us of our sins; Master, pardon our transgressions; Holy One visit us and heal our infirmities for your own name's sake.*

Oh God, you are my God for you I long, for you my soul is thirsting. (Ps 63:2).

Cast me not away from Thy presence and take not Thy Holy Spirit from me (Ps 51:13).

In my hands no gifts I bring; simply to Thy cross I cling. (From the hymn "Rock of Ages." Useful when feeling discouraged about one's ability to accomplish anything good.)

Drive out the darkness of my heart and mind. (From the Easter Vigil: "May the light of Christ rising in glory dispel the darkness of our hearts and minds.")

Shine on us who dwell in darkness and in the shadow of death, and guide our feet into the way of peace (Lk 1:79).

Hide me within your wounds and keep me close to you.
Open the path before my feet today, and help me to walk in it.

Don't worry too much about whether these prayers are ones that you wholeheartedly *feel* at the moment. Don't do a given prayer if it goes against the grain *too* much, but remember that prayer is not a report of how you presently feel, but an expression of your desire to become the person God wants you to be. The fact that you have a desire to come into deeper communion with God indicates that God is already at work in you.

In the next chapter, I turn to some of the obstacles you are likely to encounter as you begin to pray in a more sustained and serious way, and make some suggestions for dealing with them.

CHAPTER THREE

SOME PROBLEMS YOU MAY ENCOUNTER ON THE WAY

SCRUPLES, DISCOURAGEMENT, TEMPTATIONS AND DOUBTS

Once you begin to direct your steps toward God in a serious way, you should expect to encounter a variety of obstacles. Jesus counsels His followers that they must not be like the man who starts out to build a tower but is unable to finish; they must consider the cost before beginning to build (Lk 14:28). Likewise, we are advised not to put our hand to the plow and then turn back (Lk 9:62). Why is it that the would-be disciple so quickly encounters resistance? This question can be answered on several levels.

First, there is the simple fact that we are willful, proud, self-indulgent, prone to deceive ourselves, selfish, etc. In a word, we are sinful. Christian life ultimately demands quite opposite characteristics of us: obedience, humility, self-discipline, openness to the truth, and love (charity). It involves a kind of death of the self. St. Paul says, "It is no longer I who live, but Christ who lives in me" (Gal 2:20), and "I die every day" (1 Cor 15:31). Naturally this is something our old self finds very threatening, so the fact that something in us resists God is not surprising.

But in addition to the fact that we are sinful and self-willed,

65

there is also a natural fear of becoming intimate too quickly with another whom we do not yet know very well. A certain caution is appropriate when opening up our deepest heart and soul. It takes time to learn to know and trust God, and God understands this. Reason plays an important role; the image of our mind as a kind of watchdog guarding the house (Chapter Two) is apt here. Given that receptivity and surrender are central to the form of prayer outlined here, it is especially important to keep your head about you. Granted, we know in faith that God will not harm us and that we can trust Him completely, but how are we to know that what we are experiencing is in fact God? During prayer you should not try to analyze and test everything constantly, or you won't be able to let go enough for God to draw you into communion with Him. But if something feels wrong or seems to be suspicious or sinister it is appropriate to step back, tell God that you are seeking Him, and ask Him to protect you from being deceived. And in between prayer times certain trends gradually become apparent. Making the appropriate discernment will be discussed below in the sections on discouragement and doubt and in the section on guidance in Chapter Four.

Yet another level of explanation involves the action of negative spirits who seek our destruction and want to keep us from God. People often get overly sensationalistic about this topic. Many people are quite skeptical about regarding evil as personal in this way. But the belief that angels and fallen angels (demons) exist has been pretty standard among Christians throughout history, although the nature and extent of their involvement in the evil we find around us in the world is disputed. (If you don't believe in them, don't just stop reading at this point, since a lot of what I say can be translated into purely psychological terms.) I don't intend in any case to say a lot about them because excessive focus on demons can have very bad effects. For one thing it can draw them to us; we tend to draw to ourselves the things we focus on. And we can become paralyzed by fear or entangled by the "glamour of evil," or get puffed up with spiritual pride and indulge in self-dramatizing fantasies of ourselves heroically combating the forces of evil. We should, instead, humbly ask Jesus to fight them for us and go on in the Way. Still, it helps to be aware of the existence of negative spirits. Otherwise you are likely to suppose that everything that goes on in you *is* yourself. If some horrible temptation presents itself or a fierce rebelliousness sweeps through us, we may take that to be our real self, relegating our better impulses to a kind of false self — a sort of self-deception or desire to impress others. The fact is that we have both good and evil impulses. God's grace poured out through the action of the Holy Spirit in us breathes life into the good ones, while demons seek to inflame and agitate the evil ones. Just as God's grace perfects our nature, so demons also work on what is already there to try to cause us to fall away from God.

Finally, given what God offers us in Christ, it is not surprising that the path should be beset with challenges and trials. Perfect charity and being drawn gradually into ever deepening communion with God, although they are gifts, come with a certain cost (which does not mean that anything we can possibly give *merits* what we receive). It is like the man who found the pearl of great price buried in the field, and went and sold all he had to purchase that field (Mt 13:46). High and great things are not attained without sacrifice and struggle. It is not as though God is up there saying, "Now you must pay for what I am giving you." That would be the wrong way to think about it. Rather it is the nature of what we seek that requires our purification, and our purification can only be effected by following Jesus faithfully through trials. Probably none of us quite realizes what we've taken on when we start, but the same is true of any serious commitment. Would any of us enter into a marriage, for example, or have a baby, if we could see in advance all that these commitments will require of us? Jesus asks His disciples, "Are you able to drink the cup that I shall drink and be baptized with the baptism with which I will be baptized?" (Mk 10:38). They say yes, but the full meaning of this emerges only through time.

It is probably impossible most of the time, when feeling beset and confused, to determine what is coming from our own mind or our imaginations, what is rooted in our will, and what may be in part the action of negative spirits on us. A man I know used to find that every time he sat down to pray, all of a sudden he would find himself beset by all sorts of dark and spooky images that seemed to come out of nowhere and made him so uncomfortable he would often get deflected from prayer. Sometimes even things outside ourselves seem to arise and try to prevent us from taking some important step in our Christian life. A priest once told me that on those Sunday mornings when his family had resolved to go early to Mass so as to be able to go to confession, the cows would disappear and refuse to be rounded up to be milked. And I find I often fall into quarrels with my husband just before church. The best time for the Devil to stamp out a good impulse in us, of course, is when it is just beginning to take shape, and after you begin to recognize the pattern you can see what is happening and push ahead anyway, knowing that something good must be just around the corner, or you wouldn't be encountering so much resistance.

I will divide the obstacles to prayer into four categories: (1) scruples, or worries about whether you are doing it right; (2) discouragement over whether prayer seems to be "working" — perhaps you don't think you are experiencing what you should be or making sufficiently rapid progress in overcoming your weaknesses and sins; (3) temptations of various sorts; and (4) doubts of a broader sort about whether perhaps the whole thing is some sort of wishful thinking or self-delusion, or perhaps the result of some sort of negative spiritual being acting on you. Such distinctions are to some degree artificial. Direct encounters with demons are, I think, fairly rare, but in a wide sense, all that draws us away from God can be seen as the work of the Evil One.

The discussion in this chapter presupposes that you are making at least some attempt to pray on a regular basis. Prayer is essentially a practice, and not just something to be studied.

Some of what I say here may be of interest to those who are watching from the sidelines (as it were), especially the section on temptations. But I strongly recommend that you sit down and make an attempt to pray before reading this chapter — preferably using at least some of the prayers given in Chapter Two. This is because many of the issues discussed below pertain either to questions about whether you are doing it right, or about the difficult and thorny problem of integrating your experience in prayer into your broader conceptual framework — in a word, with how to *understand* what is going on. And if you have not yet had some experience of prayer, you may have the conceptual framework, but lack the sort of lived first person perspective to integrate with it.

SCRUPLES

People with high spiritual aspirations tend to be especially vulnerable to excessive scrupulosity and to worry constantly about whether they are doing things right; they constantly pick at themselves and find fault with themselves. Scruples take an endless variety of forms, but the common underlying principle is that your prayer won't work or won't be heard by God because somehow you aren't doing it right, or don't have the right motivation. And the answer to such anxieties, at the most general level, is that of course we are imperfect and our motives are mixed; that is why we need God's help. I've listed a few common worries people may have, but the list is not exhaustive.

I'm not concentrating properly. My mind is wandering.

Am I concentrating carefully enough on what I am saying? I've gotten off onto distractions too much, so I'm not really praying. The cure for distractions is a very simple one. As soon as you are aware that you are off on an unproductive distraction, simply bring your mind back to the prayers. Do *not* allow yourself to get upset or mad at yourself for your poor concentration. You don't have to start all the way back at the beginning; this quickly leads into a sort of magical way of thinking about prayer — I *have* to say all the words in order with concentration, etc. This is a recipe for disaster. Start from roughly where you were when your attention wandered if you can remember. If you can't remember just start anywhere. Since prayer is more something that God does in you than something you do, simply saying the words is an expression of your intention to pray and your openness to God's action in you. Asking God to free you from distractions can help. If something really important that you need to do that day crosses your mind and you are afraid of forgetting it, write it quickly on your writing pad and return to prayer.

Do I really mean what I am saying?

A related scruple is the worry about whether or not I really *mean* what I am saying. This could just be a worry about whether I am doing it correctly, but it starts to go deeper and turn into a worry about whether I have the correct motivations. What *is* it to "mean what I am saying"? It is easier to say what it is not than to say what it is. Meaning what you are saying is *not* a matter of having certain feelings while you speak, so do not constantly monitor your feelings or try to summon up the right sort of feelings. A prayer is not just a report of what you now feel or of your current desires.

A distinction must be drawn between "first order desires" and "second order desires." I may currently desire to hit somebody or say something horribly wounding to him or her (first order desire), but I can step back from myself and realize that I really do not want to be the sort of person who has such desires, but instead to be a patient person who maintains a steady charitable attitude towards others. The desire to be this better sort of person, then, is a second order desire — a kind of considered and deliberate desire. This type of desire is the one that is most important for prayer. God's grace can, over time, bridge the gap between our current disordered desires and our second order desires. It is enough that we *want* to want to be good and to draw closer to God. So we should pray that God will put His desires in our hearts — that He will redirect the compass needle of our souls toward the true North — toward Himself. St. Augustine said that virtue is rightly ordered love. And allowing God to transform our hearts and reorder our desires properly is one of the main goals of the form of prayer outlined here. So don't despair if you find that your desires are chaotic and not always perfectly holy. Welcome to the human race. In the *long* run, of course, we may hope that our spontaneous feelings and desires will come more into line with what we would like them to be, but these deep sorts of transformations only occur through the action of the Holy Spirit in us, and ordinarily require considerable time to be effected.

Second order desires have to do with our character ideal — with our choice of the sort of person we want to become — and thus involve desires to nurture and encourage certain first order desires, and to allow others to atrophy. Not all second order desires are good ones, however. A person who wants to become a terrorist, for example, will try to stifle his spontaneous feelings of human sympathy. I assume, for the purposes of this book, that you have a desire to be a good person, and understand what this means in roughly Christian terms, aspiring to what St. Paul calls the fruits of the Spirit — namely love, joy, peace, patience, kindness, goodness, faithfulness, gentleness, and self-control (Gal 5:22-23).

What if I fall asleep while I am praying?

This isn't always a bad thing. As the Psalmist says, "He gives to his beloved in sleep" (Ps 127:2). Just as a doctor puts a patient out in order to perform certain procedures or surgeries,

God may be able to do various kinds of deep work in us better if we let ourselves slip into a light doze, or perhaps even a deeper sort of resting in Him. (Some such thing may well be occurring when people are "slain in the spirit.") This is especially true if you are very exhausted and frazzled. Some saints have fallen into deep states of ecstasy in which they are unresponsive to sensory stimuli. Indeed, such phenomena were once viewed as not particularly abnormal. If you emerge from the state in question feeling refreshed and clear, then there is nothing to worry about. If, however, you feel heavy, muddy minded and generally confused, then you are probably just trying to run on too little sleep. Getting adequate sleep (and I mean something in the general vicinity of eight hours) is very, very important for our mental and physical health. Even strong and stable people will crack when subjected to severe sleep deprivation. Christians are in it for the long haul, and given that we are likely to be under spiritual assault when seriously trying to do God's work, we need to avoid things that needlessly weaken us and make us more vulnerable.

I ought to be able to handle things more myself and not bother God.

The idea that God is too busy to pay attention to our trivial concerns stems at least in part from being too anthropomorphic about God. Yes, it would be a burden to a human being to attend to all the minute details of your life (let alone those of all the other people in the world), but God is not limited in the ways we are. Our coming to God for help does not "bother" God. Our material needs should be brought to Him as well as our spiritual needs. Religious people often feel it is somehow unspiritual to pray for help with worldly problems. As a result we often find ourselves constantly blocked, frustrated, entangled and exhausted trying to get some sort of control over them. But if we turn them over to God and ask Him to smooth the way, they often become easier to handle; things fall into place.

This said, however, it is possible to get too obsessive about bringing every detail to God and asking the Holy Spirit which way to turn at every street corner. Getting the balance right on this takes time (see the section on guidance in Chapter Four). Pray for openness to the guidance of the Spirit, and try to respond to it. Generally speaking if you have to agonize back and forth — is it the guidance of the Holy Spirit or isn't it — then it probably is not. Nothing is too small to bring to God in prayer and He wants us to learn to depend on Him. But whether and when God chooses to give us some sort of direct guidance is up to Him. We can ask, but He is under no compulsion to give us instant answers. As the Rolling Stones put it: "you can't always get what you want; ... you just might find you get what you need." God is training us to be responsive to His guidance, but He may do this in different ways at different stages in our Christian life. And He may also lead different people in different ways.

Am I not being kind of selfish, just coming to God and wanting Him to give me comfort and help all the time?

You should not expect to have completely pure and selfless motivations. This side of Heaven our motives are always mixed, and we should leave it to God who sees the heart to make judgments about them. The very idea of having wholly selfless motives in approaching God is rather ridiculous when you think of it. We are small, frail, and desperately in need of God's love, mercy, healing, protection, and comfort. To put ourselves on an equal plane with Him and worry about whether we are perhaps being selfish in wanting this from Him is to misconceive the nature of the relationship. Do we expect an infant's love for his or her mother to be wholly unselfish? At the same time, however, we ought to want to please God and not just drink in all He nourishes us with and then go our own selfish way all day. So in that sense one's motives can be overly selfish. As our Christian life becomes more mature, our love of God should incline us to want to give back to Him.

There are, of course, certain motives you should *not* have while praying, such as a desire to manipulate God; this is both selfish and inappropriate to the nature of God and our situation in relation to Him.

DISCOURAGEMENT

I don't feel anything happening.

Jesus says, "Seek and you shall find, knock and the door will be opened, ask and you shall receive" (Mt 7:7; Lk 11:9), so you can pray with confidence that you will receive and find what you are seeking. But since God is free to act as He chooses with each individual person, it is hard to make generalizations about what sort of feelings or experiences you should expect and when. Comparing yourself with others is always a bad idea. And in any case, excessive focus on yourself and what you are or are not feeling deflects your attention from God and thus short circuits the process of prayer. Spiritual writers generally discourage people from being overly attached to what they call "consolations" — by which I think they mean feelings of sweetness, delight, joy, heightened life, peace, etc. I'm not at all sure that it is wrong to desire these so long as you do not desire only the feeling itself but rather the sort of closeness to God or apprehension of His glory, beauty and love that evoke such feelings. But don't try to psyche yourself up to feel some particular sort of consolation. And don't take the presence or absence of such feelings as a measure of whether your prayer has been successful, or regard prayer as merely a means to the end of feeling consolation.

Given the picture of the self discussed in Chapter Two, you need to keep in mind that there are many levels on which God can act in us, and the act of praying (especially using prayers that focus on receptivity and surrender) invites Him to do so. You can't expect Him to always act in ways that you can feel and understand. Trust that He is working. Like the seed that germinates deep in the earth, the new life that we receive through Christ can be at work within us long before we become consciously aware of it. Jesus says: "The Kingdom of God is as if a man should scatter seed upon the ground, and should sleep and rise night and day, and the seed should sprout and grow, he knows not how" (Mk 4:26-27). So although you may sometimes feel like the cold, sodden, bare ground in March, realize that this is only one stage of the process and wait patiently for the new living green shoots to begin to appear. Gradually you should begin to have a sense of God's presence when you pray, although often it is very subtle — perhaps simply the sense that you are not alone, a moment of inner stillness and peace, or a heightened feeling of life. For a while the experience of God's presence is likely to be intermittent, but over time it will hopefully become steadier and more constant. But I think everyone has bad days — days when their minds or emotions are too agitated to allow them to relax and let God in. Sometimes it may take a number of prayer sessions to work through things. Ask Him to direct your prayer and He will.

If you are in a particularly painful and difficult situation, bring the whole thing to God in prayer, and then try to let go of it and let Him shed His light into your heart and mind and rearrange the pieces so that you begin to understand what is going on and how the Lord wants you to deal with it. Trust and let go of your own preconceptions.

Sometimes I feel more upset after prayer than before it.

If you are the sort of person who defers emotion and represses your feelings, then when you relax in prayer some of these painful feelings may come to the surface. However, if you *often* find yourself feeling more conflicted and agitated after prayer than before, then you probably are not praying long enough or properly letting go of your problems. There was a period of years when I prayed 1-1/2 hours a day (now it is closer to 1 hour); in my experience it sometimes takes a long while to work through painful emotional problems. But you should persist in prayer until you feel at least *some* sense of increased clarity and peace. Painful feelings may not go away, but by the end of your prayer session you should feel that you are no longer completely in their grip. Formulate your problems and needs in a prayer, and then visualize yourself lifting them up to God and letting them go (if you are a visual type of person, you could imagine them going up to God like when you let a balloon go and it goes up out of sight). St. Thérèse of Lisieux sometimes thought of herself as like a child bringing a broken toy to her father. We give Him the broken pieces of our lives and gradually He returns us to ourselves whole. So hang on and plead with Him to help you, and continue praying until He does. Remember the parable of the widow who kept pestering the unjust judge (Lk 18:1-8), or the Canaanite woman whose daughter was possessed by a demon who did not let Jesus put her off but kept pressing Him to help and was rewarded for her persistence (Mt 15:21-28; Mk 7:25-30).

Prayer doesn't seem to be working; I keep messing things up.

Our habitual patterns of thought and feeling have developed over a number of years and it is not to be expected that they will disappear overnight. In fact, I have found that sometimes bad patterns seem to get worse rather than better at first. This may be a result of the fact that God's light shows up our own sinfulness more clearly than when we were turned away from Him. But also I think that the healing of deep wounds in our hearts and souls happens in the same way as the healing of a deep wound in our body. Wounds heal from the bottom up, so that although they may still look very nasty on the surface, the healthy tissue is gradually building in underneath the surface. Sometimes it almost seems that God's action *draws* the poisons to the surface in order to speed the healing — to enable us to look at the bad patterns and then let go of them.

One important thing to keep in mind when you feel frustrated with your slow progress is that *God* is the judge — not you. He sees what we do not see, and knows what He is doing in us better than we do. It may seem a sign of holiness to be hard on ourselves, but it is not. Not that we should be exactly easy on ourselves either. Rather we should refrain from passing judgment on ourselves and just keep bringing all our weaknesses and failings back to Him for help. Life is long (although we never know *how* long ours will be of course), and we must keep aiming at the ultimate goal steadily — at final perseverance and eternal life with God. As St. Paul says, "Do not pass judgment before the time" (1 Cor 4:5). We should be glad God gives us so much time, but also be careful not to waste any of it. Just keep putting one foot in front of the other and getting up when you fall and going on, as you would if climbing a high mountain. It would be easy to get discouraged if you looked at the towering height of the mountain still to be climbed, but if you concentrate on simply making one step after another, you will make progress. Realize that it all hangs on God's grace and keep stepping out, relying on that grace and keeping your eyes fixed on Jesus.

God must be really fed up with me because I keep sinning.

That we continue to fall into sins can be distressing, and sometimes we can feel that God must be totally fed up with us by now. It helps to reflect on the fact that, for all your sins up to the present moment, God has not ditched you yet. And there are comforting passages in Scripture such as the one about how "while we were yet sinners, Christ died for us" (Rm 5:8), and that "God seeks not the death of the sinner, but rather that he should turn from his wickedness and live" (Ezk 18:23). We ought, however, to be grieved at our sins and return to Him when we realize we are off the track before the wrong turn really gathers momentum. God pours out His graces in various ways in our lives. But ultimately He does want us to try to please Him and bear fruit for Him; we should not receive His grace in vain. If we do not try to please Him at least sometimes, then we are being too slack with ourselves.

Sometimes a self-imposed penance can be helpful.[36] You might give up some pleasure you enjoy for a week or a month. Or you might do some small good deed that you would not otherwise do, or perform an unpleasant duty that you would do anyway but in a resentful spirit (say, visiting a disagreeable shut-in relative) and do it without complaining as a kind of sacrifice you make for the love of God. It may sound odd to speak of refraining from complaining as a sacrifice, but it does involve denying ourselves the pleasure of indulging our resentments and venting our bad moods on others.

Are there any signs that might indicate I'm on the right track?

First, the very fact that you are persevering in prayer, and that you feel a desire or longing for God, is itself an indication that God is at work in you. Since God does not necessarily operate in the same way in everyone, it is a bit harder to say what sorts of experiences you should expect. But some good signs would be: a sense of being held by God and stilled (so your mind stops racing and you just rest in God); feelings of peace or joy; a spontaneous desire to praise God (try raising your hands slightly with your palms upward when this happens); feeling as though a kind of inner space is opening up in you (like a flower that turns toward the light and opens its petals); feeling filled and satisfied like an empty glass suddenly being filled with water (the Psalmist says, "My soul shall be filled as with a banquet," Ps 63:6); experiencing a kind of warm, golden light (this is usually subtle, but you may start to notice it at times when you are really rest-

---

[36] A penance is an expression of sorrow for sin and gratitude for the Lord's forgiveness. It is *not* a condition for our being forgiven. God forgives us freely. The penance is thus a symbolic expression of our sorrow for our sin, and there is no need to undertake extraordinarily severe penances as though this would pay a debt you owe God, and you should not do so without the approval of a spiritual director.

ing in God); your breathing changing (becoming slightly quicker and lighter or perhaps slowing down and almost stopping); a trembling feeling experienced deep within you, and perhaps slightly in your hands also; a sudden clarity that enables you to see yourself and your situation in a deeper and more honest way; or intense feelings of love. God's love flows particularly strongly through the Sacred Heart of Jesus. I puzzled for a long time over whether the love I sometimes experienced in prayer was God's love for me or my love for Him. The truth is that it is both. God puts His love in us so that it becomes our love also and in this love we are united with Him. An increased longing for God and desire to love Him more are also good signs.

Why am I not feeling the wonderful consolations I used to experience?

It is very easy to feel we must be doing something badly wrong if we have had wonderful deep experiences of the Lord's presence and action in us and these gradually happen less and less frequently. This may be just a function of the fact that there is a certain ebb and flow to spiritual life, and you may experience these again. Then again, you may not. But this does not necessarily mean you are doing something wrong. At least one reason for this sort of ebb and flow pattern is because we tend to feel a change more strongly than a steady state. When you are undergoing a major transition in your spiritual life where the Spirit is moving deeply in you, you may feel this strongly, but when God's Spirit has kind of settled in and made His home in you this can become something habitual so that you don't notice it in the same way; it has become part of the inner climate or landscape of your soul. We get all excited when the Lord speaks to us, but He is here all the time. When you come to realize this you may begin again to experience joy in His presence, as Brother Lawrence did.

Also, the Holy Spirit is sometimes poured out on us at a

particular time for the sake of some particular mission or task we are to accomplish, or perhaps just to help us meet some challenge or crisis that, unbeknownst to us, we will encounter that day. A spring is refreshed by an influx of new water when it is emptied. Likewise, when we are called to give to others in some special way, the love of God may begin to flow through our hearts to meet their needs. Ultimately, of course, God alone knows what is going on in your particular case, so ask Him to help you understand what is happening and what He wants from you.[37]

TEMPTATIONS

The Big One

The worst and most powerful temptation is simply the desire to have one's own will and not serve, obey or submit to God. The Devil's motto is *"Non serviam"* (I will not serve). This desire can sweep through you powerfully and feel as though part of you is in rebellion against God almost in spite of yourself — a kind of inner runaway horse. I think that this sort of temptation occurs precisely at those times when God is calling you into a deeper relationship with Him, so you must take advantage of such moments to return to Him, to say "yes" and move forward to a new level of life in Him.

These sorts of major turning points in one's life do not come that often, but sooner or later you will face this one, and possibly more than once. If you have already spent some part of your life living according to your own will and making a mess of things, it is helpful to remind yourself of this fact when you feel the temptation arising to do it again. One thing you can do is

---

[37] Many saints have experienced long periods of dryness or even desolation, as, for example, Mother Teresa did. And God may not disclose to you why you are going through what you are going through. We walk by faith and not by sight, so sometimes all we can do is to soldier on day by day, asking God to guide us. He leads people by different paths; what is important is surrender to Him.

say, "I will not rebel; I will not turn back." As Isaiah said, "I was not rebellious, I turned not backwards" (Is 50:5). Once I prayed, "All things come from God; all obedience is due to God; I am God's." And the temptation subsided. Confessing one's complete powerlessness to resist temptation and begging Jesus to fight for you is always a good idea. Pray, "Lord, don't let me fall."

I also find it helps to think of how very much it pleases God when we turn back to Him in spite of such temptations (Jesus says there is rejoicing among the angels over one sinner who repents). In the Psalms, God advises us "be not like horse and mule, unintelligent, needing bridle and bit, else they will not return to you" (Ps 32:9). So think of yourself as freely choosing to be docile and stay close to Him. Israel is often compared to the unfaithful bride whose love goes away early like the dew (Ho 6:4), and God expresses a kind of sorrow and regret over the cooling of her love and a longing to enter again into a relationship of love and friendship with her. So, once more, think of yourself as trying to be the faithful bride.

It is also helpful to keep in mind that the force and energy of the inner rebellion is not coming from yourself alone, but from the Devil also. There is, of course, a part of you that resists or stands against God. That is true of everyone. But what the Devil does is to go in and stir that up, magnify it, inflame it and try to persuade you that you are already lost, that this revolt is that of your true self, and that your desire to love and serve God is just a kind of shackle on the expression of your true self, perhaps put on you by others. The basic demonic strategy (which takes many forms) is to persuade you that he has already won and that you are lost. But this is a lie. You are always free to call upon God. Christ died on the cross and rose again in order to free us from the power of Satan, and only He can do this. Knowing it does not depend on me alone is comforting, I find.

In a more philosophical vein, it must be admitted that just what one's "true self" *is* is a thorny question. Jean-Paul Sartre believed that there is no such thing — that we are simply what we choose to be, and that we can at any moment choose differently. The self is a kind of "hole in being," freedom is inescapable, and to try to lay claim to a stable self is "bad faith." There is a certain truth to this, but Sartre was an atheist, and the truth in it looks very different from within a Christian world-view. In a godless universe, the inescapability of our freedom does place upon us the constant burden of choosing ourselves, our darker and more twisty desires are no less part of ourselves than our nobler ones, and there is no standard by which our choices may be evaluated as better or worse. Christians likewise acknowledge that we have freedom. We must keep choosing daily to continue to go forward in our walk with God. If you try to stop and rest on your laurels, you begin to slip backwards. There is, however, a source of value and truth other than our own arbitrary choice — namely God. Although we do not possess the "God's eye" perspective in anything like its entirety, Scripture, Christian tradition, and our own prayer life (and rational reflection, of course, as well) give us sufficient guidance to enable us to know which of the desires and tendencies we find within ourselves we should encourage and nurture and which ones we should allow to atrophy. On the basis of this knowledge, we can form stable second order desires to guide our choices from day to day. If there is such a thing as our "true self" in a more comprehensive and metaphysical sense, it is known only to God, and we should leave judgment to Him.

The temptation to turn toward your own will does not always take the form of a sudden powerful rebellious impulse. It may set in more gradually, causing us to wall God off more and more, but there is always a point at which we make a choice. I am not talking here about simple things like my desire to follow my own will in some particular thing, which I suspect we all have (*maybe* there are saints who never have such desires, but I am not in a position to know whether there are), but rather about a kind of choice of one's life direction. I don't know how many chances God gives us, though I do know He gives us more than one. But there is a certain sort of inertia that sets in as we settle into a pattern in our relationship with God, and it becomes harder to reverse direction the further we go down the road. (This is why it is unwise to decide to live a life of sin and count on a death-bed conversion — which is not to say that deathbed conversions are impossible, but just that it is unwise to risk our soul in this way.)

How do you know when you are beginning to drift into walling God off? I think that if you are honest with yourself you will know. One indication is beginning to feel a sudden distaste for prayer when you had previously been finding it satisfying and healing. Several times I have felt an aversion to prayer or a kind of shying away from my icons and pictures of Jesus, like pushing Him away. Again, this is the time you need to move forward into a deeper relationship with God. Saying, "I *will* love you, I *will* serve you, I *will* follow you, with the help of your grace" helps break through the barrier. Keep firmly in mind the fact that happiness cannot be found apart from God.

Spiritual waffling is dangerous because the stakes are high. St. James says a double minded man will receive nothing from the Lord (Jm 1:8), and Jesus frequently cautions people against turning back. Once you have made a choice for Jesus you must continue to cling to and follow your guide. There is no alternative. Jesus tells the story of how a demon had been driven out of a man, but finding the place swept and garnished, the evil spirit returned bringing seven spirits more evil than himself, and "the last state of the man was worse than the first" (Mt 12:45; Lk 11:26). If you do not put something positive in the place of the evil Jesus freed you from, something worse may befall you, as he said to the healed paralytic, "Sin no more lest something worse befall you" (Jn 5:14). I don't say these things in order to frighten you, and God does welcome our return to Him after we have drifted away from Him, so don't ever feel it is too late to return. But you need to realize that this stuff is for real, and is not just something you engage in lightly to make yourself feel better and can discard when you feel like it with no bad consequences.

If you sometimes feel that you heart is starting to turn away from God almost against your will, don't despair. Jeremiah says, "The heart is deceitful above all things, and desperately corrupt; who can understand it?" (Jr 17:9). Willfulness, selfishness and sin pervade us in deep ways, and when we begin to fully realize this, we can feel frightened and driven to despair. The Psalmist says, "My iniquities have overtaken me til I cannot see; they are more than the hairs of my head; my heart fails me" (Ps 40:12). But however wide and deep the corruption of our hearts, God's mercy extends just as widely. Only God knows our hearts in all their mysterious depths and only He can heal them. In our powerlessness we can only beg Him to put a new and right spirit within us (Ps 51:12) so that, by His grace, we can remain faithful. This, however, does not mean that we should not ask our friends to pray for us when we are undergoing temptations, for He can help us through them (see the section on intercession in Chapter Four).

The "Glamour of Evil"

Not only are we beset by the temptation to prefer our own will to everything else ("I did it *my* way" could perhaps be the inscription over the gate of Hell), but evil may also exert a positive fascination on us. The prayers traditionally used at Christian baptisms ask the person about to be baptized (or the infant's parents and sponsors) to reject not only "Satan and all his empty promises" but also to "reject the glamour of evil and refuse to be mastered by it." On the face of it there is something odd about the idea of evil being glamorous. There is, I think, always a kind of surd, incomprehensible dimension to evil; it seems irrational to choose it. The Irish have an expression, "as ugly as sin." Yet it does seem that evil can present itself in ways that make it alluring.

Being deeply evil is sometimes thought to confer "spooky powers." Hitler apparently exerted a mysterious pull on people for this sort of reason (he did, in fact, dabble in the occult). Feminist theologian Mary Daly, a self-identified witch, says she took up lesbianism (a sin against the "Godfather" — in other words the internalized or cosmic representative of what radical feminists call "heteropatriarchy") in order to acquire occult spiritual powers.[38] The "black riders" in Tolkien's *Lord of the Rings* seem to exude a mysterious and fascinating power — noble, kingly, terrifying, and evil — able to strike people's hearts with horror and despair. Some find this sort of power alluring; Frodo, himself, at one point feels this pull very strongly, desiring to rush toward them and immolate himself. (This impulse, itself, is perhaps a warped form of a deep-seated and healthy desire to give ourselves freely and completely — a desire that should, of course, be directed first toward God.) The desire for spooky power is connected with, but not the same as, a second way in which evil presents itself as attractive — namely by promising us some sort of higher and secret knowledge (*gnosis*). Adam and Eve fell for this type of lure. "Your eyes will be opened, and you will be like God, knowing good and evil." And Eve says that the tree "was to be desired to make one wise" (Gn 3:5-6).

Another variant of the "secret knowledge" temptation presents it not as an insight into higher things, but as a vision into the depths — into the squirmy horrors lurking beneath the surface of human life. Experiencing something of these depths, it is suggested, will help you feel solidarity and empathy with other human beings — to get down off your moral high horse and join the human race. Purity is presented as something cold, aloof — even, perhaps, proud and self-righteous. Transgression, it is suggested, will give you a deeper insight into human beings, a sort of fellow feeling that will make you more human or loving toward others than if you hold yourself aloof from sin. (This sort

---

[38] Mary Daly, *Outercourse* (HarperSanFrancisco, 1992), pp. 43-44. The heteropatriarchy consists in the sum of all those forces, apparently natural but in the view of radical feminists socially constructed, that sustain male dominance over women. In the version of radical feminism adopted by Daly, these include heterosexuality itself, even as an option among others.

of "sin mysticism" is most frequently applied to sexual sins.[39]) There are, of course, virtuous people who are self-righteous, but the twisted envy that lies behind the glamour of evil is particularly close to the surface here. For example, Iago, in *Othello*, sets out to destroy Cassio because "he hath a daily beauty in his life that makes me ugly."[40]

The Devil, of course, is the "father of lies" (Jn 8:44), so these temptations involve a mixture of lies and half-truths. To understand what is going on, you need to realize, first of all, that the motive that drives all these temptations is the Devil's bitter envy of human beings: "Through the Devil's envy death entered the world" (Ws 2:24). He knows he is going to Hell, and wants to take as many people down with him as he can. Envy is not a desire to possess what the other has, but rather a desire to deprive the other of it out of malice and hatred, even if you get nothing out of doing so. And what happens if we fall for the glamour of evil, desiring to be something greater than what we are, is that we throw away the real good that is ours — our peace, our purity of heart, our friendship with God — for an illusory one. And that, of course, is just what the Devil wants.

That people who give themselves over to evil to obtain spooky power have sometimes been able to exert power over others (whether through the assistance of a negative spirit or only through some ill-understood power of the human mind) seems to be true, but the further they go down this road, the more they fall under the domination of their lust for power, or the demon involved (if you prefer the supernatural explanation), so they end up enslaved rather than powerful. And the knowledge obtained turns out to be one we wish we did not have. Yes, perhaps we know something we did not know before. The transgression

---

[39] See, for example, *The Heart of the Matter*, or *The End of The Affair* by Graham Greene.

[40] Act 5, scene 1. In a similar vein, the ungodly as portrayed in the second chapter of the Book of Wisdom, see the righteous man as a reproof to their thoughts and find the very sight of him a burden because he holds aloof from their ways and regards them as unclean. They therefore decide to torture and kill him (Ws 2:12).

changes who we are and our relationship with God, so it does yield a new insight — insight into our new situation. But since the change was not a change for the better, this knowledge is not a good to be desired. God can, and does, bring good out of evil, but to deliberately do evil to get God to bring good out of it is tempting God — like throwing yourself off the temple (Mt 4:6; Lk 4:10). Besides, if you already realize that you need greater humility and appreciation of your need for grace, you don't need to sin to learn the lesson.

The Particular, Everyday Ones

Although not so cosmic in nature, the daily nitty, gritty temptations can be extremely strong and persistent. And they are never ending. Christian life involves constant struggle, like walking against a strong headwind, and as soon as you kick back a little or stop going forward, you immediately begin to slip back. At first the temptations are likely to involve powerful raw passions that are unruly and hard to tame — usually things like sex, addictions, greed or the lust for power. They get gradually more subtle but no less powerful and treacherous for all that.

In a practical vein, there are a few things to do when in the grip of temptation. The most obvious bit of advice, is: For Heaven's sake don't dwell on it in your mind or fantasize about it. Kierkegaard, in his analysis of original sin, describes the process of falling into sin as like gazing down into the abyss and being seized with a sort of vertigo that takes hold of you, draws you down, and causes you to fall down into it. The more you keep the object of your desire before your mind, the stronger the desire becomes, which is of course why saints advise us to keep God before our minds as much as possible.

Reason can also help. Reflect about what things would be like and how you would feel *after* you acted on the temptation. This puts it in perspective and it often becomes obvious that the short term pleasure or thrill you would experience if you succumbed to the temptation would be a drop in the bucket when compared with the disastrous (or at least potentially disastrous) consequences. Even apart from the way our evil actions might impact the lives of those we love, acting on bad desires strengthens the hold they have on us, and draws us into a never-ending and increasingly desperate pursuit of a satisfaction that, like a mirage, keeps receding as we approach it. Only God can satisfy the seemingly insatiable thirst of the human heart. It is perfectly alright to have desires for various things besides God. That is normal. But we can have no true good or happiness *apart from* God. So long as we are in right relationship with God we can desire and enjoy earthly things, but we should not act on desires the satisfaction of which would lead us away from God, or allow ourselves to get obsessed by them and seek in other things the wholeness and joy that can only be found in God.

Prayer, of course, is indispensable. You should confess your powerlessness and ask Jesus to fight for you. Also ask other people to pray for you. Hopefully you will have some Christian friends who do intercessory prayer. Or you might attend a prayer group of some kind if you find that it gives you the support you need, but be sure to keep up private prayer also. Otherwise you might fall into thinking that your access to God must be mediated through other people. This isn't true. He is already closer to you than you are to yourself and eager to enter into a deeper relationship with you. You need only turn to Him and make time for Him. In selecting a prayer group beware of ones that are excessively emotional in tone, or that are too dominated by one leader in ways that make you feel uncomfortable. You can always go to a Catholic church and give the priest a small donation and ask him to offer a Mass for you.[41] That is, I think, the strongest

---

[41] It has long been a practice for the faithful to bring offerings to the Mass, originally to provide for the living expenses of the priest. They may, singly or as a group, request that the Mass be offered especially for some intention. The Church holds that there is some spiritual benefit for the Mass offering intention, but there is no firm doctrine on how the fruits of the Mass are applied or received, and theologians hold differing opinions on this.

and most effective prayer. If there is a monastery near you they usually have a little box in their chapel for prayer requests and donations, and some of them will also take prayer requests by phone or e-mail.[42] Praying the rosary or the *Memorare* (see Appendix) and asking Mary to intercede for you is also helpful if you feel comfortable with these devotions.

A charismatic friend of mine gave me a "demon binding" prayer that I sometimes use when I feel particularly badly beset: "I take authority in the name of Jesus Christ over all the demons who are trying to destroy me, and I bind you in the blood of Christ that you may work no further harm against me, in the name of the Father and the Son and the Holy Spirit." I often find this really helps. Whether the effect is purely psychological or whether I am actually undergoing demonic assault I'm not sure. That there are demons and that they sometimes act on us I have no doubt, but I am a bit leery of lapsing into the sort of sensationalistic way of thinking that is constantly finding demons lurking under every bush. Still, if you find the prayer helps, use it.

DOUBTS

Doubts, of course, take many forms. I focus here on doubts about how to understand and interpret what you are experiencing in prayer, and not on doubts about basic Christian doctrines, although the two are not wholly independent of each other. For prayer, Scripture reading, and the study of Christian doctrine are important ways in which Christian faith (and with it a distinctively Christian framework, or way of viewing the world)

---

[42] For example, The Carmelite Sisters of St. Joseph in Ontario take prayer requests by e-mail (http://www.kwcatholic.org/prayerhotline.asp) and some Carmelites in Massachusetts will take prayer requests on the phone (sometimes on an answering machine and sometimes a lay volunteer will take them down) and place them on the altar and pray for them for 30 days (508 756-0186). The National Council of the Assemblies of God run a Prayer Center. You might get a live volunteer to pray with you on their 1-800-4prayer hotline, but when I call I get a recorded prayer and information on how to submit your request online.

becomes anchored, formed, or rooted in us. When we pray we seek to enter into relationship with God, but being creatures who naturally want to understand things, we also reflect about our prayer experiences, and try to fit things together into a coherent whole. We gradually grow into a deeper and richer understanding of the world in which our Christian vision permeates all our faculties — imagination, emotion, will, and mind. Although the heart (understood in the full Biblical sense) is at the core of the sort of transformation God works in us, this transformation includes also a kind of illumination of our minds, and not just a decision of the will.

However, since we are social beings, and since many people around us (perhaps even ones we are close to) do not understand the world in Christian categories, we cannot help but be affected by this, and it is normal (especially at first) to feel beset by doubts and shaky in our faith sometimes. People undergoing religious conversion sometimes experience a kind of oscillation between competing world-views; one day the world seems created and sustained by God, and the next day it all seems empty and meaningless. If someone close to you is actively anti-religious or is convinced that no sane person could possibly claim to experience God, then you will, at the very least, refrain from disclosing your experiences to that person, and quite possibly also begin to doubt yourself if you spend a lot of time around them. And even if no one close to you is hostile to religion, there is enough hostility to religion (particularly any sort of relatively traditional Christianity) in the air, that you cannot but be affected by it. There are stories of people who have maintained their Christian faith in spite of imprisonment, torture and attempted brainwashing. But without at least some Christian support, it is very difficult to resist the temptation to "go native" and conform your thinking to that of the people around you. In the rest of this chapter, I suggest lines of response to some common doubts or worries that may arise in the course of prayer. The list of doubts discussed below is by no means exhaustive; I've tried to focus on ones that you are likely to have picked up from the surrounding culture. If you were living in Iraq or Japan you would probably have somewhat different doubts.

1. Maybe it is just my imagination.

Given that deception and self-deception are possible, is there a way you can be confident that you are not a victim of them? At the most basic level, have you any good grounds for believing that you are in touch with a personal being who exists independent of you, and that it is not all just a fantasy? Making detailed discernments about whether some particular guidance you feel you got in prayer is genuinely from God is discussed briefly in the next section, and in more detail in the section on praying for guidance in Chapter Four. Here I focus on the problem at the most general level.

I think that putative experiences of God can be evaluated using some of the same sorts of reality checks that we use to tell reality from illusion in ordinary cases. In the case of experiences of God, however, the sort of third person checks possible in cases of sense perception cannot be employed, at least not in a simple, straightforward way. I can say, "Hey, Joe, come here a minute! Is that an animal moving over there or are my eyes deceiving me?" But I can't say, "I thought I felt God was telling/showing me that I need to forgive my father. Can you come here and see if you think that's what He is telling me?" A sort of broader corroboration of your experience can be attained, however, if you bring in the collective experience of the whole Christian tradition; enjoining you to forgive someone who has wronged you is "in character" for God in a way that an inner voice commanding you to kill yourself would not be. But the way in which certain putative experiences of God can be taken to be probably veridical, and others ruled out by the collective experience of the Christian tradition provides a rather looser and less precise way of distinguishing veridical experiences from the fantasies generated by our own imagination than is possible when you are trying to tell whether or not there is an animal moving over there in the bushes.

But many of the other tests we employ to distinguish reality from illusion can be employed, although the necessary discriminations are subtle and may require looking at patterns over time. Some of the marks of a reality independent of us impinging upon us are that things outside us act on us without our willing them and even contrary to our will. They are also experienced as presenting themselves to us in ways that are not always predictable and, in the case of persons, we find that they sometimes respond to what we say to them in ways that indicate that they have understood what we said to them and their reply is intelligible as a response to our question.

It is characteristic of experiences of God, I think, that they are experienced as the action of something other than ourselves upon us. They seem to come at us with an energy that is not our own. It is also the case, I think, that when we are praying God sometimes corrects, challenges, or re-directs us, or communicates things to us that are unexpected. And God's responses to our spoken or unspoken questions sometimes clearly testify to the fact that we are in contact with an intelligent being. If, however, over a long period of time, you *never* feel as though God is correcting you, challenging you, or showing you something novel or unexpected, and if everything you experience is predictable in terms of what you expected God would say to you, then this may indicate that you are erring in the direction of fantasizing rather than really listening to God.

2. *So maybe I've gotten in touch with a real spiritual being,
   but it is not God.*

One kind of doubt that you might have is, "How do I know that the being whose presence I experience when I pray is God? Maybe I will get taken over by demons, or something." This can be a serious danger for those who engage in psychic research with no solid spiritual foundation in Christ, or who dabble in the occult. Serving as a medium is particularly dangerous. But if you are using the prayers recommended here, you will be very unlikely to fall under any serious negative influence while you are doing them. For the prayers clearly invoke the God of Christian faith and place you under the protection of Jesus Christ.

The standard way of discerning whether a spirit is of God is whether you are left with a feeling of peace or not. If you come away from your prayer session feeling a sense of disquiet, anxiety, confusion, or fear, that would be a bad sign. Or if you feel over-excited in a kind of feverish way. One test I have found useful is to wait maybe five or ten minutes after your prayer session and take a good look at yourself in the mirror, particularly at your eyes. They should look clear and light, not dark and confused. Do you look like the sort of person you would spontaneously trust? No need to go peering at yourself in the mirror every day, of course, but only if you have some reason to be suspicious.

There are a few practices (besides dabbling in the occult), however, that might open you up to malign spirits, and you should avoid these. You should not expect a response from God to every question you pose to Him in prayer. He is entirely free and sovereign, and is not bound to answer every question you put to Him. (This is not to say, of course, that you should not try to listen inwardly for responses to your questions, but merely that you sometimes need to accept the fact that God is not giving you an answer right now.) If you try to inwardly discern or make out some sort of answer to *every* question — thereby treating it as a two-sided conversation between equals — you are likely to persuade yourself that you "hear" an answer all the time. If you are lucky you will just pick up things from your own imagination. But as happens with people who use Ouija boards, the responses you get may be coming from a spirit that is not of God. This is especially true if you try to get God to tell you what will happen in the future. Consulting oracles or fortune tellers has always been strongly condemned in both Judaism and Christianity.[43] I know a woman who thought she had gotten a guidance in prayer that "in a year you will not recognize yourself." She took this to be something positive, but within a year she had had a complete breakdown and was in a mental hospital.

There are also some warning signs that should alert you to the presence of some sort of negative spirit. The list is not exhaustive.

(1) Obviously, any being that tries to persuade you to kill or maim yourself is not of God. A very psychically sensitive woman who dated a friend of mine once encountered a being of light on her college campus (Wellesley). It enfolded her in its wings, and she came to worship it and got more and more entangled with it. It then began to try to get her to kill herself.

(2) If you feel a strong sense of harsh condemnation that tempts you to despair, then it is not Jesus. This is a hard one to detect sometimes. God may show you your sins with a clarity that can be painful, but if it is really God you will at the same time feel a sense that His loving presence is there with you — that He has not cast you off. The realization of the truth about ourselves should occasion sorrow and a heightened sense of our need to depend on God more, but should not lead us to despair. There is a kind of cleanness to His judgment — like a light flooding into a dark place — but without condemnation. Jesus says that the truth will make us free. And so it is. We don't need to put energy into repressing things or hiding things from ourselves any longer. God's love strengthens us so we can look at things as they are.

(3) If you feel that you are being offered special, secret knowledge or powers, this is a bad sign. Anything that puffs you up and makes you feel you are better than other people is not good. Humility should be one of the fruits of prayer. God,

---

[43] If you employ the *I Ching*, or other fortune telling devices before you become a Christian, God's grace may make use of these to help you toward Him. But once you have become a Christian you should not turn back to them.

of course, calls us to use our talents in various ways, so you may get a sense that you are specially chosen to do some particular work, but any supposed revelation that leads you to think of yourself as above others should be suspected. Do not succumb to self-dramatizing fantasies about how you personally are called to march out heroically and combat the forces of evil. Jesus alone is the victor over demons, and you should refrain from putting yourself forward in any way. Let Him fight for you.

(4) A common demonic strategy is to try to persuade you that you are already in his grip — that your real self is the one that resists God and that your second order desires to be a better sort of person aren't the "real" you (for an extensive discussion of this point see the section on temptation above).

(5) Demons, I think, cast a kind of penumbra of fear. You don't exactly perceive them, but the fear radiates into you.[44] Often this leads us to keep frantically active, running from the unnamed fear. Demons are often portrayed in paintings as lashing the poor souls in their power constantly so they can never be at rest. A lot of people seem to live in this sort of state of constant flight, and this is probably due, at least in part, to an underlying metaphysical fear or anxiety at work in them. If you are falling into this pattern, it is important, especially when you wake in the morning, not to let yourself be prodded or lashed into beginning to run right away. Stand your ground and stay in bed longer or do something slow and relaxing. Don't let all your time be torn from you. Enjoy the moment and face down the fear. To keep yourself from falling prey to frantic rushing, you might try doing every action deliberately, consciously, and in slow motion as though it were a dance, slowing your breathing down also as you do this.

(6) If any sort of being presents itself to you in a dream or

---

[44] I am inclined to think that all perception of spiritual beings usually operates in this odd, oblique sort of way. Even when the person experiences some sort of sensory image, the perception is still in a sense oblique. When the perception is of God, the penumbra is one of glory that radiates into us and produces a kind of awe or reverence.

vision (I myself am not given to visions, but some people are[45]) and you have a suspicious feeling that it is not what it claims to be, trust your intuitions. I once had a dream in which a being presented itself to me as a psychic I had once had a reading with, but it just did not feel right; the being was impersonating him, and as soon as I realized this, it vanished. There is a story about a monk who had a vision of a being of light who claimed to be Jesus but there was something suspicious about it, so he said, "Where are your wounds?" and it disappeared.

(7) Strange perceptual distortions are a danger sign. For example, suddenly feeling that you are gigantic or seeing others suddenly change shape, size, or appearance.

(8) Sometimes just feeling torn apart, pulled down, anxious, and fearful can be a sign of demonic oppression; likewise being unable to find anything and just generally feeling you are going to pieces. This, of course, can just be stress, but some prayers never hurt.

If you do feel beset by some sort of negative presence you should immediately call on Jesus to deliver you. Command it to "Stand in the light of Christ or leave," or use the demon binding prayer given at the end of the section on temptations above. There is also the short prayer that is a routine part of night prayer in the daily office: "Lord we beg thee to visit this house and banish from it all the deadly power of the enemy. May your holy angels dwell here to keep us in peace and may your blessing be upon us always. We ask this through Christ our Lord." The prayer to St. Michael is also traditional against demons: "St. Michael the Archangel, defend us in the day of battle. Be our safeguard against the wickedness and snares of the Devil. May God rebuke him we humbly pray, and do you oh, prince of the heavenly host, cast into Hell Satan and all the evil spirits who prowl about the world seeking the ruin of souls." (The story about Michael and his angels battling the Devil is found in Rv 12:7-9.) Sprinkling

---

[45] See, for example, Phillip Wiebe, *Visions of Jesus* (New York: Oxford University Press, 1997).

some holy water while you do the prayers is another thing you might want to do.[46]

Just a firm resolve to stand and fight dispels the miasma. Allowing your anger to kick in can help give you the necessary backbone. St. Teresa of Avila is reported to have made obscene gestures at the Devil. After all, we rightly become furiously angry at terrorists who destroyed thousands of innocent lives. How much more should we be angry at a being who, in full knowledge of what he is doing, attempts to warp, twist and destroy all that is good, and to draw all creation down with him into despair and death! As soon as the immediate feeling of fear subsides, return your attention immediately to Jesus. Remember how Peter started to walk on the water, but began to sink as soon as he started looking at the wind and waves instead of at Jesus who was stretching out His hand to him (Mt 14:28-31). Grasp hold of that hand and go on in the Way.

On the positive side, there are certain long-term trends that you may observe in yourself that should quiet your fears that you might be going wrong in some serious way. St. Paul lists the fruits of the Spirit in Galatians 5:22-23 as: love, joy, peace, patience, kindness, goodness, faithfulness, gentleness and self-control, and eventually some of these should become more manifest in you as you continue praying faithfully. Different people will probably notice improvement in different areas, depending on the weaknesses and bad patterns they are particularly prone to. You should, of course, pray for help with the bad patterns that are particularly troubling you, but God may also heal problems you don't even realize you have, and you may only notice months (or even years) later that something has changed. Even if your prayer experiences are quiet, subtle, and quite unlike those of St. Paul on the road to Damascus, a great deal is still going on dur-

---

[46] The prayers said while blessing holy water in the Eastern Rite Churches include a prayer against demons. The older Latin Rite did also, but the book of blessings currently in use does not. Probably different priests use different prayers, so check on this if you care. Lourdes water has not been blessed by a priest, but simply taken from the spring.

ing those quiet times with the Lord. Faith is a gift of the Holy Spirit, and over a period of time you will begin to understand everything in your life in more Christian terms, and find yourself responding differently to all sorts of situations. Sometimes it seems that, for reasons best known to Himself, God allows us to continue to struggle unsuccessfully with weaknesses for a long time, so don't set a timetable and become too dreadfully disappointed if things don't change as quickly as you had hoped. God will "complete the good work He has begun in you" (Ph 1:6) but in His own way and His own time.

The kinds of improvements in one's character that may result from regular prayer are certainly encouraging signs that you are going the right way. But there are also some signs that are particularly definitive for ruling out the possibility of demonic activity. Faith, hope and charity are the three theological virtues (so called because they direct us toward God), and are described by Aquinas as "infused" virtues — meaning that they are gifts of the Holy Spirit and not just moral excellences that we might acquire through practice. I don't think one can draw a hard and fast line between natural and supernatural — grace and nature are intertwined. But if you find yourself experiencing real joy and delight in praising God or in reading Scripture passages that praise God and Jesus His Son, or if you find yourself longing to receive the body and blood of Christ in communion, then these experiences cannot possibly be caused by evil spirits. One thing demons will *never* do is inspire you to love, praise, desire, and delight in God. St Paul says that it is only by the Holy Spirit that a person can say "Jesus Christ is Lord" (1 Cor 12:3).

Another indication that the Holy Spirit is at work in you is if you find your heart moved when you hear other people praying or speaking about Jesus from their hearts. There is a phenomenon known to musicians called the "sympathetic string" effect. If one string on a musical instrument is struck, this can cause a kind of sympathetic vibration in other strings that vibrate on that frequency or related ones. The second string does not sound as loudly as the first, but it does emit a sound also. An old Southern gospel song says: "There are many other Christians in the world today. I can feel the spirit moving when I hear them pray. And it gives me consolation when my soul is tried." And an old shape note hymn called "Devotion" says: "Oh, may my heart in tune be found, like David's harp of solemn sound!" (*The Sacred Harp*, p. 48). Interestingly, ordinary language also contains several expressions involving things like "heart-strings." The analogy between the heart and a musical instrument is thus a common one, and prayer is one important way in which our hearts become attuned to God.

At this point, you may wonder whether perhaps there are spiritual beings other than God or demons. Could you not, perhaps, get in touch with an angel, a deceased friend or relative, or some sort of spirit guide? Many people who are involved in the New Age movement attempt to contact such beings. On the whole, I think such practices should be avoided. Trying to get in touch with the spirits of the dead has always been strongly forbidden by both Judaism and Christianity. And the category of angels includes both fallen and unfallen angels (the former of course being demons). The word "angel" derives from the word "messenger" or "one who is sent." And good angels move only at God's command. A woman I know who dabbled in the occult (much to her own harm) and studied with the woman who is now the official witch in Salem, once told me that if it comes when you call it, it is not an angel. You may ask your guardian angel to pray for you if you like. But don't try to summon angels, or worse yet "spirit guides." The dangers of getting entangled with negative spirits are too great. And really there is no need to contact such beings. Whatever good we seek is in the gift of God to give us; we should go directly to the source.

3. Don't I just find the Christian God because that is what I am expecting?

With this doubt, you begin to step back from your own way of understanding the world and recognize that other people operate within different belief systems. You have not yet stepped completely outside it and adopted the perspective of the sceptic. You are still interpreting what you experience in Christian categories, but you are starting to worry about how you would justify doing so if challenged by someone raised in another religious tradition. This doubt is one that has to be handled either in a brief and sketchy way, or in a book. Needless to say, I will handle it briefly. There is a deep problem here, having to do with differences among cultures — called by philosophers the problem of "cultural relativism." We approach our experience with certain concepts and not others; the language and culture we have been shaped by cannot but affect how we experience things. I can see an airplane where an aborigine might only see some sort of strange, giant bird because I am familiar with airplanes and he has never seen one. And I am told that some cultures divide up the color spectrum in slightly different ways than we do, so that the color words they employ do not correspond neatly with ours. This problem does not affect only religious beliefs; ethics, aesthetics, politics, psychology and so on, all take different forms in different cultures.

Most of us, whether or not we were brought up as believers, have grown up in a culture permeated by Christianity (and to some degree also Judaism). Hindus and Taoists no doubt interpret their religious experiences through their own cultural and religious framework. So, the objection runs, don't their experiences then confirm their religions just as much as ours confirm ours? And if so, why should we take *our* experiences to be revelatory of the truth? Mightn't Hindus and Taoists say the same?

One attractive and simple way to resolve the problem would be to say that in spite of apparent differences, all religions turn out on a deep level to be the same, so it doesn't matter which one you choose. Unfortunately, however, this just won't hold water. Some religions are theistic (*i.e.*, believe in a supreme being), while others are not (*e.g.*, Taoism and most varieties of Buddhism). There is not even uniformity on the level of moral teachings. Not all religions teach that we should love others and follow the golden rule. Consider, for example, Thugee — a Hindu sect whose members murder random passers by as a sacrifice to Kali (the goddess of death and destruction).

In response to this problem, I will limit myself to a few brief remarks. First, belief in the truth of Christianity does not require us to deny that there is some truth in other religions, or to believe salvation is impossible for non-Christians; we can't know how widely God's mercy extends. Secondly, this book is addressed to people who have decided to at least give Christianity a try. St. Teresa of Avila said that he who has God finds he lacks nothing. And if Christian faith and practice could open such riches to her, there is no reason why they cannot do the same for us. It is enough to know that a certain path leads from where you now find yourself to something you desire in order to set out on that path; you don't also need to know that no other paths lead there.

Finally, in a more philosophical vein, there is a tendency among postmodern thinkers to view conceptual structures as necessarily distorting reality. Somewhere in the background here is an implied contrast between experiences mediated by concepts and direct or unmediated experiences that would give us undistorted access to the truth if only they were possible (as in fact they are not). This seems rather silly when you think about it. An experience that had *no* conceptual dimension would not be a *human* experience at all. God knows *us,* no doubt, in a way not mediated by human concepts, but we cannot know Him in this way. Our conceptual structures serve the positive function of enabling us to comprehend certain dimensions of reality. Obviously, no human concepts are fully adequate to the being of God. Rather, they are ways in which human minds over the centuries have reached out toward the divine, attempting to know

God. (Christians believe this reaching out is itself a result of God's work in the soul.) Relying upon revelation, theological reflection, and religious experience, the Christian tradition has developed a rich and complex understanding of God — a well-trodden path in the wilderness through which we may approach Him and grow into an ever-deepening communion of knowledge and love. That there are other paths is not surprising. That they lead to the same goal is, I think, uncertain at best.[47]

4. Intrusion of the Third Person Perspective.

Even though you have felt a sense of God's presence, it is easy to begin to doubt whether it was real afterwards. You step back and see yourself from outside through the eyes of a real or imaginary sceptic, and it all seems to evaporate.

For a start, you should be very careful about looking at yourself through the eyes of other people.[48] There is an enormous variety of people out there with deeply different world-views (i.e., basic beliefs about the nature of the world and our place in it) and it is easy to lose yourself if you allow all these different people's perspectives to define reality for you. The way things look from the outside and the way they are experienced from the inside are different, and you can't let the third person perspective intrude and rob you of the lived reality of your prayer life. You need to be faithful to your own experience and make your own judgments. Epictetus, a Roman Stoic, said: "If someone handed over

---

[47] In fact, I think that the world's religions do not all pursue the same final goal, and that none of them understands it in precisely the same way Christians do. This could be argued at great length, but I won't do so here. A valuable discussion of this is found in Fr. Joseph DiNoia's book *Diversity of Religions: A Christian Perspective* (Washington, DC: Catholic University of America Press, 1992).

[48] Strictly speaking, of course, this is impossible. You can't directly experience other people's experiences. But given that we are social animals and possess a certain natural empathy, we can go at least part way toward a sympathetic understanding of how others think and feel. If those others are particularly forceful personalities, or if they communicate their perspective through media that appeal powerfully to the imagination (such as art, literature, film, etc.) this allows their perspective to have more impact on us than it would otherwise.

your body to any person who met you, you would be vexed; but that you hand over your mind to any person that comes along, so that if he reviles you, it is disturbed and troubled — are you not ashamed of that?" I am not suggesting that you should never pay attention to the perspectives of other people and cling uncritically to what you take to be your own experiences or revelations. Just be careful about whose opinions you give weight to, especially at first, and try to seek advice from other Christians, preferably ones who seem to be charitable and reasonable people. And eventually you should also be able to enter into rational dialogue with open-minded non-believers. But there is no point in letting people who are dogmatically opposed to the possibility of religious experience define your reality for you; if they want to turn their backs on God, that is their business. You should be faithful to your own call.

A few analogies may help. Imagine for a moment that a deaf person who has never seen dancing, comes upon people who are dancing animatedly to music. The movements of the people would seem totally unintelligible to him because he does not hear the music, and he would be likely to suppose they were crazy. Or, in terms of the analogy between prayer and a dance given in Chapter Two, suppose that someone is dancing with an invisible partner. The intricate and graceful movements the dancer is going through are responses to the guidance of the invisible partner, but from the outside it would all look very strange. This analogy also helps us understand how saints are sometimes able to do extraordinary things that seem humanly impossible. For just as the invisible partner's arm holds up the dancer in positions that would otherwise be impossible, so God enables us to accomplish things leaning on Him that we could not otherwise accomplish.

5. The "Nothing But" Argument.

This is a special case of the intrusion of the third person perspective. People who are dogmatic atheists often try to ex-

plain away religion and religious experience by providing alternative explanations. They often sound very confident and as
though they have the authority of science on their side, so this
can be intimidating. But, to the extent that the science they rely
on is sound, it does not threaten faith.

The first thing that you need to keep in mind is that such
people accept a view of the world that excludes the very possibility of religious experience because they believe that there *is* nothing transcending the physical world to experience. They are not
merely arguing that on occasion you might take something to be
an experience of a spiritual being that in fact has a purely natural
cause — for example, that your perception of demons surrounding your bed last night may have been the result of the LSD you
consumed while watching *The Exorcist*, or that your vision of the
Virgin Mary telling you that women who wear short skirts are
all going to Hell may have been the product of your own over-
heated imagination, motivated, perhaps, by some sort of jealousy
or sexual frustration. If that were all they were saying, what they
say might be useful as a corrective for weeding out some fraudu-
lent religious claims (believers are, after all, not committed to
accepting *every* claim to religious experience). But they are saying more than this. They would never, in principle, accept a supernatural cause as a legitimate explanation for any experience.
They rule the believer's own lived experience and understanding
of that experience out of court at the start; you can't dialogue
with them because they are making a take-over bid.

If you do not assume there *is* no God to act upon us, what
they say looks a lot less threatening. For example, claims to understand how the brain works and to show that what is happening in religious experience is really *nothing but* some sort of
strange pattern of chemical and electrical activity in the brain
are unpersuasive. In part this is because the brain is extremely
mysterious and poorly understood, so scientists who pretend to
have it all figured out are doing a lot of bluffing. But in addition,
all our experiences are correlated with changes in the brain so

this does not put religious experience in a worse position than other experiences. And if there is a God, He could choose to communicate with us in any number of different ways, including causing changes in our brain which then cause us to experience what He wants us to. If there is a soul, He might act on the soul, which then causes changes in the brain. We don't know *how* God acts in us, but that is no reason to deny that He does.

Freudians make the other main version of the "nothing but" argument.[49] Believers, they argue, pray the Lord's prayer addressing God as "Father," and sometimes believe that they are experiencing God's love or being in some special way united with God. They believe that they stand under God's judgment, and that God forbids certain actions and enjoins others. But all this can be easily explained, say the Freudians, without invoking a supernatural cause. What is really going on is *nothing but* wishful thinking and a projection of their infantile image of their father, or perhaps regression to an infantile state in which they experienced a feeling of union with their mother. And what believers take to be God correcting them morally is really *nothing but* their own superego which derives from their internalization of parental authority figures.

First, notice that a lot of the persuasive power of these sorts of claims is carried by a pervasive rhetoric suggesting that religion is something for the weak — for those unable to face the harshness of reality as it is and needing comforting illusions to make it through the day (or perhaps the night). This rhetoric is one that many atheists employ, and it can be intimidating (especially, I think, to men, who have been socialized to regard being tough and self-reliant as essential to their masculinity).[50] We all

---

[49] For a more extended and philosophical discussion of these points, see my article "Countering the 'Nothing But' Argument" in *Faith and Philosophy*, Vol. 22 No. 4, October 2005.

[50] William James, for example, suffered from doubts of this sort. A Christian women's discussion group I was part of, found this aspect of James particularly alien. Not that women are immune to doubts, but we certainly didn't worry that it was cowardly, weak (or "unmanly" obviously) to have faith and find consolation in God.

naturally want to be treated with respect as adults, and therefore tend to shy away from things others regard as inappropriate to adults. Freud, however, assumes that a fearless pursuit of truth leads us to atheism. If, on the contrary, it leads to God, then there is nothing weak or immature about worshiping, loving, and serving that God. Christian beliefs, attitudes, and practices are altogether reasonable and appropriate if God is what they take Him to be.

Second, remember that Freud first assumed that there was no God, and then set out to find naturalistic explanations for religion and religious experience. But if you do not assume atheism to start with, a lot of what Freud says turns out to be valuable and entirely consistent with Christianity. We feel a deep need and longing for God; this was implanted in us by God Himself in order to draw us to Him. We are not entirely transparent to ourselves; our motivations are not always what we tell ourselves they are, and we can sometimes be confused about what comes from outside us and what arises from the depths of our own psyche. Like other animals we have certain hard-wired instincts, and whatever we perceive we perceive *through* the nature we have (which includes but is not limited to some deeply rooted instincts). So it is not surprising that God's action in us is experienced in ways that have been filtered through our instinctual structures — as, for example, when Brother Lawrence, John of the Cross, or Teresa of Avila describe their delight in God as like that of an infant at the mother's breast. The way we think of God is colored by and sometimes distorted by our experience of our own parents. This is because God, in revealing Himself to us as "father" in Scripture, is tapping into images we already have stored in our imaginations in order to communicate certain things about Himself, as happens also when God is described as "king" or "bridegroom," or even compared to inanimate things such as rocks, wind, fire.

As for the idea that science has somehow disproved religion, or made religious belief impossible now in the 21st Century, this is not something you need to lose any sleep over. Science has been successful in giving us knowledge (or at least the power to predict and control) certain natural processes, but it is far from being a monolithic solid edifice of uncontested truth. There are any number of things scientists are unable to explain, ranging from the simple fact of consciousness to the origin of the universe. Every system of thought in the history of the human race has had weak spots; reality is, after all, complex beyond the capacity of the human mind to completely understand. So if you have to struggle to fit things together, you are not alone.

To be an intellectually serious Christian requires swimming against the cultural stream, so you need some support from other Christians. If you were an atheist in the sixteenth or seventeenth centuries you would likewise have needed to seek fellow freethinkers to support you in your dissent from the way people around you thought. Being counter-cultural does not show that Christianity is wrong (nor, of course, does it show it is right). But don't be intimidated into thinking that the sceptics' views are perfectly consistent and rational and explain everything because they aren't and they don't.

In the next chapter, we will take a closer look at different types of prayer and explore some ways to integrate prayer into your daily life.

Chapter Four

A CLOSER LOOK AT PRAYER

Since the basic set of prayers provided in Chapter Two is intended only as a kind of skeleton or underlying structure for your private prayer time, various different types of prayer can be integrated into that structure as the Spirit moves. And prayer will begin to change your life more and more as it becomes interwoven with your daily life. This chapter is intended to give you some ideas about ways of praying that you may want to engage in. But don't look at them as more things that you have to do. Keep your prayer time leisurely and uncluttered so as to leave time for your own personal conversation with God. The growing edge of your soul is at that point where God touches you; you have to let Him meet you where you are, and not just say lots of words. So look over the suggestions below and see what you feel drawn to do. Certain things like penitence, thanksgiving and praise are standard aspects of Christian prayer generally, but other things like the Jesus prayer or praying in tongues may be right for you or they may not. You will probably find that different ways of praying will be helpful at different points in your Christian life. For those of you who are naturally inclined to be more physically expressive,[51] I've included at a few points on

[51] If you can't resist tapping your foot and moving your body a little to music, clap your hands when delighted, laugh easily, express your pleasure readily when you see something beautiful or taste something particularly delicious, are easily moved to tears, spontaneously reach out to touch a person you want to comfort, and so on, then you will probably respond more physically in prayer also, but these things are largely just a matter of personal style. Pray in whatever way comes naturally to you.

some physical gestures that might aid your prayer, but the more reserved and stoical among you should feel free to ignore these suggestions.

The Jesus Prayer

The Jesus prayer, especially popular in the Eastern Orthodox monastic tradition is "Jesus Christ, Son of God, have mercy on me a sinner."[52] Some people coordinate the prayer with their breathing — for example, breathing in on the first half and out on the second. "Jesus mercy" is a shorter version of the prayer, or just "Jesus." I usually just use the name of Jesus, and don't try to coordinate it with my breathing, though coordinating it with your breathing may be helpful if you have trouble sleeping and want to pray when you are wakeful at night. This prayer can fit in anywhere during your prayer time or as you go about your daily activities.

To speak someone's name is to invoke, call or summon that person. Think of all the ways in which you might speak another person's name. Think of a lost child calling his or her mother or someone lost in the woods or frightened and calling for help. Think of tenderly and softly speaking the name of someone you love, or pleadingly when trying to reach out to a person. You may speak someone's name to be sure they are still there (say, in the dark), or to be sure that it is indeed your spouse who has just walked in and not the Boston Strangler. One can speak Jesus's name in all these ways and many more.

Yet there is also something unique about the name of Jesus. The seventy-two disciples return from their mission reporting to Jesus that the demons were subject to them in His name, and are described as casting out demons "in His name." Even people who were not Jesus's disciples were apparently casting out de-

---

[52] This is modeled on the prayer of blind Bartimaeus: "Jesus, Son of David, have mercy on me" (Mk 10:47-48). Some people use the form "Jesus Christ, Son of the Living God, have mercy on me a sinner."

mons in His name, and the disciples were rebuked by Jesus for trying to stop them (Mk 9:38; Lk 9:49). St. Peter, in the book of Acts, when asked "by what power or by what name" he had been able to heal the cripple, replied "by the name of Jesus Christ of Nazareth... by him this man is standing before you well... there is no other name under heaven given among men by which we must be saved" (Ac 4:7-12). I once knew a man who had been in a very bad car accident, and when he saw it was going to happen he just cried out "Jesus" and went limp. He walked out of the accident unhurt, although the car was so badly damaged that the police were amazed he had survived. St. Paul speaks of "putting on the Lord Jesus" (Rm 13:1) and I think that speaking His name repeatedly can be one way of doing this. For His name has a certain life to it and can draw Him to fill us. Baptism is the most important way in which we "put on Christ." New converts are always baptized at once by the apostles in the book of Acts, so if you have not been baptized it is important to do this as soon as you are comfortable doing so.

Do not, however, think of the prayer of repeating His name in a mechanical way — a certain number of repetitions takes a certain amount of time off someone's time in purgatory (I once found a booklet in a chapel that approached the Jesus prayer in this way). Think of it as a devotion — as an expression of your longing for Him and need for Him, or as a way of recalling your mind from wandering and fixing your attention on God. His name seems to be alive and to take root in us as we speak it. It can sometimes feel almost literally sweet or pleasant to speak and dwell upon His name.

PRAYER OF PENITENCE

On days when you are feeling particularly conscious of some way in which you have fallen short of what God wants from you, this type of prayer is appropriate. The crucial thing is to resist the impulse to flee and hide from God at such times. Adam and Eve, immediately after their disobedience, hid from God, and this reaction is a natural one. But through the sacrificial death of Jesus Christ, we have been reconciled to God, so we can come to Him trusting that He loves us even in our sins and that we can be forgiven. We must humbly let Him stay close to us and support us, realizing that apart from Him we cannot hope to make progress in holiness.

Prayer of penitence may fit well just at the start of your prayer time. It also flows naturally after the verse in the Holy Spirit invocation, "Wipe the stains of guilt away," or after the line in the opening prayer, "Almighty God unto whom all hearts are open, all desires known, from whom no secrets are hid," or in the litany along with the verses from "propitiation for our sins" through "pierced with a lance," but can fit anywhere. You might want to pray Psalm 51. Certain physical gestures naturally express penitence, and some of them can be performed while sitting. One is simply sitting in His presence and hanging your head in sorrow. Remember the tax collector who "would not even raise his eyes to heaven, but beat his breast and prayed 'Oh God, be merciful to me a sinner'" (Lk 18:13). Beating against your breast with a closed fist is a common gesture of sorrow or mourning, and so is appropriate to express repentance. It is done ritually during the Catholic Mass, when, just before communion, the communicant beats (gently) against his or her breast, saying, "Lord, I am not worthy to receive you; but only say the word and I shall be healed."[53] One prayer used in some Eastern Orthodox Churches that you may want to use is: "Holy God, Holy Mighty One, Holy Immortal One, have mercy on us (three times). Most Holy Trinity have mercy on us; Lord cleanse us of our sins, Master pardon our transgressions, Holy One visit us and heal our infirmities for your own name's sake. Lord have mercy (three times)."

---

[53] This prayer is modeled on that of the Centurion (Mt 8:8).

You might sometimes feel moved to express your sorrow for your sins by weeping over them. Some spiritual writers connect this with what they call "the gift of tears." If you have, for a moment, a clear realization of how badly you failed the Lord on some particular occasion, as happened to Peter when the cock crowed (Mt 26:69-75), or a general sense of how far you fall short of what God is calling you to be, then hanging your head and weeping tears of sorrow over this is entirely healthy. It could begin to become unhealthy, however, if you dwell constantly on your past sins and weep over them excessively. You need to trust in His forgiveness. As the hymn "Rock of Ages" says: "Could my tears forever flow, could my zeal no languor know, these for sin could not atone; thou must save and thou alone. In my hands no gifts I bring. Simply to thy cross I cling." Ask Him to help you do better, pick yourself up, and go on.

Being excessively shocked and horrified by one's own sinfulness can sometimes be a subtle form of pride. Why should we expect ourselves to be perfect? Brother Lawrence says, "If I fail in my duty, I readily acknowledge it saying I am used to do so; I shall never do otherwise if I am left to myself.... It is you who must hinder me from falling and mend what is amiss.... If I fail not, I give thanks to God, acknowledging that the strength comes from Him."[54]

PRAYER OF THANKSGIVING

"Give thanks in all circumstances," St. Paul admonishes us (1 Th 5:15). All too often, this is the last thing we feel like doing. Instead, we, like the Jews at Meribah in the desert, feel like bitching and moaning. They were reproached for having done this "although they had seen my works" (Ps 95:8-9). This phrase, I think, puts the problem in the right perspective. The superficial

---

[54] Brother Lawrence, *op. cit.*, pp. 16-19.

"count your blessings" approach (e.g., "things could be worse; you could be in a concentration camp or dying painfully of cancer") has its point, but it does not get to the heart of the matter. If you worry that there is something wrong with you because you do not feel brimming over with thankfulness, it may be that you have not yet come to realize the gift that is yours in Christ Jesus. The man who could write "Neither death, nor life, nor angels, nor principalities, nor things present, nor things to come, nor powers, nor height, nor depth, nor anything else in all creation, will be able to separate us from the love of God in Christ Jesus our Lord" (Rm 8:38-39), and who described that love as surpassing knowledge (Eph 3:19) had reason to be constantly thankful. And as we begin to experience more the love of Christ, we too will have cause to be thankful in spite of trials. We can, of course, be thankful because we believe in God's love for us in an intellectual way, but thankfulness will come more spontaneously as we come to "taste and see that the Lord is good" (Ps 34:8).

Having said this, however, it is still true that we ought to give thanks to God even when we do not *feel* thankful. For we know through faith that we have been given certain gifts. To begin with, we have been given that little kernel of faith that motivates us to seek God. And as we grow more deeply into that faith, we will have more and more reason to be thankful. The "General Thanksgiving" in the *Book of Common Prayer*, summarizes some of the things we ought to be thankful for quite well. It says, "We bless thee for our creation, preservation, and all the blessings of this life; but above all, for thine inestimable love in the redemption of the world by our lord Jesus Christ; for the means of grace and for the hope of glory." If you think about it, you will be able to come up with at least some things to be thankful for in addition to these general ones: acts of kindness others have shown you or those you love, narrow escapes from danger, prayers answered, moments of warm fellowship, the beauty of nature, occasions where by God's grace you were able to touch another person's life in a positive way, for all those who have helped you along the way, especially those through whom you have been drawn to Christ. So ask God to give you a more thankful heart.

Cultivating a thankful attitude rather than a complaining one opens you to receiving more from God and orients you toward looking for ways in which God may be bringing good out of circumstances that at first glance appear entirely bad. One of the most saintly people I know makes a practice of thanking God for the terrible things that happen in her life and for the good that He is bringing out of them.

WORSHIP/PRAISE/ADORATION

"Come let us worship and bow down, let us kneel before the Lord our maker!" (Ps 95:6). Worship is the most fundamental religious act, and it is something we owe *only* to God. Remember Jesus's response to Satan in the desert when Satan asked Jesus to bow down and worship him (Mt 3:9). Adoration is likewise appropriate only to God. God is perfectly adorable in Himself and worthy of worship. An attitude of worship should pervade all prayer as a sort of background. But sometimes you may feel overpowered by a sense of awe and reverence. An old *Sacred Harp* song says of Jesus: "Sweet majesty and awful love sit seated on His brow; and all the glorious ranks above at humble distance bow" (*The Sacred Harp*, p. 362). A good prayer for expressing worship is: "Holy God, holy mighty one, holy immortal one, have mercy on us" given at the end of Chapter Two. Another good one is the *Te Deum* (see Appendix).

Physically, worship is expressed by bowing your head or even your whole body in reverence, head toward the ground, sometimes also going down on your knees as well as bending forward. (You can visualize or imagine yourself making these more extravagant gestures, but don't get up and start moving around.) Balaam describes himself as the man whose eye is opened, who "sees the vision of the Almighty, falling down but having his eyes uncovered" (Nb 24:4), and this is an interesting picture of worship. Normally when you bow your head you cannot at the same time see that which is in front of you. But since the bowing of the head in prayer is a kind of bowing in spirit, and the one we worship is not seen with the physical eyes, such physical limitations do not apply. Unlike the sort of hanging your head in sorrow for your sins described above, there is something formal and ceremonial about the bowing involved in worship. I sometimes accentuate this by holding my fingers tips together and touching them to my forehead while bowing my head.

Praise flows naturally out of worship. Many of the psalms are good for praising God — for example, Psalms 95, 103, 104, or 148. Praise is an attempt to express and celebrate, however imperfectly, the wonder, glory, and mystery of God. Language cannot capture these of course, although worshipers have tried to do so by ascribing to God things like power, honor, glory, majesty, holiness, beauty, love, goodness, wisdom and so on. Whereas worship can involve simply bowing silently before the Lord, praise is more active. There is a feeling of reaching up, pouring out one's heart to God, and delighting in Him. Some may find praying in tongues a particularly good way of doing this (see below). Praise is commonly associated with a lifting of the hands, usually at or above the level of your head mostly within the plane of the body or just a little in front of it, and tilting your head slightly upward. These gestures often come naturally when praying in tongues.

Adoration is something I do not think of so much in terms of bodily posture. There is still a background sense of bowing before the mystery of God. But adoration seems more inward turned — as though a jewel has dropped down for a moment into the center of our being (the pearl of great price), and we can for a moment delight in this free gift. Another way of thinking about this is the image of the treasure (Christ) that we hold in earthen vessels (2 Cor 4:7). Think of yourself as holding Christ and treasuring Him. Holding a crucifix or cross to your heart is another gesture that may come naturally and aid your prayer. Think about how often the saints are depicted doing this. As you continue in prayer, you may come to understand why.

Worship, praise and adoration are intimately connected, and different people may use the words differently. So don't take the above descriptions as making hard and fast distinctions among them. The purpose of this section has been only to provide some evocative images to help you enter into prayer in richer and more varied ways. You can also, of course, just say, "Lord, I worship you; I praise you; I adore you," without employing any imaginative images or physical gestures. People's styles of prayer differ and that is all right.

INTERCESSION

Most people, when they think of prayer, think predominantly of intercessory prayer. Prayer is something you do when you or someone you love are sick or in trouble. Certainly it is valuable to pray at these times, but intercession should be only a part of our prayer life and not its main point. The main point should be to enter into right relationship with God and allow Him to transform our hearts and guide us. As He works in our hearts, He can also use us and our prayers to help lift up those connected with us. Think of us as corks attached to a net floating on the surface of the water. Some corks are more closely connected to us than others, but there is a vast web of connections known only to God. If one cork pulls down, it exerts a downward pull on those most closely connected with it, but if we allow God to buoy us up, those connected with us are also lifted up along with us (to some degree at least). Or, take the analogy of the sympathetic string phenomenon in which one string sounding causes those harmonically related to it to vibrate also, although more faintly. God uses one heart sometimes to reinforce what He is doing in another. Only He knows all the connections that exist between us and other people, and we may be connected with someone we have never met. I pray regularly for "all those connected with me as you (God) see and know best." So if you feel moved to pray for someone you haven't met, either a public figure or someone closely connected with someone you have met, do it. If you find someone you know popping into your mind when you are praying, it is probably a sign that you should pray for them.

Generally speaking, it is better to bring a situation to the Lord for help without being too specific about what we are asking Him to do since He knows what would be best. In small things it is probably all right to be very specific like asking God to help you find a lost object, but even here, God may sometimes have a purpose in allowing something to get lost and stay lost. There are certain things that it is never wrong to pray for, for oneself or for others, such as a clearer vision of the truth or growth in faith, hope and charity, or for virtues like patience, gentleness or courage. Likewise praying that someone become more open to God in his or her life, or praying for someone's salvation are always good because we know that God wants these things for everyone. We should pray for healing for ourselves and others, and never for death for ourselves or others (even as a way out of suffering, since we don't know the Lord's purposes). For the Spirit of Christ is a Spirit of healing and life. When the disciples asked Jesus if they should call down fire from heaven to consume those in the village that had refused to listen to them, Jesus reproved them (Lk 9:54-55).

Don't forget to pray regularly for those who exercise any sort of religious authority — especially the priest or minister of the church you attend (if you attend one). They need our prayers as we need theirs. The stress, burdens, responsibilities and temptations that come with ministry are especially difficult, and such people are probably under at least as much demonic assault as lay people and probably more (especially if they are really effective in their work for the Lord). There is an Eastern Orthodox story about a novice whose spiritual director showed him two pictures — one of a monastery that looked beautiful, peaceful, surrounded by lovely gardens, quiet, etc., and one that had demons fiercely assaulting it and peering in every window — and the novice master asked him which was the truly holy monastery. The answer was the second one. Where God's work is going forward most strongly, that is the place where the fiercest assault will come. For that matter, if your pastor is something of a slouch, perhaps your prayers will help strengthen him and rouse him to greater fervor and faith. I once felt especially guided to pray for our pastor who was away on retreat, and perhaps it is my imagination (though I don't think so, as others noticed it too) but I noticed an increase in seriousness and devoutness in him after his return.

Once you have been praying regularly for a while, and have some Christian friends who are part of your prayer network, you may suddenly out of the blue feel that your friend is going through some sort of crisis and needs your prayers. Trust these intuitions, and really pray your heart out for the person. Don't put it off, but do it right away. Often you will discover later that there was a reason why the person needed prayers at that moment. Feeling a sudden impulse to pray for a friend is not, of course, something that need happen only with *Christian* friends, though I have noticed it particularly with those friends who are what I would call prayer partners — *i.e.*, we pray for each other regularly, and feel comfortable asking each other for special prayer support at difficult times. God can, of course, help other people simply because *they* ask Him — He doesn't *need* our prayers to sort of boost the level of energy or add to His power. But because we are interconnected already on levels we don't understand, there is a path from our hearts to theirs and back again that is already open, and God's power at work in us can also flow through these channels, or cause a sort of sympathetic vibration in them. Granted, all this sounds most mysterious, but that is because it is.

To put this point in more rational and intellectual terms,

the underlying basis for intercessory prayer is the profoundly social nature of human beings. Yes, we are saved only by Jesus Christ's sacrificial death and resurrection, and each of us must make a choice to follow Him. But we are able to understand and to make choices only because we have been taught to speak, reason, and understand both morality and the Gospel itself by other human beings.[55] Children who have been raised away from all human society ("feral" children who have been brought up, for example, by wolves), if they are not found and taught language by a certain age (I think it is around five), become unable to learn a human language adequately and therefore cannot acquire all sorts of distinctively human capacities, probably including the capacity to understand the gospel.[56]

Also, there exists a kind of natural sympathy among human beings. We normally feel a kind of pang when we see people (in real life or even in films or pictures) undergoing horrible pain, or grieving the loss of a loved one, and experience a sort of sympathetic pleasure when we see someone feeling joy — say, people being reunited with loved ones or even just having a good time in the park. Since we are already connected on some level, what touches one touches the other. This sort of sympathy is found among other species of social animals. The fear of one animal is communicated to the rest of the group for example, and sympathy is found in fairly complex forms among the higher mammals. I'm inclined to think that sympathy even operates across species. Pets seem sometimes to pick up the emotions of their owners, and we certainly feel sympathetic pain or pleasure for pets

---

[55] There may be exceptions to this. Some people may receive exceptional revelations, as St. Paul did (although even he had heard some things about Jesus and the new Way before his vision). God may, of course, reveal Himself in any way He pleases. But the ordinary way the faith is passed on is from others. St Paul asks, "How are they to believe in Him of whom they have never heard" (Rm 10:14) and also says, "Faith comes from what is heard" (Rm 10:17).

[56] This is not to say, of course, that God's mercy does not extend to such human beings. Their situation is rather like that of infants who die before baptism, or the victims of abortion. We must entrust them to God.

that we love. Sympathy, then, is natural to us as human beings, and since grace perfects nature, God's grace raises up and works through what is already present in us.

There are several places in the prayer routine outlined above where intercession fits well. Just as you sit down to pray, you could bring to the Lord people whose needs are especially on your mind. After the verse "pour forth Thy grace in every heart" in the Holy Spirit hymn is another good place to insert intercessions, and other verses may bring other people to mind, so if this happens mention them by name. Don't just focus on the person you are praying for; think of yourself lifting up the person to Jesus and letting go of him or her. If you get so obsessed by a person you are praying for that the person starts to crowd out God, this is a bad sign. (The person may be getting some sort of unhealthy hold on you.) Keep your focus on God. A friend of mine recently shared her image of intercessory prayer with me, and I found it a lovely sort of image. She said that sometimes when she feels really close to the Lord, she imagines herself as tapping Him gently on the shoulder and pointing, saying, "Look over there, Lord, at that one; please help that person."

One thing you should avoid when you do intercessory prayer is try to force God or use Him to accomplish what you want. That slides quickly into the sort of magical attitude that regards God as a kind of power, force, and energy that we can manipulate instead of a free and sovereign being who will act as He pleases. We should simply lift up the person or situation we are praying for and beg Him for help. Remain quiet, open, and receptive, so He can use your heart to touch other hearts. Reaching up and forward, palms up, is a gesture that may come naturally.

Sometimes God can use us to intercede for other people in unexpected ways, and we should try to make ourselves available so He can use our prayers at any time and in any way He chooses. You might occasionally find that when you are praying for someone, the Lord allows you for a moment to experience in a real way their darkness, doubt, despair, cynicism, or whatever it is that is provoking some sort of spiritual crisis in them. You then stand with them and pray for them from the place where they are. (The clearest case of this I ever experienced involved a person I did not know at all who was sitting near me in a church and obviously in the grip of an inner spiritual struggle, and there were clear indications that my prayer had been heard.) Standing with them and interceding for them from that place is perhaps a faint reflection of the full-bodied way in which Jesus Christ intercedes for humanity — taking on our very nature and the sufferings that our sins deserve in order to restore us to right relationship with God. In His identification or solidarity with us, He drank the cup of human suffering to the dregs, crying on the cross: "My God, my God, why hast thou forsaken me?" (Mt 27:46 and Mk 15:34). As members of the body of Christ, we participate in various ways in His perfect offering of Himself to the Father, and one way to do this is to offer ourselves to God in prayer and make intercession for others as Christ did. Not everyone is called to pray in this way, however, and it is probably best not to try to do it deliberately, since you may just be pulled down into their desperate mental and spiritual state and not be of any help to them.

Using the Litany for Intercession

Many Catholics pray the rosary as a way of interceding for someone (see Appendix). You can also pray the Sacred Heart Litany for a particular intention or for a person in need. When using it in this way, don't linger over every phrase, but move through it steadily — not at a furious speed, but at what musicians would call *andante* or a walking pace. The key thing here is to first lift up to the Lord the need or intention for which you are praying and then to see the various verses as arrows shot toward a mark. Calling on Jesus Christ by name is all we *need* to do. But when deeply distressed it comforts us to remember the wonder and richness of His heart that the Litany reveals to us, and helps us to trust in Him more. And you can use it for intercession in situations where you are too agitated to meditate. For example, I was once very angry at my mother for deep and complicated reasons and was very resentful of having to drive up to Boston and see her on a day when I could ill afford the time. So I prayed that God would fill in with His love what was lacking in mine and then did the Litany as I drove. There was a kind of urgency and desperation to my prayer and it went on against a constant backdrop of tumultuous feelings of anger and emotional pain — high above the tumult of a raging sea. Nothing seemed to be happening at all, but at one point during my visit I was moved to sit by her and hold her hand, and I could feel love flowing through me to her.

Or if you are feeling limp, dispirited, and lacking in the kind of passionate energy needed to cry out or reach out actively toward God, try praying the Litany while thinking of yourself as like a baby bird, huddled blind, naked, hungry, and helpless in the nest, waiting for the mother bird[57] to come and feed you. You can only wait and trust that she has not forgotten you and knows how to find you. It is true that baby birds make excited, little peeping sounds, but they do this only when the mother arrives, and until then they remain still and silent (after all, sounds might attract predators). When this image is the one that best fits the way you feel, the Litany will serve to remind you of God's fidelity and the sacrificial love of Christ who nourishes us with His own body and blood. The image of the mother pelican who is said to pierce her own heart and give her babies her own blood to drink (only under extremely desperate conditions of course) is one that has often been applied to Christ.

---

[57] Actually, in many species both parents feed the babies. I use the feminine pronoun to avoid grammatically convoluted sentences, but use whatever image works for you.

Intercession of the Saints

A Catholic practice that disturbs some Protestants is asking various saints to pray for you. Certainly this practice is optional; we can address God directly in prayer, and Jesus Christ is indeed the one mediator between God and man. Nonetheless, relying on the intercession of the saints seems no different in principle from asking living Christian friends to pray for you; it is effective because of the communion of saints. The Apostles' Creed affirms that "We believe in the communion of saints." What does this mean? Theologians speak of the Church Militant (Christians now alive on earth), the Church Suffering (those being purified in purgatory), and the Church Triumphant (those currently enjoying the vision of God in Heaven). All of the saved, and all those people now living who are in a state of grace, are members of this community. Just how this connection works is mysterious, but in some way the prayers and sacrifices of previous generations of Christians help us in our struggles now, and our prayers and sacrifices may perhaps help those who have died (God is outside of time, after all). So if you find some particular saint an inspiring example that you would like to imitate, you can ask that person to pray for you. Sometimes, for example, when reading the story where St. Thomas says, "My Lord and my God" (Jn 20:28), I may ask him to pray for me that I may see Jesus as he saw Him. Or a saint who has struggled with what you are struggling with may be one you feel can identify with your problem and help you, as, for example, St. Anthony is appealed to for help finding lost objects because he himself was always losing his glasses or his sermon notes.

Doubtless some individual Catholics may err in the direction of treating the saint as having himself or herself the power to grant their prayers, but the theologically correct way to understand what is going on is that we are asking the saint to pray for us. Just as you would be more likely to ask for the prayers of a friend who you think is close to God than those of another friend who is, to all appearances, mired in a life of sin, so when we want someone to intercede for us we can also turn to those Christians who have gone before us. If I am not completely certain that some particular person is in Heaven, I sometimes preface a prayer by saying, "If you are in Heaven and you can hear me, please pray for me." Or sometimes I say, "All you saints and angels pray for me." The sense that we are supported by the prayers of those who have gone before us can be a real source of comfort.

HEALING

A great deal of healing prayer goes on through special prayer ministries within churches, or through sacramental channels — in particular the sacrament that used to be called "Last Rites," or "Extreme Unction," but which is now called "Anointing of the Sick."[58] The practice of laying hands on people, anointing them with oil and praying for their healing is solidly based in Scripture (Mk 6:13; Jm 5:14). The disciples are sent out by Jesus to preach and to heal, and the apostles in the early Church anointed the sick with oil and prayed for their recovery. I focus here on private prayer, but those interested in how healing prayer ministries function should take a look at *Healing* and *The Power to Heal* by Francis MacNutt.

When we are talking about private prayer, then, prayer for the healing of another person is a special case of intercessory prayer. The basic prayers already contain verses that mention healing: "Heal our wounds, our strength renew" and "Our weakened flesh do thou restore to strength and courage evermore," and these could be good places to insert special prayers for healing of oneself or others. If you or someone you love is se-

---

[58] This sacrament used to be performed only in cases where death seemed imminent, but there has tended to be a relaxing of this rule, and some parishes have a service for the Anointing of the Sick on a regular basis. Catholics can, in any case, request that a priest come and anoint them for healing if they are seriously ill. Normally confession should precede the reception of this sacrament, and it can have very powerful effects spiritually as well as physically.

riously sick, the temptation to try to manipulate God can be very strong, and it is especially important to really let go and entrust yourself or the other person to God. When I was in Berkeley, I knew of two women who had degenerative disease affecting the optic nerve in one of their eyes. One came to a small charismatic prayer group I attended, and regularly prayed claiming and accepting a healing and thanking God for healing her. So far as I know she did not get healed. The other woman prayed quietly after Mass (at a nearby Anglican church) and said, "Lord, if you want me to be blind, you can take the other eye too." She then suddenly got back the sight in the affected eye.

That faith healings have occurred is pretty widely acknowledged even by the medical profession, but why God heals some people and not others is a mystery. I suspect each case is different, so it is hard to lay down any sort of hard and fast rules. But there are a few general guidelines that emerge from Scripture. Jesus asks the paralytic lying by the sheep gate pool of Bethzatha, "Do you want to be healed?" (Jn 5:6). And to several other people He says, "Do you believe that I can do this?" (e.g., Mt 9:28). Finally, people are rewarded for their persistence. For example, blind Bartimaeus (Mk 10:46-52) and the Canaanite woman whose daughter was possessed by a demon (Mt 15:22-28).

It might seem that of course a sick person wants to be healed, but in fact things are often much more complicated. People may feel on some deep level that they deserve their illness because of some sin they committed, and they may not even be aware that this is what is going on. Or sometimes people have gotten themselves entangled in some sort of bargain with God, offering to bear suffering for some other person (MacNutt describes a case of this sort), and so feel they shouldn't seek healing. Some people may feel that it is selfish to ask things for oneself, or that it is more holy to say with St. Paul, "My desire is to depart and be with Christ, for that is far better" (Ph 1:20). But we should be willing, as St. Paul was, to continue to work and labor in God's service until He calls us home. I believe we should always ask for life and healing. Even Jesus prayed in Gethsemane that this cup pass from Him (Mt 26:39), although He immediately submitted Himself to God's will, saying, "but not as I will but as Thou wilt." There may be cases where you feel you have a very clear guidance from God that it is indeed your time to die and be with Him. But even then it is probably a good idea to talk to a mature Christian you respect about your guidance. I'm not saying it doesn't happen, but be careful. So, in your private prayer you need to pray very hard that God will reveal to you what is really going on, and help you recognize any sort of inner blocks that you may have to receiving a healing.

"Do you believe that I can do this?" The other important thing is having faith that God can do it. Often times Jesus says things like, "Your faith has healed you" (Mt 15:22; Mk 5:34, 52; Lk 8:48; Lk 18:42), but be careful here. Always remember it is God who heals. Trust in God and not in your faith. Sometimes people think if they can psych themselves up to have really rock-solid faith then they will be healed. But that is not the point. Faith is a gift of the Holy Spirit; we can pray for it, but not give it to ourselves. "I believe, help my unbelief," prays the father of the epileptic child (Mk 9:24).

However much you believe in the power of prayer to heal, you should not neglect to consult doctors, and this may include various types of alternative medicine such as chiropractic, acupuncture, homeopathy, therapeutic massage, or nutritional and herbal medicine. God may choose to heal you through a doctor, after all, and it is not right to insist that God perform a miracle when there is a perfectly normal and efficacious remedy open to you. You should pray to be guided to the right doctor (perhaps consulting more than one), and pray about which of the possible treatment plans you should follow. Don't simply do blindly whatever the doctor says; you have a right to decide what is done to your own body, and doctors sometimes over-treat patients. But don't regard prayer as an alternative to medical treatment; they can work together.

Finally, if healing does not occur, you should not feel that there is something wrong with you — that you don't have enough faith or that God is punishing you.[59] Ask for healing, but submit yourself to God's will. We can't know what God's purposes are, and must trust that He can bring good out of whatever He permits to happen.

PRAYING IN TONGUES

This practice, common among Christians of many denominations, is one that is solidly rooted in Scripture, but is controversial among contemporary Christians.[60] Some have a horror of it and denigrate those who engage in it as "holy rollers," while others regard it as essential for living a full Christian life. I will not be dogmatic about this, since I know some very holy people who do not pray in tongues, but my own experience has been that praying in tongues has built me up, strengthened me in my faith, been an uplifting and joyful way to praise God, and an aid to intercessory prayer as well. Catholic charismatic prayer groups routinely run "Life in the Spirit" seminars in which you learn about the gift of tongues, and at the end of the seminar you are prayed over by other people to receive this gift. Having a group of mature Christians to guide and support you can be very helpful, but it is not necessary to have other people lay hands on you and pray over you to receive the gift of tongues; God dispenses such gifts as He wills.

I received the gift of tongues while sitting alone in front of the sacrament in an Anglican church. I simply asked the Lord to

---

[59] The book *Faith Beyond Faith Healing: Finding Hope After Shattered Dreams* by Kimberly Winston may be helpful for those who do not receive a physical healing.

[60] Speaking in tongues is mentioned frequently in Acts and in the writings of St. Paul. It occurred at Pentecost, of course, and the practice continued in the early Church (e.g., Ac 10:46; 19:6, 1 Cor 12:10, 28, 30; 14:5, 6, 18). Exactly what was going on in each case and whether different sorts of things went under the same name in different contexts is not certain, but at any rate the phenomenon was a common one.

give me a tongue to praise Him and started praising Him, first in words and then gradually moving out into praying in tongues (I had been attending a Catholic charismatic prayer group, so I had some idea what to expect). Imagine yourself in the presence of the angels and saints praising God. Raising your arms, palms up, in whatever position feels natural is helpful. The experience is hard to describe, but it is something like an inner spring being opened in one's heart (or rather at the deepest center of one's being, which is not identical with the physical heart) and a powerful river of praise beginning to flow forth effortlessly.[61] It is not something uncontrollable that makes you babble and fall into fits against your will. But neither is it something simply willed. It involves feeling praise welling up inside you, allowing it to do so and delighting in it — a kind of breaking open and overflowing. "Thou anointest my head with oil, my cup overflows" (Ps 23:5). It enables us to praise God with a richness and complexity beyond what our mortal minds could devise — in a way more fitting to His glory.

Interestingly, when the disciples first received the promised Holy Spirit on Pentecost, people passing by thought that they were drunk (Ac 2:15) and one could, perhaps, see the experience of praising God in tongues as analogous with inebriation. St. Paul says we have been given to drink of one Spirit, and advises us to be "filled with the Holy Spirit and not get drunk with wine" (Eph 5:18-19). Just as the more subtle, emotional, and spiritual dimensions of "eros" have been driven out of currency by the crudest ones, so also the term "inebriated" has become simply a more genteel way of saying "drunk." But the term "inebriate" has historically been used to describe some of the most sublime human experiences as well as the lowest sort of physical stupefac-

---

[61] Interestingly, this is precisely what Jesus predicts in Jn 7:38. He says that "He who believes in me... out of his heart will flow rivers of living water" and the evangelist explains that "He said this about the Spirit, which those who believed in Him were to receive; for as yet the Spirit had not been given, because Jesus was not yet glorified" (Jn 7:39). The Spirit was given at Pentecost, at which time the apostles began to speak in tongues, glorifying God.

tion. Emily Dickinson, for example, wrote: "Inebriate of air am I and debauchee of dew; reeling through endless summer days from inns of molten blue." According to the *Oxford English Dictionary*, a person might be described as "inebriate in the love of God," and Peter was described as "inebriate and made drunken with the sweetness of this vision." A trace of this older way of using the term "inebriate" is found in a verse from the traditional *Anima Christi* prayer: "Body of Christ be my salvation; blood of Christ inebriate me" (See Appendix). Since one way of thinking about our desire for God is seeing it as analogous to a thirst: "Oh God, thou art my God, I seek thee, my soul thirsts for thee; my flesh faints for thee, as in a dry and weary land where no water is" (Ps 63:1), having that desire satisfied would be like the experience of having one's thirst completely slaked — so that one's hard, narrow self has at last been broken open and filled to overflowing. Water is life giving; plants without water cannot sustain life. So the thirst for God is, in a sense, a thirst for the fullness of life; Jesus says, "I came that they may have life and have it abundantly" (Jn 10:10).[62]

Praying in tongues is not only a way of praising God. It can also be a way of expressing your longing for God or a way of reaching out toward, or pleading with God when you are asking for help or praying for someone else. Hold the person in your mind, visualize lifting them up to Jesus, and ask the Holy Spirit to help you pray for that person. The Spirit knows best what is needed, and although you may not understand the sounds you utter, God does. St. Paul speaks of the Spirit interceding for us with sighs and groans too deep for words (Rm 8:26). When praying in tongues for another person, reach up and forward as you would in intercession. Characteristically when you first receive the gift of praying in tongues you will receive one pattern of syl-

---

[62] Might it be, perhaps, that alcoholics are people who have the thirst for God especially strongly, but want to be able to forcibly break down those hard walls of the self and give themselves the fullness and delight that only God can give (as the person who masturbates wants to give himself or herself an experience that can only truly come from union with another human being).

lables which will then come forth each time you pray in tongues (some call this their personal prayer language), but if you pray in this way often, the gift will usually become more fluent and variable, although the original pattern you received does not go away but continues to hold a central place in your prayer. You may feel moved to sing softly while praying in tongues. Praying in tongues privately can occur at different points on your vocal range — from very deep and low sounds all the way up to very high frequency sounds that almost disappear from the range of hearing. Sometimes feeling moved to simply move your lips and tongue silently can accompany quite deep experiences in prayer. The key thing is to keep your attention directed toward God, pouring out your heart in praise or supplication.

There are several points in my prayer routine where I often pray in tongues. When I say, "Heart of Jesus, in whom dwells all the fullness of divinity," or "Heart of Jesus of infinite majesty," or "Heart of Jesus most worthy of all praise," I often pray in tongues. Also after "the Father's promise true to teach our earthly tongues thy heavenly speech" in the Holy Spirit hymn. Even just after a "Glory be...." No need to be mechanical about it; let it happen when you feel moved.

PRAYING FOR GUIDANCE

This is one of the most difficult problems in Christian life. I focus here on seeking guidance about what *you* should *do*[63] — not about what *other people* should do, nor about doctrinal questions, issues pertaining to Church discipline, or things like when the Second Coming of Christ will occur. Since prayer involves entering into the walk with God that He is calling us to, our central task is to clean up our own act (remember the passage

---

[63] In using the word "do" here I do not intend to limit it to outward actions of the body. We might be guided to pray for someone, or even merely to be still and rest in God.

about trying to take the speck out of your brother's eye when there is a beam in your own). Ordinarily God does not reveal to us things about other people's spiritual condition, or about what they should do.[64] These are not our business; He holds us responsible for our own intentions and actions.

American culture stresses self-reliance, taking control of your life, setting your own goals, being an autonomous individual who doesn't let others tell him what to do, and so on. We tend to think of ourselves as writing the story of our own lives. We are like artists struggling to make ourselves into the person we want to be, and fashioning our lives into the pattern we think will express who we are and fulfill us. To a certain degree, this sort of thinking is not bad. We do need to think about the kind of person that our choices are making us into. But for a Christian the over-arching fact is that God created us and that He has a plan for our lives — something that He wants us to do for His glory. I don't want to say that God has every detail planned out. We do have free will. But we have certain talents that He wants us to use — gifts given us for building up His Kingdom. We have all let Him down on occasion, but there is always work still to be done that our talents fit us to do, so we need to pick ourselves up and go on, praying that He will guide us to do what He wants us to do. This is not like being a servant or a drudge, for it is in using our talents in this way that we find happiness. "In His service is perfect freedom" (*Book of Common Prayer*).

As Christians, we should strive to do God's will, as Christ Himself came to do the will of the one who sent Him (Jn 4:24), but how are we to tell what God's will *is?* Decision making is always difficult, and often we can feel rather desperate. If only God would give us more direct guidance about what to do! Why does He so often seem to remain silent? Are we at fault? Perhaps

---

[64] If you are a priest and hear confessions, or a pastor entrusted with the spiritual guidance of your parishioners, the situation is somewhat different, although you should still be cautious about making judgments of others' hearts. See the section on "Spiritual Direction" in Chapter Five.

we are really not listening. Would we really do His will if He *did* tell us directly? Asking such questions, it is all too easy to get ourselves totally tied in knots, which of course does nothing to help us discern God's will.

Volumes could be written about how to find and recognize God's guidance. There is no easy one-size-fits-all answer, and many methods have been employed within the Christian tradition. Even the disciples struggled with this problem. For example, they prayed and drew lots in order to choose someone to replace Judas (Ac 1:24-26), and there are several instances in which they are guided by dreams from God (See Ac 16:10, for example). St. Joseph also received guidance in dreams (Mt 1:20 and Mt 2:13). Some fell into trances or had visions. See Acts 9, for example, for an account of the visions experienced by St. Paul and Ananias. St. Peter falls into a trance and has a vision indicating he should go with the men Cornelius had sent to him (Ac 10:9-16). The Book of Revelation records the visions experienced by St. John.

It is helpful, I think, to step back a little from the immediate pressure of making a decision now, and see learning to be responsive to God's guidance as one of the long-term fruits of prayer, rather than thinking of it too much in anthropomorphic and external terms like one person asking another who stubbornly won't answer. "Here I am asking you, God; why don't you tell me now?" If you keep worship of God and entering into a deepening relationship of love with Him at the center of your prayer life this will lay the foundation for becoming responsive to His will. We are like plants that need to be trained to climb up a trellis. In prayer God re-anchors our wandering hearts and minds to Him. By clinging more closely to Him, we continue to grow toward the light and are prepared to bear the flowers and fruit He wants from us. The more our hearts, minds, and wills become conformed to Christ, the more spontaneously we will be moved to act as He would have us act, so we should pray daily that He will conform our hearts, minds and wills to His own. If we get into the habit of regularly being open to God's guidance in prayer — allowing Him to direct our prayer and show us the truth — then it will be easier to be attuned to His guidance in specific decisions. Pray for docility and ask Him to put His desires in your heart.

Don't think of guidance too much just in terms of external actions. God wants us to look to Him, accept His love, worship Him, allow Him to show us the truth and transform us. This is a long, slow, work, and until we have been deeply nourished and formed by Him, we are not yet ready to rush out and climb mountains, swim the seas, and fight battles for the Lord. Rather, we should try to be small and humble. Remember the passage about accepting the Kingdom of God like a child. If you keep looking outwards and trying to get Him to tell you moment by moment what to do, but neglect that quiet, receptive time alone with Him, you are likely to rush off on ill-considered crusades and do more harm than good. There are long, slow months or even years of preparation time necessary, as was the case with St. Paul who spent considerable time in Arabia (Gal 1:17) after his initial conversion before he began his most active ministry But that preparation time is itself delightful in that it allows us to become more intimate with Him. So don't be too impatient for action; the Lord will give you plenty to do in His own time.

I think the image of the dance given in Chapter Two is especially useful for thinking about guidance. Being guided by the Lord is not like simply asking a friend for advice, but neither is it like being a soldier taking orders. A good dancer is able to guide his partner through gentle pressure and subtle signals of various kinds, and the more perfectly you are able to follow, the more the two of you can move as one. If two people dance together regularly, a kind of spontaneous sympathy or attunement develops, and ideally you will become able to anticipate your partner's next move and follow without having to be shoved. During the learning process (and we are never wholly out of the learning phase) we often need to be corrected — sometimes fairly forcefully. The Lord's guidance thus can often be particularly clearly felt when

He is correcting us — when He is opposing the direction in which our will and desires are carrying us, as a rock stands out sharply against a swiftly flowing current. This does not mean that He is not guiding us at other times, but merely that He is doing so in a more subtle way.[65] Whether or not God *speaks* to you, He is always there, and that is what is most important.

In what follows, I will first discuss some things you should not do, and then say some more positive things about seeking God's guidance and recognizing it when He gives it.

You should not expect a response from God to every question you pose to Him in prayer. He is entirely free and sovereign, and is not bound to answer every question you put to Him. And don't turn inward and try to become attuned to your feelings or desires. Unfortunately, these can sometimes be deeply disordered in ways that will require considerable time for God to heal and re-order, and they can flow with the force of a raging river or a runaway horse. They generate a sort of inertia, so we can't just turn on a dime, as it were. We need, somehow, to get distance from our own passions, especially when the decision in question involves them deeply. This is, of course, more easily said than done. But at least we need to be aware of our situation and realize that feelings are an imperfect guide. This does not mean that they should have *no* weight ever. Sometimes our intuitive feelings are right on target, so you don't want to fly to the opposite extreme and regard your feelings as having no importance at all.

Looking now at the positive side, there seems to be no limit to the ways in which God may guide us. This is, of course,

---

[65] I think this point is similar to that made by Ignatius Loyola in his *Spiritual Exercises*, in the section entitled "Discernment of Spirits." He notes that the action of a spirit on you will stand out more clearly (like water dropping on a rock with a kind of "ping") when it is in opposition to the direction that your desires and will are currently flowing (think of how the water ruffles up when a flowing stream hits a rock). But when it is in harmony with them it flows imperceptibly into the stream, as a drop of water is absorbed by a sponge. He relies on this fact in helping people discern whether they are being acted on by a good spirit or a bad spirit, but this of course requires knowing what direction you are moving — toward or away from God.

not surprising. The important thing is to put your question out clearly, let go of it, and try to be open to His answer when and if He gives it. Sometimes God may make use of other people or of purely natural phenomena (say, the splendor of the night sky, or the devoted loving care of the parents for a baby bird). St. Augustine's famous conversion story involved his overhearing the voice of a child playing nearby calling, "Take and read." Augustine experienced this as an instruction addressed to him and picked up the letters of St. Paul and began to read. It might be a conversation overheard on a bus. It might be one phrase in something you are reading that sort of jumps out at you.

Even a hostile person's criticism of you may contain a little kernel that you feel is from the Lord. Be careful here, though. Do not take to heart every criticism leveled at you. Doing so may look like a form of humility, but it leaves you at the mercy of others and easily leads to discouragement and paralysis. It is the Lord whom you need to please first and foremost. So ask Him to help you discern any kernel of truth in what critics say and to stand firm in the face of opposition and hostility when this is called for. If you are trying to live a Christian life and struggling on a daily basis to overcome your faults and do what God wants you to do, you will be in the proper frame of mind to pick up these sorts of clues. Sometimes, even when you have been wandering a long time away from the Lord and following His guidance would seem to be the last thing on your mind, you may be, on a deeper level, only a heartbeat away from conversion, and some very small thing could precipitate a massive shift in the direction of your life (as a small falling stone can trigger an avalanche).

If you keep praying for the guidance of the Holy Spirit, God will direct you in all sorts of ways, and sometimes you can see in retrospect that you were being led in some direction in ways that you did not recognize as God's guidance at the time. Or God may have had very different ends in view than the ones that you were thinking about. For example, I remember my decision to visit California in 1978. I'd been involved with a religious community of a vaguely New Age and syncretistic sort that was feeling increasingly wrong for me, but didn't know what to do. Various little things began to put the idea of California in my mind, including a story about a woman from that group who had met a wonderful husband in San Francisco (San Francisco is, of course, a rather bad place for husband hunting), a drive-away car suddenly became available, and so on. The little pointers all fell into a pattern and I went, wound up staying with an old college friend who had become a Catholic, and met all sorts of people through whose influence and example I joined the Catholic Church a year or two later (I did *not*, however, find a husband in San Francisco).

Another story illustrates how you may think that the Holy Spirit is guiding you for one reason, when in fact God has something different in mind. My husband and I were walking on an almost deserted beach, and got into an argument and he walked off separately. As I was walking I prayed the Sacred Heart Litany for help, and was soon joined by a young man to whom I lent my binoculars. I said how beautiful the birds were, and he said, "Praise God for them," and then went off. Later, just as my path and my husband's path were about to converge again, he again appeared and joined us. He began to talk to us about Jesus, and asked whether we truly accepted Him as savior, etc. Once we assured him that we did, he told us that he was practicing being responsive to the guidance of the Holy Spirit. He had, it seems, been thinking in terms of testifying to Jesus and converting us. But it was clear that the Holy Spirit had guided him to us in order to cushion our meeting and heal the rift between my husband and me.

The most common form of guidance does not involve specific words experienced as addressed to us. It is a subtle shift in the way the situation appears to us after prayer by comparison with the way it appeared before (this may require prayer over some period of time). Sometimes you may put a question out in prayer and not receive an answer, but suddenly it will become clear a little later as you are engaged in some simple habitual activity like showering, putting on makeup, or shaving that takes your mind out of gear and thus makes it more receptive. It is as though when you really let go of all the pieces, God rearranges the puzzle into a coherent pattern and it becomes clearer what you should do. At first a lot of His guidance is likely to be about how He wants you to pray and enter into relationship with Him (and the things separating us from God will differ from person to person). Perhaps I am an unusually willful person, but I, at least, find that I need to keep praying that "bend the stubborn heart and will" verse (from the Holy Spirit invocation) often.

But it is not all that uncommon to experience something like a voice speaking — words forming themselves in your mind in such a way that they seem to have a kind of energy that is not your own (unlike, for example, a fantasy that one is making up). Just as sense perception comes at us as from outside, so does perception of God. God is operating *in* us of course, but it is not *we* who are acting. Also, I have noticed that the words are often arranged in ways that are not characteristic of my own style of speaking. Biblical scholars often try to determine when two books have the same author by analyzing the style of each writer — the characteristic vocabulary and grammatical structures, the rhythm of the speech, the images used, etc. Often God uses material already in our imagination and memory, but when He speaks directly in answer to spoken or unspoken question, or just of His own free will, one senses a style not one's own. If you are never surprised by what God says, or at least caught off guard and challenged, you may be fantasizing too much. Try to avoid anticipating what He will say.

People marveled at Jesus because He taught "with authority" and not as the scribes and Pharisees did. The authority comes through particularly clearly when God is correcting you or challenging you. There is a clear sense that you are in touch with a personal being, but the experience is quite unlike that of another person giving you advice or asking you a question. Sometimes you might get words in response to a question you have asked God — usually in response to your request to understand something more clearly. Or at key turning points God may pose a question to you, as, for example, after I had fallen away from Him for many years and was beginning to turn back toward Him, I got, "Are you serious this time?"

The idea that God might speak to you may sound a bit alarming, and perhaps it should. After all, haven't some people come up with crazy things, insisting that they were revealed to them by God? If you are worried that perhaps some negative spiritual being may be at work, the suggestions offered in Chapter Three in the section on doubts may be helpful in making a discernment.

But if you are just unsure what a "guidance" means or whether you have gotten it right, try placing things you think are God's guidance to you on a spectrum ranging from those you feel confident about through those you suspect might be only your imagination to ones that seem somehow wrong or unintelligible to you. Do not act on a "guidance" when big things are at stake unless you feel pretty confident that it is right, and use your common sense. Talk with someone you trust. Let things settle for a while. Cross check them. Does the putative "guidance" seem to be of a piece with previous guidances? Does it cohere with what you know or reasonably believe about God from the Christian tradition as well as with your knowledge about the world drawn from everyday life? People do have auditory hallucinations, so don't tie yourself in knots over every little thing. If it is really important, God will make it clear. Trust Him.

Another mark of genuine guidance is that it cuts right to the heart of the issue and brings clarity and peace. In my experience, at least, God does not waste words and ramble on and on. A communication is always put in the simplest bare bones sort of way. In fact, the Lord's ability to cut through all the verbiage and rationalizations and confusion and reveal the truth of the situation is evidence that it is, indeed, the Lord. There are, of course, special cases. Some mystics report longer and more complicated communications from the Lord, and people with prophetic vocations may receive fairly lengthy revelations. But I think the more usual case is that one receives actual verbal guidance fairly rarely. Even many very holy people have received their central guidance for their lives in only a few words. For example, St. Francis was told to "Rebuild my church," and Mother Teresa felt Jesus say "I thirst," and she interpreted this in terms of His thirst for souls, and this touched off her lifelong vocation to bring souls to Christ.

Sometimes, also, it seems that God wants us to take responsibility for a decision and does not direct us what to do. For example, a woman who was praying about whether to marry a particular man, was told by the Lord that "he has been very wounded." The Lord was present with her, and wanted her to make an informed choice, but left the decision to her.

The practice of asking God for signs is one that many Christians have had grave reservations about. Generally speaking, the more open-ended your request is, the better. Simply ask God for some sign and then be open to ways in which He may be using events or people or even natural occurrences to communicate with you. There is the case of Gideon and the fleece, but it not altogether clear that his repeated asking for signs from God was something the author of Judges approved of (Jg 6:36-40). It involves a kind of testing God to require that He give you signs of a particular form. It is not for us to specify *how* God should reply to our questions. Some of the forms that devotion to St. Thérèse of Lisieux have taken, for example, verge on superstition. If someone gives you a rose out of the blue, then that is taken to be a sign from God that your prayer has been heard. I know someone who tried to structure the request for signs by saying if the next rose he received was red it was a sign he should marry and if it was white it was a sign he should go into the priesthood. This sort of precise structuring of how God is to reply is, I think, improper.

Even drawing lots or flipping coins after praying is probably not a good idea. The apostles drew lots to determine who should replace Judas to fill up the number of the Twelve Apostles (Ac 1:26), but this was a unique case. I take bluebirds to be signs of happiness and on occasion have taken seeing one to be a sign that I should take a particular course of action, but I worry that this verges on superstition. If I see one spontaneously one day when I am feeling sad, I may take it as a good sign — a sign of God's presence and love. That is probably all right. But if I make some specific decision turn on whether or not I see a bluebird on a particular day, that crosses over the line into being a kind of testing of God. We cannot demand that God answer our questions in our terms.

INTEGRATING PRAYER INTO YOUR DAILY ACTIVITIES

So far I have focused on how to use the time when you sit down and devote yourself fully to prayer. This kind of concentrated prayer time is necessary to allow God to work deeply in your heart. But obviously it is also desirable to remain in a prayerful state of mind as much as you can as you go about your daily activities; St. Paul says we should "pray constantly" (1 Th 5:17). And Brother Lawrence advises us to try to be attuned to God's presence at all times, and to lift up our hearts to Him often in little acts of love and worship. But given all the distractions and stresses of modern life, keeping our focus on God can be difficult. Brother Lawrence said that he eventually came to feel no difference between formal times of prayer and other times. He could remain calm and joyful and focused on God even in the midst of his work in the kitchen, with people calling for various things and banging pots and pans. But many of us have jobs that demand a higher and more complex level of mental and emotional involvement than cooking, and it is a lot harder to integrate prayer into these activities than it is to do so with an action you can perform with minimal attention.

During the formative period of monasticism, and still to-day for the most part, monks and nuns tend to do simple sorts of manual work that are fairly easy to integrate with prayer. This may be one of those areas where our situation is sufficiently un-like that of those operating within the monastic tradition that we cannot simply transfer their methods to our jobs in the twenty-first century, though you might try repeating the name of Jesus, or "Jesus I love you" aloud or mentally as a kind of background to whatever you are doing. Singing or humming a favorite hymn or devotional song as you work can also help to keep God in mind.

Even if you find it hard to pray while doing your job, you should pray before you plan all your daily activities, pray for help with a project when you start it, cry out for help when you hit rough spots, and offer your work to Him. I've found that on mornings when I stay at home and work at my computer after prayer I can often recover a prayerful state of mind fairly easily at least for several hours after my morning prayer. But once I am out and doing things, battling with traffic, teaching, doing er-rands, dealing with difficult people, checking things off my list and trying to keep in mind all the things I need to do, it is much harder.

One thing you can do is to try to say regular prayers at certain hours. This is a common practice among practitioners of many religions, and serves to recall your attention to God at least briefly. Many people recite some sort of morning prayer. Or you could just say something brief when you first wake up, such as "Praise to you Lord Jesus Christ." The Angelus (Appendix), is traditional at noon (also 6 a.m. and 6 p.m. but I think most people do it only at noon), and many Christians try to briefly remember Jesus's sacrificial death on the cross at 3 p.m. (the time He died on Good Friday according to Scripture) and to thank Him (I sometimes say the part of the Sacred Heart Litany that pertains to His sacrifice on the cross at that hour if I remember). Saying a short prayer before meals is also traditional, thanking

God and asking His blessing on your food and on those you are sharing it with (if you are sharing a meal).

The Catholic Church has a long tradition of reciting daily what is called "The Divine Office," a rotating set of psalms and prayers and readings for the various seasons of the Church year. There is a multi-volume version used by religious orders, and a shorter one called *Christian Prayer* for those who do not have so much time to say it.[66] (I don't say it very often, since *I* find other types of prayer more fruitful and my time is limited, but you might find it helpful.) The prayers of the Office are recited or chanted in monasteries at a number of different times of day, and certain Scripture passages are recited daily at morning prayer and evening prayer. Night prayer is quite short, and is a good way to end the day. The last moment of the day is important, so you should say some short prayer before sleep (such as the Lord's Prayer) or one of the prayers suggested in the Appendix for bedtime. Many people do an "examination of conscience" at bedtime, reviewing the day briefly and asking God's forgiveness where they have sinned or fallen short. I find it easier to review the previous day at the start of my morning prayer session because at night I tend not to be very clear headed, and get bogged down in analyzing and worrying about everything.

One of the monastic hours of prayer is called "Vigils" and it is recited in the middle of the night. Some people find this a particularly good time to pray. When everyone else is asleep and all the bustle and noise is stilled, being alone with the Lord can feel intimate in a special way. If you are particularly given to doing intercessory prayer, you might sometimes feel the Lord wants you to get up and pray for someone in the night. And if you wake up feeling fearful, beset, torn apart, and unable to calm your mind, it is best to actually sit up for a while and pray. When we are lying down we are more vulnerable to spiritual assault. So

---

[66] These can be obtained from Catholic Book Publishing Corp. in New York. (On their web page click on "Liturgy of the Hours.")

instead of taking a sleeping pill, try getting up and praying until you feel calm and sleepy.

Dead time spent waiting in places, riding in busses, subways, trains, or driving the car (when your route is familiar and the traffic is not too heavy and moving at a fairly constant speed — be careful here) can provide a good opportunity to say some memorized prayers. Say the rosary using a finger rosary, sing a hymn or two, or pray spontaneously, bringing whatever is on your mind to God and asking His help and guidance for whatever you are about to undertake. When you are driving alone on the highway you can pray in complete privacy, so this is a good time to really pour out your heart to the Lord. A Japanese student of mine remarked with surprise that he found a lot of Americans scream in their cars (the Japanese do not do this). So if you find your car a safe place to cry and scream — to let out your feelings and say whatever is on your mind — then incorporate these patterns into your prayer life. You can say whatever you want to the Lord, and even express anger at Him. But don't make it like a quarrel with a loved one that ends with your storming out and slamming the door. Always leave the lines of communication open, and ask Him to help you understand what is happening, to show you the truth, to stay with you and guide you.

Another valuable thing to do is to figure out at what time of day you tend to feel most irritated, downhearted, frazzled, etc., and make a point of praying at that time. For example, you might make a practice of stopping by a church on your way home from work if that is a low time of day for you.[67] It can take a lot of discipline to resist rushing home and collapsing in your favorite chair with a drink, or perhaps simply entering into a frantic rush of trying to pick up kids and feed your family. But I've found that on those occasions when I force myself to stop by the church and pray, the Lord really uplifts me, enables me not to dump the problems of my day on my husband, and sometimes I've felt

---

[67] I find it especially comforting to pray in a church where the Blessed Sacrament is kept reserved.

as though we were surrounded by a kind of warm and peaceful presence the whole rest of the evening. Even five minutes of really heartfelt prayer can make an enormous difference.

Try to anticipate problem situations and prepare yourself with prayer before you go into them. For example, if you are about to get on the highway Columbus Day weekend in New England, you should anticipate traffic jams and prepare yourself to be patient in spite of them. If you are going to the house of someone whose spouse irritates you terribly, pray before you go that God will help you be charitable and not rise to the bait and get into an argument. Or better yet, pray that the Holy Spirit will help you see that person as God does, and also that He will move that person's heart to act on his or her better impulses. Also, if you find that there is a particular time of day when you feel low and irritable and likely to blurt things out and lose your temper, try to fit some prayer and quiet time in around that time (for me this tends to be late afternoon and just before bed).

Prayer can also avert quarrels or facilitate patching things up after one. Quarrels with family members or those you live with usually fall into certain patterns in such a way that they tend to escalate. As soon as you realize that the pattern is setting in, and before you are completely in the grip of anger, try to say a prayer that God will step in and break the pattern and keep it from getting out of control. This works best if you can get into a different room from the person you are quarreling with[68] and allow a little cooling down time before you interact with them again.

I recommend the practice of asking God to bless and help whoever is sick or injured when you see an ambulance go by. Pray before important meetings, presentations, lunches with friends, interviews, before you set out on a trip, or before you enter into

---

[68] In a pinch you can just go in the bathroom and close the door. Kneel down if you are feeling especially desperate. I've taken to saying the *Memorare* (Appendix) at such times and found that this has helped a lot, but any prayer you are comfortable with is fine.

any sort of dangerous situation, and remember to thank Him when things go well. I pray that the Holy Spirit will guide me and my students before I go in to teach a class. If you see a very sad looking person on the street or in a bus, say a prayer for him or her. Thank God when you have a narrow escape from some danger or when something unexpectedly good happens. Praise Him when you are struck by something especially beautiful. Don't ever feel that you are away from God, that what you are doing or thinking or feeling is hidden from God, or that He is indifferent to what happens to you (remember the passage about how not even a sparrow falls to the ground without His knowing it). As Brother Lawrence puts it: "You need not cry very loud; He is nearer to us than we are aware of."[69] If you feel a sudden impulse to pray at any time, by all means do it. Don't put it off. Prayers don't need to be long, elegant, or beautifully worded. Just natural and heartfelt. A brief moment of loving attention to the Lord is often all that is needed.

Some spiritual writers say that prayer eventually begins to go on continuously in our hearts, even when we are not aware of it. This is a comforting thought, though I don't know how we could tell whether it is true. But it makes a certain sense. For if, as St. Paul says, we are temples in which the Holy Spirit dwells, and the Holy Spirit prays in us, for us, and with us, then prayer could be going on when we are asleep or distracted with other things.

In the next and final chapter, we will look briefly at some of the ways in which we can nurture the new life of faith that has been planted in us, and avoid choices in our daily lives that are likely to undermine, block, or weaken that faith.

---

[69] Brother Lawrence, *op. cit.*, p. 48.

CHAPTER FIVE

CHRISTIAN LIFE

Although a lot of lip service is given to Christianity, being faithful to genuinely Christian values is counter-cultural in many ways. So we need to give thought to how the new life that has been planted in us through faith can be nourished and tended. We want to be like the case of the seed that fell on good soil and brought forth thirty-fold, sixty-fold, and a hundred-fold (Mt 13:8, 23) rather than those where it fell on the path and got eaten by birds, on the shallow soil so that it died when the sun came out and scorched it, or among thorns (the cares and pleasures of the world) that choked the plant so it proved unfruitful. Assuming that you are at least trying to live a good life in accordance with Christian principles[70] and that you have some sort of regular prayer routine in place, you need to look at the way in which other choices you are making in your life may be helping you draw closer to God, or perhaps getting in the way of your relationship with Him.

What movies do we watch? What do we read? To whom do we go for help when we feel we just can't cope any more? Who do we spend time with? What do we do for fun? How should

---

[70] As noted in the Introduction, this is a book on prayer and not a book on Christian ethics or moral theology. You should, of course, try to come to better understand Christian moral teachings and live in accordance with them. If you are finding it hard to accept them in some particular case, you should pray for enlightenment, seek help and advice from a mature Christian you trust, and perhaps look at some books on Christian ethics or moral theology.

we handle our anger? Our loneliness? Our fears? Not only can prayer bring about changes in our lives — for example, that meeting you dreaded so much may have gone better because you prayed about it beforehand — but also our little daily choices can have an effect on our prayer life and relationship with God. To live a life pleasing to God and to do the work He put us here to do should be the over-arching goal in terms of which everything else is evaluated.[71] Our faith must pervade our lives and not just exist side by side with all our other concerns if it is to provide the anchor we need amid life's storms. This doesn't mean that we shouldn't have a variety of interests and activities, but only that we should keep God at the center in all we do.

THE CARE AND FEEDING OF YOUR IMAGINATION

One important choice we make concerns our exposure to things that feed and stimulate our imaginations. The imagination is very important in prayer. It is sometimes said that "you are what you eat." What you put into your body provides the raw materials out of which it is built, and thus has enormous consequences for its structure and functioning. Certain nutrients are necessary for the proper functioning of our brain, muscles, or hormonal system, for example. Toxins can become stored in our tissues and interfere with the proper functioning of our body or even cause diseases. Similarly, what we put into our imagination enters into its structure and affects its functioning. Much of our imagination is already formed by the fact that we live in the physical world, in a certain time and place, and are the sorts of creatures we are. Therefore there we have a lot in common with all other people everywhere and from every time. Our experiences of the

---

[71] St. Paul describes himself as running a race to obtain an imperishable wreath, and says, "I pommel my body and subdue it, lest after preaching to others I myself should be disqualified" (1 Cor 9:24-27).

sky, the sun, the stars, the weather, the pull of gravity on our bodies, the sea, plants, animals, flowers, of eating food, of childbirth, of being raised and nurtured by other human beings, of hunger, thirst, sexual desire, pain, and so on, already provide a rich background vocabulary out of which the imagination can construct poetry, stories, paintings, and so on.

In trying to understand something of God and His intentions toward us or to communicate our experience of God to others, we naturally make use of these sorts of imaginative images. God is compared in Scripture to light, a rock, an eagle, a father, a warrior, a king, and a nursing mother, to name only a few such images. And Jesus draws on a number of imaginative images in trying to teach us about God. The Kingdom of Heaven is likened to a mustard seed (Lk 13:19), to yeast (Lk 13:21), and to a pearl of great price (Mt 13:46). Shepherds and sheep figure importantly in the parables, and He compares Himself to a mother hen longing to gather her brood under her wings (Mt 23:37).

Our imaginations, however, are also affected by the fact that technological advances have brought within reach of the average American a dizzying array of stimuli that would have astounded people in previous generations. Not only have we access to books from distant times and places, but we can listen to all sorts of music by pressing a button, see what is happening all around the world (or in the depths of the ocean) on television, watch a huge variety of different sorts of movies, shop for all sorts of enticing products, or access pornography just by hitting a few keys on our computers, all without leaving our homes. What we nourish our imaginations with is important. It will affect our spiritual lives by generating a sort of background climate — a mood that permeates our minds and wills also. Are you doing the equivalent of stuffing yourself with junk food?

The first and most important thing we should do is to nourish our imaginations with good Christian music, art, and literature in addition, of course, to regular reading of and reflection upon Scripture. St. Paul says: "Whatever is true, whatever is honorable, whatever is just, whatever is pure, whatever is lovely, whatever is gracious, if there is any excellence, if there is anything worthy of praise, think about these things" (Ph 4:8). This need not, and indeed should not, lead us to engage in rosy fantasies or to blind ourselves to the reality of human evil and suffering. The best Christian music, art and literature has the depth and power to speak to us in our times of need precisely because it shows us that the human spirit, sustained and forti-fied by God's grace, can triumph even in the darkest and most difficult circumstances. After listing some of the sufferings that Christians face (tribulation, or distress, or persecution, or fam-ine, or nakedness, or peril, or the sword), St. Paul tells us that "in all these things we are more than conquerors through Him who loved us" (Rm 8:35-37). Many people throughout history have shown heroic courage, integrity, generosity, and self-sacrifice in their lives. Many Christians have held onto hope and been faith-ful to their Christian calling even in the most terrible circum-stances. Reading or seeing movies about such people (especially ones that are realistic about the temptations and weaknesses they struggled with) can be helpful.

There is, of course, also an enormous amount of literature on prayer and the spiritual life. It is not a bad idea to read some of the great spiritual classics, but be careful not to keep comparing yourself to the authors, or try to squeeze your own spontaneous way of relating to God into the sort of pattern they followed. I have found that the most useful way to use such books is often to just have them around and pick one up when you feel moved to and open it. Again and again I have found that I turn to a passage that really speaks to my current situation (remember St. Augustine's conversion experience), but that if I then sit down and try reading the whole book, I get lost in the scroll work and don't find it helpful at all.

Not all that is good in the world is Christian, although Christians do hold that God is the source of all goodness; He created the world, and said, "It is good." So there is a wide variety of good things out there with which to feed our imaginations. So, be an omnivore and nourish your imagination with what is good and beautiful and true wherever you encounter it. But keep a special place for that which draws you more deeply into communion with God through Jesus Christ — that which deepens your faith and enables you to appreciate His love and His glory more.

On the negative side, there are two problems that we face. The first is that the magnitude of human suffering and sin is so great that if we open ourselves to too much of it we may become overwhelmed with sadness and horror, and react with excessive anger, cynicism or despair which are likely to disable us from doing the good that we might do. Our ancestors encountered all the same sorts of sufferings and sins that we do, but had to cope only with their own local ones and not those of the whole world. The second is that there are people out there who are deliberately manipulating our imaginations, emotions, and sexuality for their own profit. These problems require different solutions.

Some people are more sensitive than others, but we all need to be careful to limit our exposure to things that have a debilitating emotional impact on us. If you find yourself waking up with horrors in the night, feeling constantly fearful, or getting increasingly angry and cynical about the world in general, you probably should avoid exposure to upsetting things you can't do anything about. Getting information from emotionally cooler media such as newspapers (choosing one that doesn't feature sensational crimes on the front page every day), the Internet, or weekly news magazines can help. When bombarded with grim images of violence, mangled bodies, women screaming in grief over their husband's dead bodies, the distorted bodies of starving children, and so on, it is easy to get so overloaded that we shut down our natural sympathetic response to human suffering.

We each need to rationally assess what *we* can do to alleviate human suffering. We can all pray, vote, and give at least something to charity. To make wise decisions about how to spend your charity budget, you really only need to know the basics. What is the nature and extent of the problem, and what, precisely, does the charity asking for your money intend to do about it? You may be able to give some time to working on local projects that address the needs of people suffering within your community. Is the Lord, perhaps, calling you to some sort of active apostolate like those of Dorothy Day or St. Frances Cabrini or to go into politics as a vocation? But once you have decided what you are called to do, keep your energies focused on that. Don't take on the sufferings of the whole world.

Yes, you should know if there are dangers that are likely to impact you directly, but most of them aren't. And there is a certain value to reading good literature that gives some insight into human nature — even into the squirmy depths of the evil that the human heart is capable of. You don't want to just hide your head in the sand; Christians are supposed to be wise as serpents and innocent as doves (Mt 10:16). We need to know what sort of world we are living in if we are to act effectively in it. How much you should expose yourself to images of evil will vary depending on your particular vocation and temperament. But you should never take pleasure in evil,[72] and if you find that such feelings are creeping in (be honest with yourself!) when you read or watch certain types of things, by all means stop reading or watching them. Watching a violent movie or a "tear-jerker" may enable us to let out our feelings of anger or sadness in a way that releases the inner pressure we were feeling from suppressed emotions and makes us feel better. I think it is better to release these in prayer because God can heal us in a deeper way, though a certain amount of catharsis is probably okay. But if what you find exciting and pleasant is the evil or degradation itself, this is the sort of thing people can get addicted to in ways that poison the imagination and open them to all sorts of bad things. To use a common slang expression, "Don't go there."

---

[72] "Love does not rejoice at wrong, but rejoices in the right" (1 Cor 13:6-7).

The problem of people who intentionally manipulate you for their profit is morally simpler; no good comes out of this at all, and we ought not to let them get their hooks into us. But avoiding such manipulation is difficult. A lot of what looks like harmless entertainment is pervaded by very shallow worldly values that convey an image of "the good life" inimical to the Christian one — one pervaded by a sort of superficial glamour, or what St. John called "the lust of the eyes and the pride of life" (1 Jn 2: 15-17). Advertisers know how to exploit our insecurities, fears and sexuality in order to get us to buy their products, and pornographers are especially skilled at finding ways to turn us on. We are all vulnerable. The *I Ching* says that the best way to combat evil is to make energetic progress in the good, so keeping our focus on God as much as we can, and allowing Him to transform our hearts is central. But we make this more difficult if we invite others to come and sow weeds in our garden. Cares and pleasures of the world and desires for other things can choke out the Word so that it proves unfruitful. And that is just what advertisers do — they attempt to create and stoke desires for their products, constantly holding out the hope that if only we buy what they are selling we will be satisfied. Of course we never are.

We should clear some quiet space for the Lord, and not gossip and talk frivolously too much, or overstimulate ourselves with constant music or television. Don't crowd your mind. Silence is important; indeed it is essential to the spiritual life. Things deepen and develop in our minds and hearts when we give them space. A quiet walk in a beautiful place, or even just sitting on your porch or in a park or garden soaking up the beauty and perhaps reading something you find restful and inspiring helps quiet the mind. Some people find some simple repetitive task like knitting or embroidering soothing. Others find driving alone on the highway a good time to be quiet and alone. If you are an urban person, sitting quietly in a sidewalk café and letting the world go by can provide space for reflection.

One important way to find an environment that will facilitate the growth of the new life given us through Jesus Christ is to find a community to worship and pray with. Pray that the Lord will lead you to the one that is right for you. Christian friends who love you and pray for you and encourage you are a great blessing. It is good if you can also do fun things together with them — laugh, talk, hike, picnic, dance, sing, share a good meal, etc. We all have a need for friendship and fun, and there is no reason for Christians to be glum; we have a lot more reasons for being joyful and taking pleasure in the good things of God's creation than other people do.

SEEKING HELP

There are times, however, when we feel we need guidance from a wiser and more experienced person — times when we feel confused, beset, and just unable to cope. One way that this need for guidance has been traditionally met among Christians is to have certain mature members of the community, sometimes called "elders," available to counsel others. More formally, religious orders require members to have spiritual directors in addition to their regular confessor (who is expected to give a certain amount of advice and direction in the confessional), although the idea that it is appropriate for lay people to have spiritual directors was not common in the pre-Vatican II Church, and thus some older priests might view a request for spiritual direction as a bit odd. But pray and keep your eyes open, and if God wants you to have a spiritual director, you'll find one. The Eastern Orthodox Churches have placed special emphasis on the role of such people (called "starets"), accord them far greater authority than is customary in the Western Church, and have a more informal way of selecting them. Some Roman Catholic churches and many Protestant churches have lay pastoral counselors and sometimes couples who do marriage counseling.

And there are psychotherapists trained in a variety of different schools of thought who are available to help you work through your problems. Since a person we have opened ourselves up to on a deep level is able to exercise quite a bit of influence on us, it is important to make choices about who to go to for help in a prayerful way and to proceed cautiously. God may make use of a spiritual director or a therapist in healing and guiding us, just as He may make use of doctors in healing our physical problems. But remember that it is ultimately God who heals, and keep bringing everything back to Him in prayer. There are a few pitfalls to watch out for, however, so I sketch below a few pros and cons of various paths you might take in seeking help.

Spiritual Direction

If you feel you need some sort of assistance or direction, begin by praying that the Lord will lead you to the right person to help you, and keep your eyes and ears open. A spiritual director must be a serious and mature Christian. There is no need for the person to be a priest or minister. Not all priests or ministers have the charism of being good spiritual directors, and another ordinary Christian who has had to cope with problems like those you are facing and is a little more mature in his or her Christian life may be right for you. And you may outgrow one spiritual director, go a while without one, move to another, etc. Try not to get too desperately dependent on any one person. This can be hard, but trust that God will give you what you need.

Whether or not you are led to a spiritual director, remember that ultimately Jesus Christ is and should be your spiritual director. The proper role of a spiritual director should be to help you to discern the way God is trying to lead *you*. There are a number of pitfalls that may arise in relationships of spiritual direction, so be cautious and go slowly. A good spiritual director should be a person who believes that the Holy Spirit is already at work in *you* and not just in him (or her). You should get the feeling when you are with your director that he (I'll use "he" for simplicity, though it could be a woman) is reflecting about what you say carefully and not jumping in too quickly to pass judgment or label everything. Like Mary, a good spiritual director will hold things in his heart quietly waiting for the Lord to illuminate their meaning. Of course, a director sometimes has to be authoritative, and say, "Yes, that is a sin," or "This relationship is one you need to break off." But if you feel someone is trying to take you over, steer clear of him. I have no reference to this study, but I am told that psychologists and clerics (of all religions) had the highest scores on a test designed to measure people's desire for power over others. Be suspicious of anyone who has a theory of what stages you have to go through in what order and how long it will take, and what the perfected person should be like. No two saints are the same. (An analogy, here, might be the case of a woman I knew who had been seriously injured by a chiropractor who set out to make her back conform to his idea of the ideal curve and shape instead of working with the natural structure of her back.)

Besides the danger of falling in with a director who has tendencies toward taking you over, the other main danger is talking too much about your religious experiences and/or adopting an overly analytic attitude toward them. One's relationship with God is intensely personal and intimate. You don't want to talk too much about it at first while it is still fragile and new. Seeds germinate underground and need to take root and become strong before they are ready to come fully into the light. Jesus compares the Kingdom of God to yeast that leavens the whole lump of dough, and the Holy Spirit works subtly in us in ways we do not understand. It is best when baking a cake not to be constantly opening the oven and looking in to see how it is doing. Prayer is an ongoing conversation with God; you have to let some things remain implicit and wait for the Lord to make them clearer. So, although your spiritual director needs to know enough to ascertain that you are generally on the right path, you don't want to share everything. Anything that causes you disquiet, or alarm, or that seems in any way sinister should of course be brought to your director. But don't spill your guts too much or analyze things to death. Some of the energy and vitality of your inner life can be drained and its power defused if you let it flow out too soon; let it work in you slowly and deeply and trust that God Himself will bring to completion the good work He has begun in you. You should pray for the guidance of the Holy Spirit (for you and your spiritual director) before your meetings, and then trust that you will be guided to share what the Lord wants you to share (for whatever reason) and not what is still germinating and taking form. If your spiritual director gets too involved in your ongoing prayer life, there is always the danger that you will edit things to please him and force your experiences to fit into his categories. Besides, God wants there to be a part of us that belongs to Him alone — a kind of inner secret garden. Intimacy requires this sort of private space in order to develop.

Psychotherapy

If you are thinking of consulting a therapist, pray beforehand that you will be guided to the right one, and pray before each session. Opening oneself up to a therapist has the same sorts of dangers as spiritual direction. Certainly it can sometimes be beneficial to talk to a good therapist, but you need to retain your distinctively Christian categories of thought, and be aware of some of the ways in which current trends in psychotherapy may be at odds with Christian faith.

First, and most obviously, many contemporary schools of therapy are indifferent or hostile to religion, and a therapist with negative attitudes toward your faith can easily have the effect of undermining it, sometimes in subtle ways. You are entitled to know at the beginning of therapy what your therapist's views about religion are, so ask. You don't necessarily need a therapist who shares your religious beliefs, but he or she should at least have genuine respect for them — and I mean active respect, and not just a grudging "Well, if it makes you feel better...."[73]

Secondly, although you may be able to gain self knowledge and think things through in a rational and constructive manner with someone who has the benefit of extensive clinical experience, you should use your own judgment both about the sort of person the therapist is, and about yourself. Be willing to admit (if it is true) that, for example, your motivation may not have been what you thought it was on some occasion, but don't accept the therapist's suggestions unless they seem to you (after honest reflection, and perhaps also prayer) to be correct. The same is true, of course, with a spiritual director; don't accept everything uncritically. Getting insight into your motivations through therapy can work well together with regular confession (if your denomination practices confession) to help you focus on areas where you are especially in need of God's grace.

Third, some therapists encourage people to root around in their memories and re-experience their traumas, but this can be disastrous. Repression occurs to protect us from the pain that certain memories may cause us and digging things out before the person is strong enough to cope with them can make them unable to function. Yes, we need at some point to allow these to come to the surface and deal with them, but timing is important. If you have a regular prayer life and entrust yourself to God, I think He will bring such things to the surface (either in prayer or through other events in our lives) at the right time. Once they have come to the surface, there are different possible ways of dealing with them. Forgiveness looms especially large in any Christian way of coming to terms with abuse or neglect we may have suffered as children. And really deep early traumas require God's healing touch. I went once to a support group for people who were victims of such traumas, and remember in particular one older woman who talked about her attempts to love and heal her inner child, visualizing herself holding and comforting

---

[73] Many churches can recommend Christian therapists. One particularly good organization is Paul Vitz's Institute for Psychological Sciences, 2001 Jefferson Davis Highway, Suite 511, Arlington, VA 22202.

the wounded child within. Such attempts to bootstrap ourselves can't work; we *are* the wounded child and so cannot heal ourselves. We need God.

Another way in which some types of therapy go off in a direction that Christians should be leery of, is by placing too high an emphasis on gaining control and becoming "empowered." Sometimes this is conjoined with the New Age idea that there is a perfect self within us already that we need to find and affirm. Obviously Christians shouldn't let their daily lives get totally out of control, but we need to resist the ideas that empowerment is the goal, or that we are perfect already. American culture, in general (and not just the therapeutic culture), is in terrified flight from such unpleasant realities as our vulnerability, fears, loneliness, brokenness and sinfulness, from old age and from death. We want to feel safe and in control. But this is possible only for a few people and only for short periods of time. As God tells the man who had been accumulating more and more wealth and is finally feeling comfortable and secure, "Fool, this night your soul is required of you" (Lk 12:20).

We spend large portions of our lives dependent on others (as children and in old age), and accidents or sickness (physical or mental) may reduce us to helpless dependency at any moment. Any form of therapy that encourages us into the illusion of complete self sufficiency and empowerment will draw us away from the right sort of relationship with God and collapse like a house of cards under the blows of any serious misfortune. The Lord told St. Paul, "My strength is made perfect in weakness" (2 Cor 12:9). The Christian's motto, perhaps, should be: *Strength through dependence.* Enduring strength can lie only in God who sustains us, and the more we can look our own neediness and helplessness in the face and run to Him for help, the better we can weather life's storms.

One final area where contemporary therapy and Christianity exist in some tension is in the way they think about self esteem. Many psychologists are concerned to strengthen their patient's sense of self esteem, and some Christian writers express horror over this, and counter by saying that we need quite the opposite — namely a good robust sense of our own sinfulness. I am not happy with this way of expressing the Christian position, and think that both parties could learn from each other.

Christians need to take account of the fact that we live in an age where an increasing number of people have grown up without the faithful and loving support of their parents or other adults. Many have been abandoned by one of their parents (usually their father), and/or been abused physically, sexually or emotionally. Many have received insufficient attention and care due to their parents being stressed and overburdened and working long hours, or been subjected to emotional manipulation that has scarred them badly in a number of ways. Perhaps they were made to feel responsible for too much (as children, they were perhaps called upon to function as parents to their siblings or perhaps even their parents, for example) so they constantly felt blamed. Or their parents may have tried to control them through guilt manipulation rather than through clear rules and rational authority.

There have always been problems in families, but the disintegration of the extended family, and the pressures on the family caused by our current economic system have added a whole new level of stress. Also, since families are now much smaller, parents have a larger emotional investment in each child. Looking at lives of various saints, I've always been struck by how many of them came from very large families. If you have nine children, you are likely to have more of a live and let live attitude. At least some of them will turn out in ways that make you feel that you have successfully handed on your values to the next generation. But if you have only two, your chances are much slimmer. Having so much of your parents' hopes and ambitions invested in you can be extremely difficult and make you feel that you are not loved for who you are but valued only to the extent that you satisfy their ambitions for you.

In short, many people today have a very weak sense of themselves and feel they are deficient, defective, guilty — often in vague and ill defined ways. These sorts of wounds and burdens are not just the result of their sins (we are all sinners, of course) but the result of things that were done to them. They can incapacitate people for living happy, productive lives, and interfere with their spiritual lives as well. Therapists correctly perceive their need to be freed from these self-destructive attitudes, and therefore try to help them to love and think well of themselves — in other words to develop self-esteem.

But what is the proper sort of self-esteem, and what should it be based on? Here, I think, Christians have something unique and important to say. We have a *reason* for taking ourselves to be valuable. God created us in love and has redeemed us through the blood of His Son Jesus Christ. Whatever our faults and failings, God loves us with a love that surpasses all understanding. Therapists can, perhaps, help us realize some of the roots of our neurotic agonies and reason ourselves out of them to some degree. And that can be helpful. But they can't give us the unconditional love and acceptance that God can give. Nor can we give it to ourselves. Talk about "learning to love yourself" has a point and may help some people refrain from self-damaging behaviors. But if we are looking for a grounding for our sense of self, we can't give ourselves that any more than we can heal the wounded child within. The self cannot step into the place of God.

Lacking a grounding for a healthy sense of self-esteem, some therapists and educators lapse into shallow ways of puffing up our self-esteem that the patient can see through all too easily. I am reminded of a Doonesbury cartoon where a kid comes home from camp with an armload of ribbons and trophies. Upon questioning it turns out he got one for not missing too many archery practices, another for showing up at camp the right day, another for remembering his computer password, and so on. The father says, "You must feel very proud of yourself," and the kid throws one of the trophies over his shoulder and says, "Yeah, right." The father then turns to the mother and says, "You didn't tell me it was a self-esteem camp."

Christian humility requires us to have as much as possible God's perspective on ourselves. Denigrating ourselves or denying the talents we do have is false humility. Ideally what the Christian should be aiming for is forgetfulness of self. Granted, this can be hard to attain when we are in intense emotional pain, but try pouring out your heart to God in prayer when you feel that way. Many of the Psalms are examples of how to do this, and you might find it helpful to pray one of them (for example, Psalms 22, 88, 6, and 102). And Psalm 139 is one you might find comforting when in distress. If we keep our focus on God and on trying to do His work we can move forward. Whatever facilitates this is good, and the self-understanding gained in therapy can help to a degree. But beware of getting lost in the swamp of endless self-analysis. God created us to live actively (and activity here includes prayer) turned outward toward Him and our neighbors rather than sinking back into ourselves. Granted, God acts upon our inmost being, but it is a transcendent God who breaks into the natural order and gives Himself to us in Christ as a free gift of grace. *We* are not God.

RIGHT RELATIONSHIP WITH OTHER PEOPLE

Having our hearts rightly disposed toward God is integrally connected with the way in which we relate to other people. For it is one and the same heart involved in both cases. As our hearts grow into right relationship with God, this will affect how we spontaneously respond to other people. But the connection goes both ways. The attitudes we adopt toward other people can affect our relationship with God. Nursing anger and resentment toward others and refusing to let go of old wrongs, for example, are attitudes likely to damage us and block us off from God.

Forgiveness

Forgiveness may seem simple, but it is not. It is something we can choose — at least at the level of wanting to want to forgive[74] — but not something we can do ourselves. Grace and freedom are both involved. In order to forgive, you must decide that you want to stop holding the wrong the person has done against him or her, and then beg God to give you the grace to do it. He won't let you off until you do. We all know what it is to hold something against a person — to go over it in our mind, to obsess about it, to work ourselves up into feelings of anger and self-pity, or erect a wall of hostility in our mind and heart. We, as it were, cast them into the outer darkness and want to leave them there.

But forgiveness is not optional for Christians. It is there in the Lord's Prayer: "Forgive us our trespasses as we forgive those who trespass against us." We *must* forgive because we have been forgiven. Remember the parable about the servant whose master forgave him a huge debt who then went out and throttled a fellow servant who owed him a tiny fraction of that, and how severe the master's punishment of that servant was (Mt 18:29-32). You may forgive grudgingly — under duress, as it were — complying reluctantly with God's command. But His grace can move in and help you. Our capacity to forgive others flows from God's love and forgiveness toward us and the grace He pours into our hearts when we accept that love and forgiveness, and it is our obligation to pass this on to others. If we remain hard-hearted toward them, this impedes the action of the Holy Spirit in us, which is intended, after all, to flow out from us to others in loving actions and words. So we should ask God to help us love others as He loves us (and them).

A little forgetfulness can be very helpful when you are struggling to forgive someone. If you keep remembering and

---

[74] Although at the deepest level even this desire to forgive is itself the result of the action of God's grace.

brooding about the wrong done you, your feelings will keep getting churned up and letting go will be almost impossible. So try to put it behind you and not look back. Of course we don't have perfect control of our thoughts, but we can try to redirect our attention to something else when we start obsessing about it. An unforgiving attitude keeps you entangled with the one you cannot forgive; when you do finally let go, you will feel a tremendous sense of freedom. Maybe not right at first, but gradually.

In a way, however, forgiveness is easier than some people make it out to be. You don't have to feel all warm toward the person, or put yourself in a position where you let them hurt you again. You should, of course, allow them room to change — give them the benefit of the doubt. If their behavior changes, then the relationship may be healed and resumed, but you aren't called to be a masochist or a doormat. There may, of course, be special cases where you feel called to allow yourself to be repeatedly hurt as a kind of witness of faithful Christian love, but generally this is not healthy for either you or the other person. You shouldn't wish evil to those who have injured you, or try to harm them. Instead, you should love them in the sense that you will their good. And if the occasion arises you should act in ways that further their good. But their *true* good, of course, is their salvation, and since this would include recognition of their sins, repentance, and conversion, this makes it a bit easier to pray for their good.

It is easiest to forgive, of course, if the person comes to you and apologizes and intends not to repeat the offense. But what if they don't apologize, and show every intention of doing it again given the chance? Scripture gives us examples of both kinds of forgiveness. The directive in Matthew to forgive seventy times seven times makes no mention of any apology (Mt 18:21-22). But the parallel passage in Luke does. In that passage, Jesus says "If your brother sins, rebuke him, and if he repents forgive him; and if he sins against you seven times in the day, and turns to you seven times, and says, 'I repent,' you must forgive him" (Lk 17:3-4). But Jesus's prayer from the cross, "Father forgive them, for they know not what they do" (Lk 23:34), was not spoken about repentant sinners, nor was St. Stephen's "Lord, do not hold this sin against them" as he was being stoned to death (Ac 7:60). Certainly you should try to protect yourself and others against harm, and perhaps even act strongly to accomplish this. But don't harden your heart against anyone in a final sort of way; pray for their good and let go of it.

Judging Others

Another problem afflicting most spiritually serious people is the tendency to feel judgmental toward those who are enmeshed in various sins — often, although not always, those sins we ourselves are tempted to commit. It is, however, our business to see to it that *we* respond to God's call and not to oversee other people. As St. Paul puts it, "Who are you to pass judgment on the servant of another? It is before his own master that he stands or falls.... Each of us shall give account of himself to God" (Rm 14:4). One of the most wonderfully freeing things about Christianity is the truth that God alone can judge the human heart. Thank God. What a burden off us! Someone's *actions* may be objectively sinful, but only God knows the other person well enough to weigh all the possible mitigating factors and discern the true intention of his or her heart. Unless the person performing the act knows that the action is wrong and freely chooses it, we are dealing with a case of wrongdoing, but not yet sin. And since most people rationalize themselves into doing bad things, it is difficult for anyone but God to determine with any certainty whether the person is genuinely confused about what is right or whether he or she is engaged in self-deception. So leave judgment of the person to God.

Indeed, we are not the final judge of our own motives either. This might sound frightening. We imagine, perhaps, God ferreting out our impure motives and punishing us. But ours is a God in whom mercy and truth are met together. Purification of our own motives is not in our power. But that doesn't mean it is all hopeless and we are doomed. Rather, it points to our need for God. Her accusers tried to trap Joan of Arc at her trial by asking her whether she thought she was in a state of grace.[75] If she said no, she would be confessing that she believed herself to be in mortal sin, and if she said yes she would be guilty of presumption. Her reply was perfect. She declined to pass judgment on herself at all, saying, "If I am not in a state of grace, I pray God place me in it; if I be in it, I pray God keep me so."[76] So leave judgment to God and pray like mad.

What we need to avoid, then, is passing any sort of final judgment on people — saying they are bad people. Yet we need to avoid this without abandoning our conviction that some actions are morally wrong. This can be tricky. We often have friends, family, neighbors or co-workers engaging in the actions in question, and don't want to condemn them, so we hesitate even to say the action is wrong. We need to keep two things in mind here.

First, God loves them even in their sins. Try praying that God will help you see the other person as He sees him. This may yield surprising results sometimes. Once, shortly after I joined the Catholic Church, I ran into some men dressed as nuns outside the Castro Street BART station in San Francisco. They called themselves "the Sisters of Perpetual Indulgence." I was, of course, horrified. But I prayed that God would enable me to see the man in front of me (a bearded man who called himself "Sister Boom Boom") as He saw him. And I had a feeling of an intense love probing the man, searching for any chink or crack through which it could enter in. On a more mundane level, I've taken to asking God to help me see my fellow communicants at Mass as He sees them, and am sometimes amazed and delighted at the wonder of His love — that He can love all these people

---

[75] To be in a state of grace is to be in a state of friendship with God such that one could only fall out of it through one's own fault.

[76] Mark Twain, *Joan of Arc* (San Francisco: Ignatius Press, 1989), p. 341.

whom I would, if left to myself, have found boring, stupid, ugly, pitiful, irritating, etc. His love casts a warm glow over all of us — so unlovable, and yet so much loved.

Second, associating with people who do things that are morally wrong is inevitable, and if you are honest with yourself, you will realize that you do too. In any case, you can't get yourself off the hook just by being easy on other people; we all stand under God's judgment.

Correcting other people

Some people, inspired by Scripture passages admonishing us to bring back those who have strayed from the Lord, and telling us that we must "preach the word, be urgent in season and out of season, convince, rebuke, exhort" (2 Tm 4:2) go around reproaching others for their sins. St. James says that "whoever brings back a sinner from the error of his way will save his soul from death and will cover a multitude of sins" (Jm 5:20). Sometimes you may indeed be called to speak to someone about a sinful pattern they are caught in. But be careful. Pray about it a long time before you do so. Tell the Lord that if He wants you to be the one to talk to this person, He will provide an opening for you to speak. You don't need to wait for the person to ask your opinion point blank, but you should only speak if there are some signs that the person is open to it. Some such signs would be, for example, if the person expresses uncertainty, doubt, confusion, or dissatisfaction with his life as it is.

When you do discern an openness, don't jump in with both feet; be delicate. Gently ask some questions to get a sense of how they understand the problem. People who are entangled in some serious sin probably already feel a bit uneasy and guilty, and fear being condemned. If they feel condemnation from you they will become defensive and close up again. Remember Jesus and the woman taken in adultery. He said to her "...neither do I condemn you. Go, and do not sin again" (Jn 8:11). And if Jesus who was sinless refrained from condemnation, how much more should we who are ourselves so vulnerable by reason of our own sins refrain from condemning others. The goal, after all, is to lead them to realize their need to turn away from their sins and toward God. Just throwing the law at them is likely to send them into despair and probably drive them deeper into their sins. A friend of mine once said, "If you haven't heard the gospel preached in love, you haven't heard the gospel." Love and law go together in Christianity. There may be occasions where rather forceful chastisement of a fellow Christian is appropriate, but usually only where that person is some sort of public figure who is giving scandal by his or her behavior, or abusing a position of authority in ways that deeply injure innocent people.

Anger

Being angry is not a sin. Letting it eat you up is. There is a healthy anger. In some situations a person who did not feel anger would be morally defective, as for example, when you see vulnerable and innocent people preyed upon by those who rob or corrupt them. Jesus said, "Temptations to sin are sure to come; but woe to him by whom they come! It would be better for him if a millstone were hung round his neck and he were cast into the sea, than that he should cause one of these little ones to sin" (Lk 17:1-2. See also Mt 18:6 and Mk 9:42). Jesus was angered by the hardness of heart of those who were watching and trying to entrap Him when He was about to heal the man with the withered hand on the Sabbath (Mk 3:5). Anger is also appropriate if someone treats you with contempt (you are, after all, created in the image of God and thus have a certain dignity that should not be violated). Or if a workplace, college, or institution of any sort with which you are connected is placed under incompetent and corrupt leadership, deteriorates in its ability to perform its function, and gradually turns into a war zone around you, with people you care about becoming embittered, withdrawn, emotionally damaged and twisted up inside, made ill and so on, you would be right to feel angry over this. Anger, in moderation, can sharpen the mind and energize you into action to correct the wrong, stand up for yourself, or act to change the situation in some way.

So be angry; but then pray over it and calmly sit down and reflect about what lies in your power to do to correct the situation (either by stopping the person doing the damage, or binding up the wounds of the victims) and resolve to do it. When you have done all you can, however, there is no point brooding over it, and you have to try to live around it. "If you are angry, let it be without sin. The sun must not go down on your wrath; do not give the devil a chance to work on you" (Eph 4:26-7). Keep the situation in prayer, begging God to correct it, and be open if He guides you to do something about it. But picking at it and stoking the fires of your anger just keeps your emotions boiling which interferes with clear thought as well as with contemplative prayer, and is likely to blind you to both the needs of others around you and the little openings toward good things that may offer themselves — opportunities for friendship, growth, enjoyment, etc.

SIN AND SUFFERING

We are bound to sin and to suffer in this life. No one since the Fall, except for Jesus (Catholics and many other Christians would say Mary also) has ever been sinless. This is not to say that we can never choose to avoid sin. Of course we can. But to *never* sin is not within our power. And in a fallen world we cannot escape suffering. We do, however, have some choice about whether we let sin and suffering cause us to pull back from God, or whether, on the contrary, we allow them to draw us closer to God.

Sin

There are two attitudes you don't want to fall into with regard to your sins. On the one hand, you shouldn't be astonished and so horribly upset you that you crawl away and hide from God like Adam and Eve in the garden (Gn 3:8). We now have Jesus Christ who reconciles us with God. To expect perfection of ourselves is unrealistic and often a manifestation of pride. And this is true both at the level of motivation and action. We should take to heart the verse from the Holy Spirit invocation (Chapter Two): "Where thou art not man hath naught, nothing good in deed or thought, nothing free from taint of ill." I don't think this means that there is absolutely *nothing* good in us (as strict Calvinists believe), but only that true purity of heart is beyond our power to attain by our own efforts. Our knowledge of our own hearts is very shallow and imperfect; our motives are not always what we think they are, and when we manage to overcome one sinful pattern, another will crop up. Our souls are rather like the famous Augean Stables. One of the trials of Hercules was to clean out these stables, which had been full of horses and other livestock for a very long time. The labor was humanly impossible, but Hercules succeeded by diverting a river so that it flowed through the stables, washing them clean. The Holy Spirit here is analogous to the river. So get over the idea that *you* have to purify your heart — and even more get over the idea that you have to do so as a first step toward God. You could spend the rest of your life shovel in hand, and wind up with the stables no cleaner.

On the other hand, you don't want to get complacent, abandoning the quest for holiness and just coasting along figuring that God will forgive you, so what's the big deal. God is not a vindictive and irrational tyrant. But neither is He an indulgent parent who allows us to do whatever we please. Even on the human level proper parental love is not merely indulging the child's every whim. It is *because* God loves us that He sets out rules and standards for us to follow (see Psalm 119 for a beautiful celebration of God's law and how it is a lamp to our feet).

I've said some things already about how recognition of our sinfulness might be a barrier to prayer (Chapter One) or a source of discouragement (Chapter Three). I confine myself here to a few positive suggestions addressed to those who find that awareness of their sinfulness makes them inclined to flee from God.

First, make an effort to inform yourself about just what is and is not a sin. Go to someone whose spiritual advice you trust, look over some books on Christian ethics or moral theology, and of course pray that God will show you what needs changing in your life. You may be tormenting yourself needlessly about something which is not a sin. And you may be overlooking something which is a sin.

If you had a harsh, condemning, and unsound theological education, you may, as a result, be prey to neurotic anxiety and guilt (exacerbated, perhaps, by emotionally manipulative child-rearing practices that your parents used). You may have been taught that even having sinful thoughts and desires is something you should feel horribly guilty about, even if you don't act on them. No desire as such is sinful unless deliberately entertained or acted upon. If you obsess about a desire to do something sinful, take pleasure in fantasizing about it, and so on, then you have crossed over the line into sin (although the sin is less grave than actually acting on the desire). But that such thoughts go through your mind means nothing. A spiritual teacher once said that you can't stop the birds from flying over your head, but you can stop them from making nests in your hair. Some people have even been taught that just having sexual thoughts and desires is sinful.[77] This, of course, is not true and is a recipe for disaster, especially if hammered into vulnerable adolescents who are naturally beginning to feel intense and confused sexual longings that may be frightening to them already.

---

[77] This is by no means only true of Christians. Lots of people intuitively feel this way. Perhaps this is because sexual passions tend to be powerful and hard to control, and can lead people to behave in irrational and destructive ways.

It may be, however, that you are committing a sin, even a serious one, without realizing it. For example, the sins we commit in gossiping about others and running them down behind their backs tend to be neglected in favor of the hot sins like anger or lust, but the damage they do is immeasurable. If you are inclined not to take such sins seriously, take a look at the Letter of James (1:26, and 3:1-12). The usual pattern is that over time, as God heals us, some sinful patterns fade away, and we become aware of others that we hadn't seen before. Let God guide the process. If you belong to a church that practices sacramental confession, take advantage of this. Sacraments are channels of grace, and can help us progress more quickly.

Second, awareness of our sinfulness can actually draw us closer to God, when we reflect upon the fact that God's love for us is so great that He can and does love us in our sins (and for this reason, we must try to love others in their sins). Let Him do this; don't put your sins between yourself and God and not allow you to receive His love because you think you don't deserve it. Of course we don't deserve it, and we don't need to. He loves us not because we are good, but in order to make us good.[78] We should show our gratitude for His love by trying to make some return to Him for all He gives us, but that is a different matter. As St. Paul said, "While we were yet sinners, Christ died for us" (Rm 5:8). This fact is worth meditating on deeply. Think how easy it is, when you perceive clearly some particular sinful pattern in another person's life, to feel hard and cold toward them — to feel superior and look down on them. But God sees through the ugliness of the sinner and loves in him the creature He created for communion with Himself. The more we realize the depth of our sinfulness, the more we should appreciate Christ's love — a love that covers our sins — that overwhelms us with its immensity and richness. St. Paul prays "that Christ may dwell in your hearts through faith; that you, being rooted and grounded in love, may

---

[78] I owe this way of putting the point to Rev. Mark Moore.

have power to comprehend with all the saints what is the breadth and length and height and depth, and to know the love of Christ which surpasses knowledge, that you may be filled with all the fullness of God" (Eph 3:18).

Third, awareness of our sinfulness can also draw us toward God when it makes us realize our need for His help. It is only by running to Him for help that we can do better. I sometimes think of us as like airplanes with a kind of structural defect (original sin) that results in a constant tendency to crash, except that God's grace can keep us on course. An old Lenten hymn I sang as a child puts it well: "Teach us with Thee to mourn our sins and close by Thee to stay..... Teach us, O Lord, in Thee to fight, in Thee to conquer sin" (*1940 Hymnal*, #59). American religion tends to err in the direction of Pelagianism — the heresy which taught that we can become virtuous without grace. Of course, we can't separate grace and nature by inspection, and we need both to depend on God's grace and step out and act as well. But, the more we depend on God and trust in His grace, the more progress we will make. Ask for His help, quietly pick yourself up, and go on.

Finally, we should beware of getting bogged down in excessive focus on our sinfulness or on our struggle for purity, or for that matter even our own salvation. Not that we shouldn't care about these, of course, but a certain amount of self-forgetfulness is appropriate for Christians. This can take different forms, and ideally they should all become manifest in us as we grow in Christ. Obedience is a good starting point; we can grow in holiness through doing His work. I am told that there is a Monty Python movie in which God comes down and appears to some people, and they all start groveling around crying, "Oh, woe is me, I am a sinner!" God complains that every time He comes down here trying to get people to *do* something, they all start groveling and bewailing their sinfulness. There is work to be done in the world, and God has given us each certain talents and spiritual gifts that He wants us to use for building up His

Church and for the coming of His Kingdom. Imperfect as we are, we are the ones called to do this work, and it won't get done if we spend all our time picking over ourselves. Some sort of balance is needed, of course, between outward action and reflective self examination. Christians who *never* engage in honest and unsparing examination of themselves and their motives, sitting in God's presence and asking Him to show them the truth, can do real harm, especially if they are given to being horribly judgmental about others.

Ideally, of course, our obedience should be from the heart — obedience out of love, and not just a sort of resentful submission out of fear of punishment. Jesus, Himself, was obedient to the Father out of love, and it is this sort of obedience we should emulate.[79] Love of God, then, is another thing that can take us out of ourselves. Brother Lawrence expresses a laudable kind of self forgetfulness grounded in his love of God. He says that whether he is saved or lost, "I shall have this good at least that 'till death I shall have done all that is in me to love Him....' Let Him do as He pleases with me; I desire only Him and to be wholly devoted to Him."[80] A passionate love for God, then, for His glory, His beauty, His holiness, and for the coming of His kingdom animated Jesus Himself, and by His grace it has been able to stir the hearts of His followers throughout the centuries. We should ask God to give us this sort of dynamic love that can carry us out of ourselves towards Him.

Suffering

Why there is so much suffering in a world created by a good God, and why He allows it to continue are questions that have exercised philosophers and theologians for centuries.

---

[79] So much did Jesus love the Father that He regarded doing God's will as something that sustained Him like food. He said, "I have food to eat that you know not of... my food is to do the will of Him who sent me, and to accomplish His work" (Jn 4:34).

[80] Brother Lawrence, *op. cit.*, pp. 14-15, and 38.

So don't worry, I'm not going to attempt to answer them here. When undergoing suffering, there is only one thing that really helps — knowing that God is there with you.[81] The Greek gods were thought to live in endless bliss, free from all pain and death, forever young, feasting and drinking wine, engaging in romantic adventures and so on. Christians believe in a God who has entered into time and history and as a man endured the sorts of sufferings we do. Jesus' name before His birth was prophesied to be "Emmanuel" meaning "God with us" (Mt 1:23). God the Son came down into our darkness, took on the density of flesh and blood, and endured the pain of human experience. For this reason, He can give us rest and comfort in our sufferings.

Some favorite Christian hymns express well the way people have experienced God's presence and comfort amid their sufferings. "In the Cross of Christ I Glory" contains the verse: "Bane and blessing, pain and pleasure, by the cross are sanctified. Peace is there that knows no measure; joys that through all time abide" (*1940 Hymnal*, #336). "How Firm a Foundation Ye Saints of the Lord" represents Jesus as saying: "I will be with thee, thy troubles to bless; and sanctify to thee thy deepest distress" (*1940 Hymnal*, #564). And in "Crown Him with Many Crowns," it is said of Jesus, "who every grief hath known that wrings the human breast; and takes and bears them for His own that all in Him may rest" (*1940 Hymnal*, #352). Jesus drank the bitter cup, underwent the baptism of pain, endured betrayal, humiliation and death, and confronted the demonic realm when He "descended into Hell" (as the Creed tells us). He can thus be with us and support us through whatever darkness, sorrow or suffering we may have to endure. This doesn't necessarily mean that your physical pain will disappear (although of course God may see fit to take it from you), or that grief and sadness will simply melt away at once. But whatever is troubling you, it will become bearable when experienced with Jesus. This can happen in any number of ways. If it is

---

[81] A good book on suffering is Cardinal Basil Hume's *The Mystery of the Cross*. Recently reprinted by Paraclete Press.

the suffering of someone you love, He may give you that little bit of inner detachment necessary to deal with it. He may open up a new level of peace at the center that gives you a feeling of being anchored in the storm. Or a quiet joy in His presence. Whatever is needed is what He will give.

Suffering has a salvific role in Christianity, for it was through the suffering He endured that Jesus Christ accomplished the work of our redemption. And we who have been baptized into Christ have been baptized into His death so that we may also share in His resurrection. Thus suffering is not an unmixed evil. God can bring good out of it, and there seem to be some goods that can only be brought about through suffering. There is an old pre-Vatican II expression that gets a lot of people's hackles up: "Offer it up." This means that you should take your suffering and offer it up to God. This expression is naturally infuriating when said in a smug manner by someone who is either inflicting suffering on you, or at least not lifting a finger to help you, and it can easily be perceived as a brush off and an indication that they are indifferent to your sufferings. Hence you should probably avoid using the expression. But when properly understood, there is something right and important underlying it. If Christ's suffering is salvific, and you ask Him to unite your suffering with His own, then your suffering can also be salvific.[82] (I think we should ask Him to unite our sufferings with His; this is not something *we* can presume to do.) Mother Teresa of Calcutta understood this well. Her Missionaries of Charity have a large

---

[82] The practice of offering one's suffering in union with the suffering of Christ may be connected to the puzzling passage where St. Paul says, "In my flesh I complete what is lacking in Christ's afflictions for the sake of His body, that is, the church" (Col 1:25). This is puzzling because on the face of it, it would seem that nothing could possibly be lacking in the sufferings of Christ. After all, Christians believe that He is God incarnate, and that He made full, perfect, and sufficient atonement for the sins of all the world. How, then is anything lacking? I am not a theologian, so I approach this question with trepidation. But the way I think of it is parallel to the way I think about intercession. If, indeed, we are members of the mystical body of Christ, we share in His mission of redemptive suffering. So, if we pray that God will unite our sufferings with those of Christ on the cross, they participate in the redemptive power of Christ.

network of co-workers who by reason of physical infirmity cannot do active service for the poor, but who participate in her work through prayer and patient endurance of suffering.

Popular piety and theology can get a bit out of sync here. Some people talk as though offering up one's suffering for some particular purpose is like an economic transaction — so many units of suffering produce so many units of grace or merits that can be cashed in against whatever they are praying for (sort of like spiritual "green stamps"). They may even offer to bear suffering for some other person — for their conversion or healing. I don't believe we should ever ask for suffering (enough comes to us without our asking for it), and certainly we should not try to bargain with God. But there is nothing wrong with asking Jesus to unite your sufferings with His own, give you patience to bear them, let them bear fruit in some way for the coming of His Kingdom. It is our intention that good come out of our suffering that matters, and our offering it for some person or intention is alright. We can always ask God. But we should not try to control or manipulate Him, even through prayer. This can drift into a magical way of thinking about prayer, as a kind of "spiritual technology."

I've found that thinking this way about suffering has helped me in little things as well as big ones. To take a simple example, traffic jams drive me crazy. My impatience and frustration get more and more intense the longer I am in one, until I'm positively writhing with irritation and anger. I've started trying to bear this aggravation patiently and asking Jesus to unite my suffering with His and to bring some good out of it (sometimes I specify a person or situation especially close to my heart). I then put soothing music on the radio, breathe deeply, say a few prayers or sing a few songs or hymns, and resist as long as I can the impulse to let my aggravation take me over. To my surprise, I've found that I can now patiently and even cheerfully endure traffic jams that would have caused me to "go ballistic" a few years ago. (I sometimes still hit the breaking point if it is a *very* long

traffic jam, but I can hold out a lot longer.) This is because I feel
that God is accomplishing some good through my patient endurance; my suffering and self denial are not wasted. This helps
motivate me to struggle against being emotionally self-indulgent
and complaining too much. Offering suffering in union with the
suffering of Christ, then, is a kind of prayer.

THE HOPE TO WHICH WE ARE CALLED

Suffering is easier to write about than the joy and glory of Heav-
en because we have more experience of it. There was a period of
several years when I attended church on Good Friday but not on
Easter; I found it easier to believe. All the same, it is an essential
part of Christian faith that there is something after this life. We
do not hope in Christ for this life only (1 Cor 15:19), and a truly
Christian life must be one enlivened by the hope that the deepest
longings of our hearts will one day be satisfied in God. Scripture, however, provides only glimmers and hints about what to
expect after death.[83] In a way this is not surprising. An old priest
I knew, who had been at a number of deathbeds, said to me,
"The other side is so close you can almost touch it. But you can't
know it." I confine myself here, therefore, to doing two things
— saying how we should *not* think about the afterlife, and con-
necting it with the central theme of this book.

   Christians do not view the afterlife as involving only disembodied souls. We believe in the resurrection of the body
(Apostles' Creed — see Appendix). Just what the resurrected
body is like is quite mysterious. Jesus's resurrected body still bore
the wounds of His crucifixion, was able to come through walls,

---

[83] The main place where Jesus speaks about the afterlife is at the Last Supper. See John
14-17. There are other scattered references in the Pauline writings and also in what is
sometimes called the Apocrypha (these are some books of the Bible accepted as ca-
nonical by Catholics but not by Protestants). 1 John 3:1-3 also contains an important
text on the subject.

ate fish, was not recognized at first by people who had known Him well, breathed on the disciples, vanished suddenly, and so on. It just does not fit into our categories. But, then, you wouldn't expect it to. The doctrine of the resurrection of the body testifies to the permanent importance of the body — something that was alien to the Greeks and most other pagan cultures who thought that the soul, at death, simply shed the body and continued to exist in a disembodied state. Christians believe that the God who created us to start with will also give us resurrected bodies, for unlike angels human beings are by nature embodied beings. Like Jesus, we must undergo death in order to come at last to the resurrection, and this is effected only by God's power.

The Christian notion of the afterlife does not fit other popular pagan models either. We do not believe that the soul will simply disintegrate and be scattered. Nor do we believe that our souls will be dissolved back into God or the world soul or cosmic mind. We believe that we will continue to be the same individuals we are now, albeit mysteriously transformed. For each of us was created to glorify God in our own unique way — to add our voice to the eternal chorus of angels and saints praising God. Finally, the afterlife will not be a static state, but rather a dynamic one in which all our faculties will be engaged and satisfied. "Then shall I see and hear and know all I desired and wished below; and every power find sweet employ in that eternal world of joy" (*The Sacred Harp*, p. 48).

Trying to state positively what we hope for after this life, Christians will usually say "union with God." The central theme of this book has been the way in which prayer can facilitate God's transforming work in our hearts, redirecting eros (the compass needle of our souls) toward Himself. For God alone can satisfy the deepest longings of our souls, and the union with Him that we will attain in the beatific vision will do just this. But how are we to understand this "union"? The union with God that we long for has both a cognitive and an affective dimension, although the object of our desire can never be *fully* grasped by either our minds or our hearts. Knowledge and love both involve a kind of union with their object[84] and they are intertwined; one cannot love that which one does not know to some degree at least, and the more we know God the more we will come to love Him. St. Augustine describes it thus: "There we shall rest and see, see and love, love and praise. This is what shall be in the end without end."[85]

Union with God is not something that destroys our freedom. God does not take us over and turn us into automata or robots. If God wanted robots, He would not have created us with free will in the first place. Union involves freedom on both sides. God freely gives Himself to us in Christ. We, then, freely choose to receive that gift (with the help of God's grace, of course) and to reciprocate by giving ourselves to Him. "The offering of a free heart will I give Thee and praise Thy name O Lord, because it is so comfortable" (Ps 54:8-9, King James version). Duality will not be wholly gone, for delight comes from the flow between our souls and God — the simultaneous giving and receiving.

Union is something that involves God living in us and our living in God (or more specifically, in Christ), and although this is something we can experience to some degree in this life, it will be realized fully only in Heaven. Jesus, in His discourse at the Last Supper as recorded by John, says, "Abide in me, and I in you," and goes on to compare the disciples to branches that cannot live except they abide in Him, the vine (Jn 15:4). There are a number of passages where He speaks of God's indwelling in us, sometimes said to be through His Spirit (the Holy Spirit), sometimes He says, "I and the Father will make our home with him" (Jn 14:23), sometimes He speaks of His (Jesus's) life in us (see, e.g., Jn 14:20). However we understand the roles of the various

---

[84] This may seem more obvious in the case of love. But in knowledge also the thing known has a kind of existence in the knower. If I am looking at a tree, that tree has a kind of existence in me, as it would not have in a stone placed at the same spot where I am standing.

[85] *The City of God*, Book XXII, section 30.

persons of the Trinity, here (and a discussion of this would lead us quickly into very deep theological waters), the general point remains the same. God in some very real sense dwells or lives in us. And it is as members of the mystical body of Christ that we ultimately are reconciled and united with God.

The term "living *in*" has a spatial connotation that is hard to avoid, but it can be confusing. St. Augustine, toward the beginning of the *Confessions*, frequently expresses wonder that God in His vastness and glory can be contained in our little hearts, but delights in the fact that indeed it is so. God is in us and we are in Him. Nelson Pike, in his book on mysticism,[86] calls this phenomenon "double containment," and it is, indeed, a baffling notion. How can it both be true that we hold Jesus in our hearts and that He holds us in His heart? One way of understanding it, and one that some of the mystics studied by Pike suggested, is to think of ourselves as sponges that become saturated with God as we are immersed in the vast sea of God's love. Another analogy is to think of ourselves as increasingly permeated by God's light which purifies, refines, and raises us up, or relatedly to think of the Holy Spirit as a kind of fire that kindles the fire of love of God in our hearts, and burns away our sins and impurities. Some such analogies are unavoidable, but we need always to keep in mind also the personal nature of God.

Ultimately, of course, no image is adequate to the mystery. Desire, in any case, is central to the notion of union as I understand it. For God implants a desire for Him in our hearts, and this desire becomes deeper and more powerful as we grow in the Christian life. He satisfies the desire, and in its satisfaction we are given the grace of a new level of desiring Him. Union with God in its fullness then will be spending all eternity with God, who will endlessly satisfy our desire for Him and call us to new and deeper levels of desire and enjoyment of His being and His love. It is not something static; the desire we have for God will

---

[86] Pike, *Mystic Union.*

not just be satisfied totally all at once. Since God is inexhaustible, our desire for Him must be also capable of limitless growth. Union with God in Heaven, then, will be a dynamic growing into deeper union without limit and without end. This then is the desire of our hearts, and the hope to which we are called.

APPENDIX

THE CREEDS

Apostles' Creed

I believe in God, the Father almighty, creator of heaven and earth. I believe in Jesus Christ, his only Son, our Lord. He was conceived by the power of the Holy Spirit and born of the Virgin Mary. He suffered under Pontius Pilate, was crucified, died and was buried. He descended to the dead. On the third day he rose again. He ascended into heaven, and is seated at the right hand of the Father. He will come again to judge the living and the dead. I believe in the Holy Spirit, the holy catholic Church, the communion of saints, the forgiveness of sins, the resurrection of the body, and the life everlasting.

Nicene Creed

We believe in God the Father, the Almighty, maker of Heaven and Earth, of all that is seen and unseen. We believe in one Lord, Jesus Christ the only Son of God, eternally begotten of the Father, God from God, light from light, true God from true God, begotten, not made, one in Being with the Father. Through him all things were made. For us men and for our salvation he came down from heaven: by the power of the Holy Spirit he was born of the Virgin Mary, and became man. For our sake he was crucified under Pontius Pilate; he suffered, died, and was buried. On the third day he rose again in fulfillment of the Scriptures;

he ascended into heaven and is seated at the right hand of the Father. He will come again in glory to judge the living and the dead, and his kingdom will have no end. We believe in the Holy Spirit, the Lord, the giver of life, who proceeds from the Father and the Son. With the Father and the Son he is worshiped and glorified. He has spoken through the Prophets. We believe in one holy catholic and apostolic Church. We acknowledge one baptism for the forgiveness of sins, we look for the resurrection of the dead, and the life of the world to come.

SOME USEFUL PRAYERS

The Lord's Prayer

Our Father who art in heaven, hallowed be Thy name. Thy kingdom come. Thy will be done on earth as it is in heaven. Give us this day our daily bread. And forgive us our trespasses as we forgive those who trespass against us. And lead us not into temptation, but deliver us from evil.

[For thine is the kingdom, the power and the glory, for ever and ever. Amen]

(This is the one prayer that unites all Christians, as it was given us by Jesus Himself. The brackets were added because this phrase does not appear in the most ancient Scripture manuscripts and seems to have been added at a much later date.)

Anima Christi

Soul of Christ, sanctify me; Body of Christ, be my salvation; Blood of Christ, inebriate me; Water flowing from the side of Christ wash me clean; Passion of Christ, strengthen me; Kind Jesus hear my prayer; Hide me within your wounds and keep me close to you; never let me be parted from you; Defend me from the evil enemy and call me at my death to the fellowship of your saints that I may sing your praise with them through all eternity. Amen.

St. Ignatius' Prayer

Lord Jesus Christ, take all my freedom, memory, understanding and will [I add "imagination, emotion, and sexuality"]. All I have and cherish you have given me. I surrender it all to be guided by your will. Your love and your grace are enough for me. Give me these Lord Jesus, and I ask for nothing more. Amen.

The *Te Deum*

We praise thee, O God; we acknowledge thee to be the Lord. All the earth doth worship thee, the Father everlasting. To thee all angels cry aloud; the heavens, and all the powers therein; to thee cherubim and seraphim continually do cry, Holy, Holy, Holy, Lord God of Hosts; heaven and earth are full of the majesty of thy glory. The glorious company of the apostles praise thee. The goodly fellowship of the prophets praise thee. The noble army of martyrs praise thee. The holy Church throughout all the world doth acknowledge thee; the Father, of an infinite majesty; Thine adorable, true, and only Son; Also the Holy Ghost, the Comforter.

Thou art the king of glory, O Christ. Thou art the everlasting Son of the Father. When thou tookest upon thee to deliver man, thou didst humble thyself to be born of a virgin. When thou hadst overcome the sharpness of death, thou didst open the Kingdom of Heaven to all believers. Thou sittest at the right hand of God, in the glory of the Father. We believe that thou shalt come to be our judge. We therefore pray thee, help thy servants, whom thou has redeemed with thy precious blood. Make them to numbered with thy Saints, in glory everlasting.

O Lord, save thy people, and bless thine heritage. Govern them, and lift them up for ever. Day by day we magnify thee; and we worship thy name ever, world without end. Vouchsafe, O Lord, to keep us this day without sin. O Lord have mercy upon us, have mercy upon us. O Lord, let thy mercy be upon us, as our trust is in thee. O Lord, in thee have I trusted; let me never be confounded. (*Book of Common Prayer*)

(This magnificent prayer of praise is traditionally recited as part of the Divine Office on Sundays and solemnities. It is also used on especially important public occasions, such as the election of a Pope or a victory in war, or used privately in thanksgiving for deliverance from danger or death.)

Morning Prayer

O Lord, our heavenly Father, Almighty and everlasting God who has safely brought us to the beginning of this day, defend us in the same with thy mighty power, and grant that this day we fall into no sin, neither run into any kind of danger, but that all our doings, being ordered by thy governance, may be righteous in thy sight. Through Jesus Christ our Lord. Amen. (*Book of Common Prayer,* p. 592)

Evening Prayer

Lighten our darkness, we beseech thee O Lord, and by thy great mercy defend us from all perils and dangers of this night; for the love of thy only Son, our Savior Jesus Christ. Amen. (*Book of Common Prayer*)

Before Bed

Lord, we beg thee to visit this house, and banish from it all the deadly power of the enemy. May your holy angels dwell here to keep us in peace, and may your blessing be upon us always. We ask this through Christ our Lord. Amen.

Guardian Angel Prayer

Angel of God, my guardian dear; to whom His love entrusts me here, ever this day [night] be at my side to light and guard, to rule and guide. Amen.

Food Blessings

Bless, O Lord, this food to our use and our lives in Thy service. Give food to the hungry. May we who have bread hunger for Thee. Keep us mindful of the needs of others. Amen

Bless us, O Lord, and these Thy gifts which we are about to receive from Thy bounty, through Christ our Lord. Amen.

Before Communion

Almighty God, I approach the sacrament of your only begotten Son, our Lord Jesus Christ. I come sick to the doctor of life, unclean to the fountain of mercy, blind to the radiance of eternal light, and poor and needy to the Lord of Heaven and Earth. Lord, in your great generosity, heal my sickness, wash away my defilement, enlighten my blindness, enrich my poverty, and clothe my nakedness. May I receive the bread of angels, the king of kings and Lord of Lords, with the humble reverence, the purity and faith, the repentance and love, and the determined purpose that will help to bring me to salvation. May I receive the sacrament of the Lord's body and blood in its reality and power. Kind God, may I receive the body and blood of your Son our Lord Jesus Christ, born from the womb of the Blessed Virgin Mary and so enter into His mystical body and be numbered among His members. Loving Father, as on my earthly pilgrimage, I receive your beloved Son under the veil of a sacrament, may I one day see Him face to face in Glory, who lives and reigns with you and the Holy Spirit, one God for ever and ever. Amen. (Prayer by St. Thomas Aquinas)

After Communion

Almighty God, ever living, all loving, all powerful Father, I thank you for that even though I am a sinner, your unprofitable servant, not because of my worth but in the kindness of your mercy, you have fed me with the precious body and blood of your Son our Lord, Jesus Christ. I pray that this Holy Communion may not bring me condemnation and punishment, but forgiveness and salvation. May it be a helmet of faith, a shield of good will; May it bring me charity and patience, humility and obedience, and growth in the power to do good. May it be my strong defense against all my enemies, visible and invisible, and the perfect calming of all my evil impulses, bodily and spiritual. May it unite me more closely to you the one true God and lead me safely through death to everlasting happiness with you. And I pray that you will lead me, a sinner, to the banquet where you, with your Son and Holy Spirit are true and perfect light, total fulfillment, everlasting joy, gladness without end, and perfect happiness to your saints. Grant this through Christ our Lord. Amen. (St. Thomas Aquinas)

The Memorare

Remember, O most gracious Virgin Mary, that never was it known that anyone who fled to your protection, implored your help or sought your intercession, was left unaided. Inspired by this confidence, to you I fly, O Virgin of virgins, my Mother. To you I come, before you I stand, sinful and sorrowful. O Mother of the Word Incarnate despise not my petition but in your mercy hear and answer me. [Your intention.] We know our prayers will be heard through your intercession, Amen.

Easter Vigil Prayer

Christ yesterday and today, the beginning and the end; alpha and omega. His are the seasons and the ages; to Him glory and dominion through endless ages. Amen. By His wounds, holy and glorious, may He guard and preserve us. Christ the Lord. Amen.

Glory Be

Glory be to the Father and to the Son and to the Holy Spirit. As it was in the beginning, is now and ever shall be, world without end. Amen. [or "as it was in the beginning, is now and will be forever. Amen."]

The Hail Mary

Hail Mary, full of grace, the Lord is with you. Blessed are you among women, and blessed is the fruit of your womb, Jesus. Holy Mary, Mother of God, pray for us sinners now and at the hour of our death. Amen.

(For the Protestants among you, it is worth noting that this prayer is highly scriptural. The first sentence is the angel Gabriel's greeting to Mary at the annunciation (Lk 1:28), and the second is Elizabeth's greeting to her at the time of her visitation (Lk 1:42). The title "Mother of God" was given to Mary quite early on in Christian history (at the Council of Ephesus in A.D. 431). What title we give Mary is not just a matter of how we view *her*, but also of how we understand Jesus, and the question was discussed at that Council in the context of broader Christological questions.)

The Angelus

This prayer is often done in an answer and response form. I'll put the responses in italics.

The angel of the Lord declared unto Mary
And she conceived by the Holy Spirit
Hail Mary, full of grace, the Lord is with you. Blessed are you among women, and blessed is the fruit of your womb, Jesus.
Holy Mary, Mother of God, pray for us sinners now and at the hour of our death. Amen
Behold, I am the handmaid of the Lord

Be it done to me according to Thy word.
[Hail Mary done in response form.]
And the Word was made flesh
and dwelt among us
[Hail Mary again.]
Pray for us Holy Mother of God
That we may be made worthy of the promises of Christ
Pour forth, Oh God, we beseech Thee, Thy grace into our hearts, that we, to whom the incarnation of Christ Thy Son was made known by the message of an angel, may, by His passion and cross be brought to share in the glory of His resurrection, through the same Christ our Lord. Amen.

Hail Holy Queen

Hail Holy Queen, Mother of Mercy, our life, our sweetness and our hope. To thee do we cry poor banished children of Eve. To thee do we send up our sighs, mourning and weeping in this valley of tears. Turn, then, most gracious advocate, thine eyes of mercy towards us, and after this our exile, show unto us the blessed fruit of your womb, Jesus; Oh clement, oh loving, oh sweet Virgin Mary. Pray for us Holy Mother of God, that we may be made worthy of the promises of Christ. Amen

The Rosary

On the cross pray the Apostle's Creed, on the first bead an "Our Father," on each of the three beads say a "Hail Mary" praying for faith, hope and charity. Recite a "Glory be" on the last single bead. Then go around all five decades, saying an Our Father on the first bead, ten Hail Mary's and then a Glory be. After the last Glory Be recite a Hail Holy Queen on the little metal medal.

This is the basic structure, but you are supposed to meditate on certain mysteries as you do it. There are any number of good books on the Rosary,[87] so I will merely list the mysteries here and leave it to you to pursue ways to do the meditations on your own. *The Joyful Mysteries*: The Annunciation, Mary's Visit to Elizabeth ("the Visitation"), the Birth of Jesus, the Presentation of Jesus in the Temple, and the Finding of Jesus Teaching in the Temple. *The Luminous Mysteries*: Baptism of Jesus, the Wedding Feast at Cana, the Proclamation of the Gospel, the Transfiguration, the Institution of the Eucharist. *The Sorrowful Mysteries*: Jesus's Agony in the Garden of Gethsemane, the Scourging at the Pillar, the Crowning with Thorns, the Carrying of the Cross, and the Crucifixion. *The Glorious Mysteries*: the Resurrection, the Ascension, the Descent of the Holy Spirit, the Assumption of Mary into Heaven, and the Coronation of Mary as Queen of Heaven in glory with all the saints.

St. Jude Novena

St. Jude, apostle of Christ, the Church honors and prays to you universally as the patron of hopeless and difficult cases. Pray for us in our needs. Make use, we implore you, of that powerful privilege given to you to bring visible and speedy help where help is needed. Pray that we humbly accept the trials and disappointments and mistakes that are a part of our human condition. Help us to see the reflection of the sufferings of Christ in the trials and tribulations of our lives. Let us see in a spirit of great faith and hope the part we even now share in the joy of Christ's resurrection and which we long to share fully in Heaven. Intercede for us, that we may again experience that joy in answer to our present needs if it is God's desire for us [mention your intention]. We know our prayers will be heard through your intercession, amen.

Lord Jesus Christ, we thank you for all the graces and favors you have given us through the prayers of your apostle Jude

---

[87] For example, *The Rosary: Contemplating the Face of Christ*, with introduction and reflections from Pope John Paul II (Pauline Books and Media, 2003), or *The New Rosary in Scripture* by Edward Sri (Servant Books, 2003).

Thaddeus. Great apostle St. Jude, we thank you for your intercession in response to our prayers. We will always be grateful to you. Continue to intercede for our needs and in our difficulties, and be with us particularly at the hour of death, that we may face that decisive moment with courage and serenity. Amen.

(These prayers are to be said for nine consecutive days. Don't think of this practice as some kind of magic, but as simply structuring your request and disposing you rightly to receive what you are asking for. Traditionally done in desperate cases.)

A Commendatory Prayer for a Sick Person at the Point of Departure

O Almighty God, with whom do live the spirits of just men made perfect, after they are delivered from their earthly prisons; we humbly commend the soul of this thy servant, our dear brother [sister], into thy hands, as into the hands of a faithful Creator, and most merciful Savior; beseeching thee, that it may be precious in thy sight. Wash it, we pray thee, in the blood of that immaculate lamb that was slain to take away the sins of the world; that whatsoever defilements it may have contracted, through the lusts of the flesh or the wiles of Satan, being purged and done away, it may be presented pure and without spot before thee; through the merits of Jesus Christ thine only Son our Lord. Amen. (*Book of Common Prayer*, 317)

A Commendatory Prayer when the Soul is Departed

Into thy hands, O merciful Savior, we commend the soul of thy servant, now departed from the body. Acknowledge, we humbly beseech thee, a sheep of thine own fold, a lamb of thine own flock, a sinner of thine own redeeming. Receive him [her] into the arms of thy mercy, into the blessed rest of everlasting peace, and into the glorious company of the saints in light. Amen. (*Book of Common Prayer*, p. 319)

ANNOTATIONS/REFLECTIONS ON
THE PRAYERS GIVEN IN CHAPTER TWO

Introductory Remarks

Because this book is intended to help you enter into your own walk with the Lord, I have suggested a basic structure for your prayer time and encouraged you to develop your own way of working with the prayers. I believe that God will meet you where you are, and work with what is already present in you. But having used these prayers over a period of years myself, I have developed some ways of understanding and entering into them that I think might be helpful to others, especially those who do not have much background knowledge of the Christian tradition. So in what follows I have broken down the prayers from Chapter Two and offered reflections, explanations, or meditations on each verse or line, putting the prayer itself in italics and my comments in regular type.

I don't recommend that you just sit down and read this from beginning to end; there is a lot of material here. Regard it as a resource you can dip into as the Spirit moves, and go over small chunks of it at a time slowly and thoughtfully. When you are doing the prayers, you may find yourself particularly drawn to some part of the prayers, and therefore you might want to read the reflections I offer on that. Or perhaps you find some of them incomprehensible and some explanation of their meaning might help you enter into them better. So flip to the place where I discuss those verses. Likewise if some parts of the prayers leave you cold, looking at some of the suggested meditations or reflections might help them come alive for you.

I. OPENING PRAYERS

Make the Sign of the Cross while saying slowly and reflectively:

Two natures in one person: Jesus Christ true God and true man, three persons in one God; I pray in the name of the Father and of the Son and of the Holy Spirit. This formula comprises the very heart of our Christian understanding of God, so we should approach it reverently. What a treasure to have been given this in faith to hold in our hearts and contemplate! We can never fully grasp (comprehend) it, but it can in some sense grasp and form us. So concentrate carefully on the meaning each time you say it.

God come to my assistance; Lord make haste to help me. Sometimes I feel like the lepers who stood far off crying, "Jesus son of David have mercy on us!" Sometimes I feel more like I am knocking on the door of a beloved friend and joyfully anticipating his coming to meet me. But a sense of one's desperate need for help and confidence in His eagerness to help us should be in the background. An Orthodox prayer I sometimes use here is "Help us, save us, have mercy on us; for you are good and a lover of mankind." Truly our situation *is* desperate without Him, and until we really recognize and experience this we tend to drag our feet instead of running towards Him.

Glory be to the Father and to the Son and to the Holy Spirit. This prayer contains the essence of Christian worship — giving glory to God, understood as Father, Son and Holy Spirit — three persons in one God. I try to think carefully of the persons of the Trinity. One feels something different when addressing God as Father, Son or Spirit. The creation story in Genesis displays the creative power of God; reflecting on Jesus's passion and resurrection shows God at work redeeming us, and the Pentecost story (Acts 2) shows the sanctifying power of the Holy Spirit descending on the apostles.

As it was in the beginning, is now and will be forever. Sometimes I substitute "now and forever and unto ages of ages, Amen" as some Orthodox do, just because I like that form, conveying as it does the timelessness of God. Or "the God who is, who was, and is to come at the end of the ages," or "as it was in the beginning, is now and ever shall be, world without end. Amen."

Next comes the prayer from the *Book of Common Prayer* (p. 67) that has become so pivotal to me. I break it down line by line.

Almighty God unto whom all hearts are open, all desires known, and from whom no secrets are hid. This is an extraordinarily powerful opening to prayer. First it notes that our skin is not a boundary in any absolute sense. The idea that I am in here and can keep all else out is an illusion. Human beings are inherently permeable to the action of spiritual beings, so we had better be sure we align ourselves with the good ones. Second, it invites Him to enter in and know us more deeply. Psalm 138 speaks about God knowing the haughty from afar, and we don't want it to be that way with us. We want Him to know us intimately. He too wants this. Since nothing is hidden anyway, we might as well let the doctor come in and see the extent of our brokenness and sinfulness so that healing can begin. There was a woman at the court of Mary Queen of Scots who was wrongly thought to be pregnant and therefore disgraced. In fact, she had a tumor, but would not allow herself to be examined by a doctor and, of course, died. The point is merely that the doctor can't heal if we won't let him touch the sore spots. Short prayers I add at this point are things like, "Search me, know me, try my heart; see if there be any wicked way in me; cleanse me of my secret sins and lead me in the everlasting way; give me contrition for my sins and show me the truth." If you are feeling really brave, pray "Make me defenseless before you, God." I suppose this should be scary, and on occasion it is. But once one gets over the worst of it, it is a relief to have someone who can know us as we truly are, and still love us and remain by our side.

Cleanse the thoughts of our hearts by the inspiration of Thy Holy Spirit. We should thank God for *wanting* to cleanse the thoughts of our hearts. He could, after all, have left us to die in our sins. A number of images or metaphors are used in Scripture for the Holy Spirit: fire, wind, breath and a dove. But we must not forget that the Holy Spirit is a person. Jesus says, "The Counselor, the Holy Spirit, whom the Father will send in my name, He will teach you all things and bring to your remembrance all that I have said to you" (Jn 14:26). The word "inspiration" is important. God breathed into the nostrils of Adam and he became a living soul. Adam did not receive the Holy Spirit, since this was given only through Jesus, but the analogy is there with the reception of a new level of life. "The wind blows where it wills and you hear the sound of it, but you do not know whence it comes or whither it goes; so it is with everyone who is born of the Spirit" (as Jesus tells Nicodemus in Jn 3:8). Try being open to God's breathing His life into you so that you become filled with new life. For we live not only with our own life but with His. A hymn from the *1940 Hymnal* (#375) contains some lines you might fruitfully use to meditate on: "Breathe on me, breath of God; fill me with life anew. That I may love what thou dost love and do what thou wouldst do.... Breathe on me breath of God, until my heart is pure, until with thee I will one will, to do or to endure; breathe on me breath of God, till I am wholly thine; till all this earthly part of me glows with thy fire divine."

That we may perfectly love Thee and worthily magnify Thy Holy Name. God is deserving of perfect love, but we have nothing perfect to give Him — certainly we are not capable of perfect love. The Holy Spirit is given us so that we may love God with His very own love! For the Holy Spirit is/brings that love, and enables us to praise God and love Him in a way that we as mere mortals could never do. Jesus tells us that God is seeking people to worship Him "in Spirit and in truth" (Jn 4:23), and surely it is the Holy Spirit that is meant here. So worshiping Him in this way pleases Him; it is also the highest joy we can experience. That God is actually *seeking* people to worship Him is wonderful. What we most long to do is what He most wants us to do.

For the "worthily magnify Thy Holy Name" part, think of the *Magnificat*, where Mary uses that term. "My soul magnifies the Lord" (Lk 1:46). What does this mean? We should ask her prayers to help us do it as she did. In part it means "proclaim the greatness of the Lord" (more modern translation), but there is more, I think, and she can help us. It somehow involves the Lord becoming manifest in us.

Through Christ our Lord. Amen. Quick remembrance that all good things are given through Him and that He is Lord.

II. HOLY SPIRIT INVOCATION

Oh come, creator, Spirit come and make within our souls Thy home. Supply Thy grace and heavenly aid to fill the hearts which Thou hast made. In Genesis the Spirit of God is described as "moving over the face of the waters" at the time when "the earth was without form and void, and darkness was upon the face of the deep" (Gn 1:2). And when Jesus appears to the disciples after the resurrection and says "receive the Holy Spirit" He breathes upon them (Jn 20:22). Life and breath are, of course, closely connected; it is the Spirit that gives life (Jn 6:63). "Make me your child, to be always the dwelling place of your Holy Spirit and in no way the dwelling place of evil" (Ukrainian Rite prayer). Or pray, "Drive out the darkness of my heart and mind." The fact that God is the creator of our hearts accounts for the fact that He knows them in all their mysterious depths far better than we do ourselves, and that His coming there is in some way natural or fitting. Yes, this occurs only as a result of God's free gift of grace, but when He comes, He comes as one for whom the place has already been prepared in the very fibers and inward being of our hearts. They were created for this and so His presence comes as rain upon parched ground rather than as something alien.

Oh gift of God most high, Thy name is Comforter whom we

acclaim fountain of life and fire of love and sweet anointing from above. First, of course, the Spirit is always a gift and a free gift. Describing the Holy Spirit as "Comforter" is a very rich image, conveying both the idea of consoling us and binding up our wounds, and also the power of the Spirit to strengthen and build us up. The images of fountain, fire, and sweetness are various ways of trying to express what happens when God's Spirit moves in us. Jesus tells the Samaritan woman that the water He will give will become in us a spring of water welling up to eternal life (Jn 4:14).

The Spirit manifested Himself as tongues of fire at Pentecost. John the Baptist says that there is one who will come after him who will "baptize you with the Holy Spirit and with fire" (Mt 3:11). Jesus, Himself, says, "I came to cast fire upon the earth" (Lk 12:49), and numerous prophets and saints describe themselves as feeling as though they were on fire (*e.g.*, Jr 20:9). So reflect on these Scripture passages as you pray this verse.

Sweetness is a particularly interesting way in which people sometimes experience the Holy Spirit. In our rather puritanical culture, the idea of enjoying God doesn't come naturally to many people. They think that pleasure and sin are closely connected. Chocolate deserts are described as "sinfully delicious," etc. Religion for them is about being stern and self-denying — curbing their passions, renouncing earthly pleasures of all sorts, and being obedient to God's commands. Certainly Christians should not be overly sensual and self-indulgent. But God does want us to find pleasure in beholding His glory and praising Him. "Delight in the Lord, and He will give you your heart's desire" (Ps 37:4). "You have put into my heart a greater joy than they have from abundance of corn and new wine" (Ps 4:8). "Taste and see that the Lord is good" (Ps 34:8). "With great delight I sat in his shadow, and his fruit was sweet to my taste. He brought me to the banqueting house, and his banner over me was love" (Sg 2:3-4). Even Thomas Aquinas, hardly a wild sensualist, speaks of the delight of the soul contemplating God overflowing to the senses.

The ancient Jews, living in a very dry, hot climate, put oil, often sweet smelling oil, on their skin and hair. This was called anointing themselves. But anointing had a religious use also. Kings were anointed with oil to confer upon them the reality of their kingship, and prophets also received an anointing for their prophetic mission. Isaiah says, "The spirit of the Lord is upon me, for He has anointed me to bring good tidings to the afflicted" (Is 61:1). Anointing can sometimes be given to accomplish special tasks (e.g. 2 Ch 22:7). The sacrament of confirmation includes anointing with oil to give us additional gifts of the Spirit to do God's work in the world.

The sevenfold gift of grace is Thine, Thou finger of the hand divine; the Father's promise true to teach our earthly tongues thy heavenly speech. Describing the Holy Spirit as the finger of the hand divine emphasizes the fact that the Spirit reaches out to us, makes contact with us, and that certain gifts flow to us from and through this Spirit. The seven gifts of the Holy Spirit are wisdom, understanding, counsel, fortitude, knowledge, piety and fear of the Lord. I usually just reflect on the fact that God is pouring all sorts of gifts into my heart, far beyond anything that I can conceive, and do not focus on the specific gifts.

The part about how the Father promises to teach our earthly tongues heavenly speech is a good occasion to ask God for the gift of tongues. "Come thou fount of every blessing; tune our hearts to sing thy praise." Try visualizing yourself praising God together with all the angels and saints. A kind of reaching out occurs through which we try to praise Him more and more fully and appropriately to His glory. Just before the *Sanctus* in the Mass there is a prayer which says that "we join with all the choirs of heaven as they sing for ever to your glory." The verses on the saints and angels praising God from the *Te Deum* would be good to meditate on here also.

Thy light to every sense impart; pour forth Thy grace in every heart. Our weakened flesh do Thou restore to strength and courage evermore. In imparting His light to all our senses, God enables us to perceive Him by attuning them more finely and raising them up to a spiritual level. No doubt we also have inner senses and faculties for responding to God on levels that we are not aware of. It is like the seed that germinates under the ground while we sleep and rise again and again and gradually the seed takes root and grows until it shows above the ground, eventually becoming a large plant (Lk 13:19) and bearing fruit. But even our ordinary senses can be attuned more to Him, or at least they can echo, reflect, or show forth what is occurring in our souls so that it becomes more understandable to us. When praying "Pour forth thy grace in every heart" I often insert a few prayers for people I know who are in particular need of God's grace and for all Christ's church that we may make Him manifest in the world more effectively. The prayer for strength and courage is appropriate here, since it is the work of the Holy Spirit especially to strengthen us to go on in the Way and give us the courage to witness to our faith in the world. The Negro spiritual "There is a balm in Gilead" has a verse "Sometimes I am discouraged and think my work is vain; and then the Holy Spirit revives my soul again." This is a good point at which to entrust ourselves with all our weaknesses to the Lord, realizing that without Him we can do nothing.

Oh most blessed light divine, shine within these hearts of thine and our inmost being fill. In praying this I am always aware of the mysteriousness of my "inmost being" and how only God can fully know it. St. Paul speaks of our having the treasure of Christ's life in "earthen vessels" and I like to think about how much God does in us in ways that are secret and unknown to us. This verse goes over some of the same ground as the previous ones. Light serves as a metaphor for God's action. God is described as light in scripture. "God is light and in Him there is no darkness or shadow of turning" (Jm 2:17). You may sometimes feel surrounded by a warm, golden light at moments of intense prayer when your eyes are closed. I used to try to figure out whether there was a purely natural cause for this — such as turning my head upward so that more light fell on my closed eyes, or a ray of sunlight. It may or may not matter, since one cannot clearly distinguish natural from supernatural in any case, and God can make use of entirely ordinary events to communicate with us. But I do think this occurs sometimes when no natural cause can be found. It is quite subtle — I'm not talking about the sort of thing St. Paul experienced on the road to Damascus. Light seems to exist at a higher level of vibration — not perhaps a bridge between the physical and the spiritual, but at least a metaphor for this. People have often observed that saints and holy people seem to radiate a kind of light (which is the reason why they are portrayed with halos). For example, Moses's face shone when he came down from the mountain after talking with God, and Hasidic folk tales describe particularly holy rabbis who appeared to be surrounded with light when they were praying.

Where Thou art not man hath nought; nothing good in deed or thought; nothing free from taint of ill. This verse is particularly helpful to me in moments of emptiness, desolation, or disappointment with my own sinfulness because it brings home to me the depth of my own helplessness and consequently my total dependence on God. I am able to remain quietly in hope, knowing that only He can rescue me. I may not be able to reach out and grab onto Him, but He can always reach out and touch me and the more I realize my own powerlessness and need for Him, the more receptive I become to His action in me. The failure of my own attempts at bootstrapping myself, at conquering my faults, or going out and driving the forces of evil into the sea (à la Joan of Arc) appears to me then to be exactly what is to be expected. Even those of my motivations that appear good and holy are all too often tainted by romantic self-dramatization or an inflated image of myself and my powers. Why should I suppose otherwise? Complete dependence on Him should ultimately become the most natural thing in the world to us.

Heal our wounds, our strength renew; on our dryness pour Thy dew; wipe the stains of guilt away. God, of course, does all sorts of things in us, beyond all we can ask or know or conceptualize in any way. But this verse and the next one give us at least some images to work with. We acutely feel our wounds sometimes. Things fester and hurt. We feel less than whole. We don't feel like we can go another step. We are weary. We feel dry, hard, blocked, hemmed in, exhausted. We feel unclean and unworthy and unloved. The images in this verse speak to us of the power of God to change us — to make us more alive, gentle, clear, free, strong — to lift the burdens from our shoulders. That is the work of the Holy Spirit.

Bend the stubborn heart and will, melt the frozen, warm the chill; guide the steps that go astray. This verse really applies to us all. It is easy to pray for the conversion of those people — those sinners over there. You should pray here, of course, for people you know who seem to have gone badly astray. But we are all hard and stubborn of heart. We must bring our hearts to Him for healing and trust that He can do it. This has to do with what I called above second order desires. It is enough that we desire to desire God; that we want to be less willful. God's grace can bridge the gap between us as we are (stubborn of heart and beset by temptations) and what we long to become. When we feel we are falling into some temptation we should pray for help and ask Him to deliver us from our own willfulness — to bend and soften us and make us more supple to move at His direction like the dancing partner. Pray this verse whenever you are tempted to take the bit in your teeth and go your own way.

On the faithful who adore and confess Thee evermore, in Thy sevenfold gift descend. You may feel that your faith is shaky, but don't worry. You have at least that germ of faith to seek God. How blessed we are to have that germ of faith. God can and will deepen and broaden that faith as we continue to pray for this gift. The term "confess" here has nothing to do with the practice of confessing one's sins. To "confess" one's faith is to assert it over and against heresy, or in the face of hostility. And to be truly faithful, we must be prepared to do this. Pray for conversion of heart of all Christians so that we may be more faithful to our calling. Adoration of God is what we hope to spend eternity doing. "God has highly exalted him and bestowed on him the name which is above every name, that at the name of Jesus every knee should bow,... and every tongue confess, that Jesus Christ is Lord, to the glory of God the Father" (Ph 2:9-11).

Drive far away our spirit's foe; thine own abiding peace bestow. Where Thou dost go before as guide, no evil can our steps betide. An Orthodox prayer says, "Our hope is the Father; our refuge the Son; our rampart the Holy Spirit." Here I think of the Holy Spirit as a sort of rampart — as though He spreads a tent over me that keeps out the darts of the Evil One. I dwell secure in a protected space, and God's peace surrounds and fills me. Even though all sorts of evil things are trying to get at me, they are powerless against the Holy Spirit. The old folk hymn says, "What a blessedness, what a peace is mine, leaning on the everlasting arms."

The Spirit not only provides protection, but He also is leading or guiding me to go forward in the right way. Being protected from evil does not mean that we will be protected from all suffering. The Lord's Prayer says "Deliver us from evil" not "Deliver us from suffering." For suffering of itself does not separate us from God and may draw us closer to Him. But evil does separate us from Him, and is therefore more to be feared.

There is a verse in "Glorious things of thee are spoken" that says, "With salvation's walls surrounded, thou mayest smile at all thy foes" (*1940 Hymnal* #385). If you think of the foe as the Devil, it would seem risky to go so far as to smile. Shouldn't we have a reasonable fear of him, and not, perhaps, provoke him to anger at us for not taking his assaults seriously enough? But I think the Lord does want us to have that rock solid a trust in Him. A cat will only lick its paws and wash its face if it feels comfortable and secure, and if a cat really trusts you it may sometimes lick its paws while you are holding it. So we should be like that cat — so safe and secure in Jesus's arms that we can calmly wash our paws without any fears at all.

Through Thee may we the Father learn, and know the Son and Thee discern, who art of both and thus adore, perfectly for evermore. St. Paul says, "The Spirit searches everything, even the depths of God. For what person knows a man's thoughts except the spirit of the man which is in him? So also no one comprehends the thoughts of God except the Spirit of God.... We have received the Spirit which is from God, that we might understand the gifts bestowed on us by God. And we impart this in words not taught by human wisdom but taught by the Spirit" (1 Cor 2:10-13). We should ask the Holy Spirit to reveal to us more of God's nature that we may worship Him in spirit and in truth, and be drawn into His very life.

III. SURRENDER PRAYER

Dear Heavenly Father, please help me now and throughout this day to surrender to you more than yesterday. Help me to receive you and allow you to dwell in me more deeply than yesterday. Help me to live in you and for you only, more today than yesterday.

Surrender involves allowing God to act in us. Pray: "Lord take me and make me your own." It is both a giving and a receiving, and at a deep level the two are inseparable aspects of the same thing. Surrender is something God can effect within us at levels we don't even know about. It is not exactly something that we can *do*, though some of the images offered in Chapter Two may help dispose us rightly toward God — for example the one of the ground that is receptive to softening showers and warming sun. But our surrender to Him is ultimately His gift to us. Allow Him to draw you to Himself; allow the desire for Him to take root in you. "Rivers to the ocean run, nor stay in all their course. Fire ascending seeks the sun, both speed them to their source. So a soul that's born of God, pants to view His glorious face; upward tends to His abode to rest in His embrace" (*The Sacred Harp*, p. 84). Larger bodies exercise a gravitational pull on smaller ones, as the earth exerts a pull on the moon and the sun exerts a pull on the earth. Might it not be the same on the spiritual plane, so that a vast spiritual being exerts a kind of attraction or pull on a small one? This is, of course, metaphorical; God does not occupy space and so isn't "big" or "large." Yet the analogy with the sun and the planets points to something very profound; He is, in truth, that true sun around whom we must move,[88] held in our orbits by His love and grace, praising Him joyfully throughout eternity. For this we were created.

Receiving can require humility. We like to think that we have somehow deserved the good things that come to us. Consider, for example, how often advertisers tell us we deserve this or that comfort or luxury. They don't just say, "You've got the money; you've got the power; so, go out and indulge yourself." But God gives us what we can never deserve or repay; the appropriate response, therefore, is thankfulness and praise.

"As therefore you received Christ Jesus the Lord, so live in Him" (Col 2:5). What is it to live "in" God? Jesus says, "I am in my Father and you are in me and I in you" (Jn 14:20). St. Paul says, "It is no longer I who live, but Christ who lives in me" (Gal 2:20). Believers are often described as members of the body of Christ. The easiest way to understand this, perhaps, is to meditate on the analogy Jesus gave at the Last Supper: "I am the vine, you are the branches. He who abides in me and I in him, he it is that bears much fruit" (Jn 15:5). To live for Him is to refer all that we do back to Him; to offer it to Him and to seek to please Him.

---

[88] Interestingly enough, Nietzsche, the influential Nineteenth Century prophet of "the death of God" (whom he says we killed) uses this very analogy to describe the world without God: "What did we do when we unchained this earth from its sun? Whither are we moving now? Away from all suns? Are we not plunging continually? Backward, sideward, forward, in all directions? Is there any up or down left? Are we not straying as through an infinite nothing? Do we not feel the breath of empty space? Has it not become colder? Is not night and more night coming on all the while? Must not lanterns be lit in the morning?"

IV. LITANY OF THE SACRED HEART OF JESUS

Mercy

Underlying the litany is our cry for mercy. A feeling of total helplessness and need should accompany the plea for mercy. God *is* mercy. His mercy is like the sun shining steadily, but clouds can drift between us and that mercy, or perhaps we might be turned away from it as half of the earth is at any moment turned away from the sun, so we pray that the clouds may be dispelled, that our hearts may, by His grace, be turned toward Him, so that His mercy may shine through. St. Faustina visualized mercy as two rays of light streaming from Jesus's heart, one red and one white (symbolizing the blood and water that flowed from Jesus's side when the soldier pierced it with a lance). That mercy flows from Him in this way is not inconsistent with God's being also just; His light discloses our sinfulness and need for mercy. His mercy should work a real change in us, and not just be regarded in a legalistic way as God's letting us off from punishment.

Lord have mercy; Christ have mercy; Lord have mercy. Christ hear us; Christ graciously hear us. These lines link the terms "Lord" and "Christ." That the Jesus whom they called "Lord" was also the Christ, the Messiah, the Son of God, was something that dawned on the disciples slowly. This is a wonderful occasion to meditate on the confessions of faith of Peter (Mt 16:16), Martha (Jn 11:27), and Thomas (Jn 20:28) and recall the words they used and the circumstances in which they were uttered. Beg them to intercede for you that you may see Jesus as they did.

God the Father of Heaven have mercy on us; God the Son redeemer of the world have mercy on us; God the Holy Spirit sanctifier of the faithful have mercy on us. Holy Trinity one God have mercy on us. People tend to say that the Trinity is incomprehensible and generally don't think too much about it. Certainly I don't claim that it is easily comprehensible, but I think it is important to think about it; God has, in a sense, revealed His nature to us — given us His name in a way we could never have discovered on our own. We think of the Father most strongly as the source of all being — of all creation springing forth in joy from His creative act — and of God redeeming us in Jesus Christ, the co-eternal Son through His incarnation, passion and resurrection. And the Holy Spirit moving over the waters at the creation, breathed out upon the disciples in John 20:22, or poured out upon the apostles at Pentecost. Yet the three persons are also one. I think of different notes in a chord of music sounding together, or some sort of perfect dance. Pray: "I bind unto myself this day the strong name of the Trinity, by invocation of the same, the three in one the one in three" (from St. Patrick's Breastplate). This prayer can strengthen our trust in God in wonderful ways.

Heart of Jesus, Son of the Eternal Father, have mercy on us.

Jesus as God's co-eternal Son:

Reflect here about the Scripture passages describing Jesus's baptism (Mk 1:11; Mt 3:17; Lk 3:22) or the transfiguration (Mt 17:5; 2 P 1:17) where God calls Jesus His Son. Or the words of the Nicene Creed describing Jesus as "begotten of the Father before all worlds, God from God, light from light, true God from true God, one in being with the Father." Jesus, Himself, says, "No one knows the Father but the Son and anyone to whom the Son chooses to reveal Him" (Mt 11:27; Lk 10:22). From the *Te Deum,* pray: "Thou art the king of glory O Christ; Thou art the everlasting Son of the Father."

Heart of Jesus, formed by the Holy Spirit in the womb of the virgin mother, have mercy on us.

Jesus in Mary's womb:

This is one of my favorites. Try to visualize Jesus's development in the womb, starting from the tiniest zygote. When the eternal God, creator of heaven and earth chose to manifest Himself to us, He came so silently, so secretly, so delicately and softly — yet with such power. The fetus develops rapidly and in complex and beautiful ways. It is so delicate and vulnerable, yet the woman's whole metabolism and hormonal balance is affected in very powerful ways from the start of pregnancy, and in a sense it is the fetus who is in control of the process. The changes in her body are for the sake of the child. So, also, the coming of God into our hearts is subtle and intimate, yet very powerful.

Pray that Jesus be formed in you also in whatever way He chooses. This is absolutely central to Christian life. We are supposed to become new creations, formed in His image. "We know that when He appears we shall be like Him for we shall see Him as He is" (1 Jn 3:2). St. Paul says we shall "bear the image of the man of heaven" (1 Cor 15:49), and that "we are all, with unveiled face, beholding the glory of the Lord, and are being changed into His likeness from one degree of glory to another" (2 Cor 3:18). It is good at this point to ask Mary to pray for you that you may say yes to God as fully as she did and allow Him to form Himself in you in whatever way He wills. For He is formed in us by the action of the very same Spirit who formed Him in her womb (although not, of course, in the special unique way He was in Mary's womb).

Heart of Jesus, substantially united to the Word of God, have mercy on us.

Jesus as Word of God:

St. John tells us that "the Word became flesh and dwelt among us full of grace and truth; and we have beheld His glory, glory as of the only Son from the Father" (Jn 1:14). We could meditate on this verse fruitfully for a thousand years without exhausting its richness. Reflect also more concretely on the actual heart of Jesus and how His heart — the core of His being — was one in being with God the Father, since He was true God and true man, God shining forth in human flesh. St. James says, "Receive with meekness the implanted word which is able to save your souls" (Jm 1:21). We should ask that He, the Eternal

Word, be implanted in our hearts, and that our hearts be like the good soil in which the Word can take root and bear much fruit. The image of our hearts as like a ground in which the seed of new life has been planted is a feminine one, and it pervades the New Testament. We must allow our substance to be transformed and restructured and raised up. Or one can perhaps think of His heart as becoming planted in our hearts, beating with them, taking root there.

Heart of Jesus of infinite majesty, have mercy on us.

His Divine Majesty:

There is a *Sacred Harp* hymn I have come to like especially with the line "Sweet majesty and awful love sit smiling on His brow, and all the glorious ranks above at humble distance bow" (*The Sacred Harp*, p. 362). Think also of the line from the new version of the Latin Mass, "*in conspectu divinae majestatis tuis,*" "In the face (or sight) of Thy divine majesty." Or "in the sight of the angels I will sing Thy praise." Visualize all the host of Heaven — angels and saints — praising Him and falling down before His divine majesty. Majesty is not a term we use much these days, but its associations with dignity and royalty and splendor make it a rich term to use to describe Jesus — like the sun shedding its rays of glory in all directions. An old hymn by St. Ambrose of Milan addresses Jesus Christ thus: "O splendor of God's glory bright, O Thou that bringest light from light... O Thou true Son, on us Thy glance let fall in royal radiance." Psalm 29 is a good one to reflect on for a sense of God's majesty. It speaks of the voice of the Lord as "full of majesty... the voice of the Lord makes the oaks to whirl and strips the forests bare, and in his temple all cry, 'Glory!'"

Heart of Jesus, sacred temple of God, have mercy on us.

Temple of God:

A temple is a place where God dwells and is worshiped. Jesus describes His body as a temple, when He says, "Destroy this temple and in three days I will raise it up" (Jn 2:19). As Christians we are members of the mystical body of Christ, and thus we are living stones being built into this temple (1 P 2:5). St. Paul says, "Do you not know that you are God's temple, and that God's Spirit dwells in you?" (1 Cor 3:16-17). So we should pray that our human hearts, like that of Jesus, will be places where God dwells and is worshiped. Hopefully this can become habitual, so that a sort of inner worship goes on continually — perhaps even when we are not aware of it.

Heart of Jesus, tabernacle of the Most High, have mercy on us.

Tabernacle:

This term was used by the Jews to describe the special tent used for worship that they carried around with them in their wanderings. It had an outer tent and an inner tent called the Holy of Holies into which the priest went only once a year taking the blood of sacrificed animals which he offered for his sins and those of the people. In it was a golden altar of incense and the Ark of the Covenant which contained the tablets of the law (ten commandments), some manna, and Aaron's rod which budded. Cherubim of glory were sculpted overshadowing the mercy seat. This was the center of the community's religious life, for it was here that Yahweh was present to His people.

Christians believe that Jesus Christ brought to fulfillment what was foreshadowed in the Jewish blood sacrifices, and rendered them no longer necessary for us by the shedding of his own blood (see Heb 9-10). The tabernacle as the place of presence flows naturally into the more complete dwelling of God with us through the incarnation. St. John says that "the Word became flesh and dwelt (was "tabernacled") among us" (Jn 1:14). Jesus, then, opens to us the way into the "holy of holies" now understood as Heaven. The tabernacle in modern churches that is used to store the consecrated host can be seen as analogous to the Jewish tabernacle, and, drawing on this analogy, angels are often sculpted on or near the tabernacle kneeling in worship.

Heart of Jesus, house of God and gate of Heaven, have mercy on us.

Gate of Heaven:

If God is fully in Christ, there is a way open to Heaven through the heart of Christ — that is, through the core or center of His being. In being called into the heart of Christ we enter upon the way to Heaven. We are never fully in Heaven here, of course, but may be granted glimpses.

Heart of Jesus, burning furnace of charity, have mercy on us.

Charity:

Jesus is often pictured with flames coming out from the top of His heart, representing the burning love He has for us. It is so much deeper and wider than we can imagine. Sometimes I think of how the earth has a molten center, and through cracks in the earth's surface we may for a moment have a glimpse of the depths — a kind of pulsing furnace. How vast is the love of which we let in only in little droplets. Yet even so the effects of this in our lives and the lives of others can be vast. They carry a kind of resonance of the real thing — the fullness of God's love for which we thirst so. We should pray that this fire be communicated to our hearts, consuming our dross, refining us, and enabling us to love more as He does. The disciples on the Emmaus road, after Jesus revealed Himself and disappeared, said to each other, "Did not our hearts burn within us while He talked with us on the road and opened to us the Scriptures?" (Lk 24:32). We should pray to *be* love as He is love (this was the prayer of St. Thérèse of Lisieux), and not just to *have* love.

Heart of Jesus, abode of justice and love, have mercy on us.

Justice and Love:

For a while I used to find this one less moving. Somehow justice sounds cold by contrast with the more nurturing and loving side of Jesus. Yet it is central to our life with God that we allow His judgment to stand. We allow Him to search us, to reveal our sins to us in the light of His love, and to stand firmly as the Truth against which we are measured. Without this, faith could degenerate into "feel good" religion. God's mercy is clear-eyed in the sense that He looks on us as we truly are. He is not an indulgent father who is blind to our sins and failings; He looks at us in the full light of day and loves us all the same. "As a father pities his children, so the Lord pities those who fear Him. For He knows our frame; He remembers that we are dust" (Ps 103:13-14).

Heart of Jesus, full of goodness and love, have mercy on us.
God's Goodness:

This verse rounds out the vision of the last one on how there is both justice and love in Christ. For we are reminded that the various traits of Christ are all bound together and are deeply and pervasively manifestations of goodness. All He does is for the good. God alone is good (Lk 18:19). So although there is judgment, it is all for the good. Our good, but also a deeper and fuller good that goes beyond our vision or understanding. His justice shows us the truth about ourselves, but His goodness and love extend just as widely as His justice, so we must not fear His judgment.

Heart of Jesus, abyss of all virtues, have mercy on us.
Christ's Unfathomable Heart:

This verse has an odd sound to the modern ear, in that it uses the word "virtue" in a way we don't ordinarily use it. Think of being virtuous as having various kinds of excellence or perfection rather than as being a goodie two-shoes who never breaks the rules. An abyss can be thought of either in terms of depth (as in the "burning furnace of charity" verse) or it can be seen as a kind of endless regression from the heart of Christ back to the heart of the Father. I have a picture of a painting that shows God the Father with His arms up and out to the side, and Jesus on the cross, smaller and in front of Him with the line of His arms in front of the arms of the Father and forming the same pattern (with the Holy Spirit being pictured as a dove). Jesus Christ is the hand God stretches out to sinners, and there is a kind of endless depth to His heart; for through it and in it God reaches out to us. One can never plumb the depths, but we should try somehow to feel our way toward the Father through the Heart of Christ. Perhaps like when we see something, our attention is not directed at what happens on our retina, but reaches out toward the object that is the source of the light. Wave upon wave of light and being radiates from the heart of God through Christ to us.

Heart of Jesus, most worthy of all praise, have mercy on us.

Praise:

Here it is useful to ask the Holy Spirit to pray in you, and with you and to help you more fittingly praise God: "Praise befits the upright" (Ps 33:1). St. Paul speaks of offering "a sacrifice of praise" (Heb 13:15). Praising God is partly a matter of the will, but it is also something that God brings forth from our hearts. "Oh may my heart in tune be found like David's harp of solemn sound" (*The Sacred Harp*, p. 48). Praise is a spontaneous and natural reaction to the manifestation of God's glory. Since we are to spend eternity praising God the activity itself must be delightful. "In every joy that crowns my days, in every pain I bear, my heart shall find delight in praise or seek relief in prayer" (*The Sacred Harp*, p. 143). The gift of tongues can help here; it enables us to feel more of a sense of exultation in praising God.

Heart of Jesus, king and center of all hearts, have mercy on us.

Christ the King:

Reflect on passages like "Be lifted up ye ancient doors that the King of Glory may come in" (Ps 24:7-10). He must enter our hearts as king: "By thine own eternal spirit, rule in all our hearts alone" (*1940 Hymnal*, #1). Monarchy is not a common form of government these days, so the imagery of kingship may have lost some of its richness for us, but images of kingship, majesty, thrones, etc. pervade the imagination of many of those who wrote the Scriptures. And perhaps the scarcity of available icons of kingship in our culture has contributed to the popularity of related themes in fantasy literature. In *The Lord of the Rings*, for example, the whole third book is entitled "The Return of the King" and a close reading of the text (by contrast with the movie which conveyed this poorly) reveals a lot of very rich imagery surrounding the kingship of Aragorn. The King is perhaps what Jung would call an "archtype" that is deeply imbedded in the collective unconscious of the human race, carrying with it images of splendor, light, and a kind of overflowing graciousness — a giving beyond all measure. The king also embodies and radiates authority.

This triumphal and glorious image of kingship needs, however, to be balanced by a proper understanding of the peculiar nature of Christ's kingship. When questioned about His kingship by Pilate, He said, "My kingship is not of this world" (Jn 18:36). And the title "Jesus of Nazareth: King of the Jews" was one that Pilate had inscribed on the cross.

In what sense is Jesus at the center of all hearts? God is already at our center by way of desire — we long for Him from our hearts — but through prayer He comes to be at the center also by way of enjoyment. The heart is unfathomable and mysterious, and at some level He is at work in our hearts long before we realize it. So perhaps our hearts know Him better than our minds. But still, I think it is necessary to invite Him to be at the center each day more deeply.

Heart of Jesus in whom are all the treasures of wisdom and knowledge, have mercy on us.

Wisdom:

This is a verse I am constantly drawn to, probably because I am a philosopher, and the word philosophy in Greek means "love of wisdom." The treasures of wisdom and knowledge are hid in

Christ (Col 2:2-3). Think of the longing for wisdom so often expressed in Proverbs and Sirach and the praise they accord to her. Wisdom is something deep and holy and mysterious, and involves the heart and not just the mind. "Teach us to number our days that we may get a heart of wisdom" (Ps 90:12). St. Paul describes Christ as "the power of God and the Wisdom of God" (1 Cor 1:24). He also makes the striking claim that we have the mind of Christ (1 Cor 2:16). Wisdom is one of the seven gifts of the Holy Spirit; we must pray for it.

Heart of Jesus, in whom dwells all the fullness of divinity, have mercy on us.

Divinity:

This verse is from Colossians 1:19. "All the fullness of divinity" indicates that He is fully God. This is something that sets the human mind reeling if you try to think about it. "We behold the glory of God in the face of Christ" (2 Cor 4:4). How can the glory of God fit into a human heart? Yet that is the mystery of the incarnation before which we can only bow our heads and worship, exclaiming along with St. Thomas: "My Lord and my God!" (Jn 20:28).

Heart of Jesus, in whom the Father is well pleased, have mercy on us.

Perfect Obedience:

The mystery of the love between the heart of Jesus and the heart of the Father is, I think, another one of those unfathomable things. God calls Jesus His Son (see "Son of the Eternal Father" above). Through His perfect obedience and self-abandonment to the Father, Jesus was able, on the cross, to offer that "full, perfect, and sufficient sacrifice, offering and oblation for the sins of the whole world" (*Book of Common Prayer*). Through this we are saved. This is a helpful verse to meditate on when we start to slip into having an Atlas complex — trying to carry the weight of the world on our shoulders. Our salvation is, and can only be, the work of God Himself in Christ.

Heart of Jesus of whose fullness we have all received, have mercy on us.

Sharing in His Divinity:

When combined with the last two verses, this is rather earth-shattering. For if the fullness of God dwells in the heart of Jesus, and we receive of the fullness of His heart, then we receive of the fullness of divinity. Not *all* the fullness, but *of* the fullness. There is a teaching about deification in Catholicism. "May we come to share in His divinity who humbled Himself to share in our humanity" (from the Mass prayers). This may sound frightening — as though we might be suddenly blasted by all the fullness and power of God and obliterated as individuals. No. He wants us to be with Him in eternity — to raise us up and purify us — which could not occur if we ceased to be the persons we are. The appropriate prayer then is thanksgiving for all the fullness He has lavished on us so far, and longing for greater fullness. Brother Lawrence cried often that we are to be pitied, who content ourselves with so little when God has infinite treasure to bestow, and that when God finds a soul with a lively faith He pours His graces and favors into it like a torrent.[89]

Heart of Jesus, desire of the everlasting hills, have mercy on us.

Nature's longing for Christ:

This is a particularly poetic verse. St. Paul says that all creation is groaning and longing to be made new in Christ (Rm 8:22), for the fall of the angels and human beings has affected nature as well. The desire we feel for God is so deep that it is rooted in the whole of nature itself. Or, perhaps, the longing that nature has for healing and sanctification reaches up through human beings since we are the only ones who are in the image of

---

[89] Brother Lawrence, *op. cit.*, p. 42.

God in the appropriate way to be able to cry out to Him. I tend to visualize mountains and hills, although the places I pray do not look out on any, and cry out to God for and with them, feeling the brokenness and incompleteness of our world so in need of God. The thought that our longings are rooted in and shared by even inanimate nature is an inspiring idea. When Jesus was riding into Jerusalem amid hosannas just prior to His crucifixion, some of the leaders told Him to order the people to be quiet. He replied, "If they were silent the very stones would cry aloud" (Mt 21:9). Praise is a spontaneous and natural response to the manifestation of God in Christ, and all nature shares in this. The winds grew calm at His command. And all nature was stricken with grief at His death: it became dark at the three o'clock hour when He died, and there was an earthquake.

Heart of Jesus patient and most merciful, have mercy on us.

Patience:

Think of how patient and merciful He has been already, through all your defections, coldness and ingratitude, and thank Him for this. It always comforts me a lot to think of how He has stuck with me through so much already, that surely I can trust Him to continue to do it now. If the things I have already done have not driven Him away, then He is *very* hard to drive away, and nothing short of persistent and deliberate rejection would do it (if persisted in until death). So I pray that He won't let me ever try to drive Him out of my heart again. I guess that is a prayer for final perseverance, but it sounds more poetic this way and easier to understand what is happening in us.

Heart of Jesus, enriching all who invoke you, have mercy on us.

Christ's boundless generosity:

This one is comforting also, especially when you have been having trouble really feeling His presence. For it assures us that no matter what we may feel or not feel, He does actually enrich those who invoke His heart. Something is occurring when we pray this prayer. Sometime down the line we will understand and see what He has been doing, but for now we must just trust Him.

Heart of Jesus, fountain of life and holiness, have mercy on us.

Life-giving Water:

Here we reflect on the heart of Jesus through the image of drinking from a spring or fountain. Meditate on Jesus's encounter with the Samaritan woman. She came to the well at midday when other women would not be there because she was a social outcast. Jesus tells her: "Every one who drinks of this water will thirst again, but whoever drinks of the water that I shall give him will never thirst; the water that I shall give him will become in him a spring of water welling up to eternal life" (Jn 4:13-14). Pray: "Oh God, thou art my God, I seek thee, my soul thirsts for thee; my flesh faints for thee, as in a dry and weary land where no water is" (Ps 63:2). Recognize the way in which you are like that dry and weary land, and long for the living water only He can give. How often we keep going back and back to the same wells that fail to satisfy us rather than turning to Him who can give life-giving water! In receiving this we truly receive the life of God which transforms us.

Heart of Jesus, propitiation for our sins, have mercy on us.

His heart offered for us:

The next six verses draw attention to a whole new and wonderful dimension of the Sacred Heart. For they tell us that the heart of Jesus in all its richness, joy, beauty and glory, was offered up as a propitiation for our sins. To propitiate means to appease or placate an offended power — to win or secure God's favor by an offering. We have, by our sins, offended God, and Jesus's offering of Himself to God reconciles us with God. We must allow ourselves to be taken up into Him so that He can carry us and our sins to the cross with Him. The more deeply we become incorporated into His body, the more full and complete our healing and salvation become. Theologians have understood propitiation in different ways. Some think in terms of Jesus Christ's taking God's wrath upon Himself to deliver us from it, while others (distressed by the kind of image of God that this way of thinking implies) emphasize instead Christ's victory over the powers hostile to humanity through His perfect self abandonment to the Father's will.

Heart of Jesus, loaded down with opprobrium, have mercy on us.

Enduring ridicule and contempt:

We tend, I think, to focus more on Christ's physical suffering. But equally painful, or perhaps even more painful, was the scorn, reproach, ridicule, and contempt He endured. Being "dissed" — disrespected, put down, and treated with contempt is in some ways far worse than physical pain, especially when — as in the case of Jesus — one is treated in this way by people to whom one has been kind and loving. Think of His loving heart enduring all that spitting, abuse, mocking, and so on. Think of all the people who turned on Him so savagely. Like the suffering servant in Isaiah He did not hide His face from shame and spitting. Whatever you do, don't shrink from contemplating this aspect of His suffering because it makes you feel guilty that your sins are so awful that He had to endure this. Think, rather how great His love for us is that He was willing patiently to endure all this for our sake. When you feel unjustly humiliated or put down, offer your humiliation along with His; try to find a kind of union with Him in humiliation.

Heart of Jesus, bruised for our offenses, have mercy on us.

Enduring pain:

This is along the same lines as the previous one, only it calls attention to the actual physical pain and bruising of His body. The suffering servant song in Isaiah says: "He was bruised for our iniquities; upon him was the chastisement that made us whole, and with his stripes we are healed" (Is 53:5). I've often felt a lot of healing of my emotional (and occasionally physical) hurts when I allow them to well up during this verse and visualize Christ's suffering for us, asking Him to unite my sufferings with His own.

Heart of Jesus, obedient to death, have mercy on us.

Abandonment:

When facing some particularly bitter loss, emptiness or deprivation, this is a good one to meditate on. It is the climax of His passion; think of Him breathing out His spirit on the cross. In breathing out His spirit He was giving us a priceless gift. He went all the way to the bitter end for us, handing over His spirit to the Father in obedience and love (for God and for us). Like Christ, we must allow ourselves to be emptied out or poured out even unto death. He said before His passion, "My soul is exceedingly sorrowful even unto death" (Mt 6:28). Yet in His death is victory over sin and death. We have to go through death to the resurrection, and let go completely of even what we most desire.

Heart of Jesus, pierced with a lance, have mercy on us.

His pierced heart:

Visualize Jesus as He is depicted on the cross with Mary and John standing by the cross, and the blood and water flowing from His side when the soldier pierced it with a lance. These symbolize the foundation of the sacramental life of the Church, namely the water of baptism and the blood of the new and everlasting covenant. As the old Protestant hymn puts it: "there's power, power, power, power, wonderworking power, in the precious blood of the lamb." The priest mixes wine with water before consecrating it in the Mass. It was only through being pierced that all that was in His heart could flow out to us. Just as lovers are portrayed as having their hearts pierced by Cupid's arrows, so also Jesus's heart was pierced for love of us and ours too must be pierced by His love. Many mystics have experienced a kind of piercing of their heart in prayer. This, I think, is a sign that the person's heart is no longer like a walled city; the wall has been breached and the Lord can now open the door from within. You might pray the *Anima Christi* prayer here.

Heart of Jesus, source of all consolation, have mercy on us.

Consolation:

This one flows naturally from the preceding one, since the blood and water flowing from His side are the source of our consolation through baptism and the Eucharist. People can console one another sometimes, but ultimately and most fully it is God's love that does so, and that love is most visible in His pouring out His very life blood for us on the cross.

Heart of Jesus, our life and resurrection, have mercy on us.

Resurrection:

It is no longer we who live, but Christ who lives in us. We have died with Christ and live now because He lives. And we will be raised with Him on the Last Day. Jesus said, "When I am lifted up from the earth, [I] will draw all men to myself" (Jn 12:32). "Thou hast opened paradise, and in Thee Thy saints shall rise" (*1940 Hymnal*, #89).

Heart of Jesus, our peace and reconciliation, have mercy on us.

Restored to friendship with God:

At the Last Supper Jesus says: "Peace I leave with you; my peace I give to you. Not as the world gives do I give to you" (Jn 14:27). And in His post-resurrection appearance to the disciples on Easter evening, the first thing He says is, "Peace be with you" (Jn 20:19). So these are good passages to reflect on here.

Think of how alienated we all were from God, and how Jesus has by His passion, death, and resurrection effected our reconciliation with God. Not all Christians understand this reconciliation in the same way. Some Protestants hold that we are simply covered by Christ and His blood, so that when God looks at us He sees His Son. Luther said grace is like snow falling on dung. On the Catholic view, we are genuinely transformed more and more into His image; the change is internal to us (this is called "deification"). Regardless of how we think about the way in which reconciliation is effected, Christians all agree that in Christ we have been genuinely restored to friendship with God in spite of our continuing imperfections and sins.

Heart of Jesus, victim for our sins, have mercy on us.
Sacrificial Victim:

This verse is like the "propitiation for our sins" one, but has a more concrete and emotional tone which invites us to recall the details of His passion. The term "victim" has taken on a somewhat unfortunate tone in our society, where so many people and groups seem to be trying to outdo each other in claiming victim status. So return, instead, to the scriptural sources: Isaac on the point of being sacrificed by Abraham, or the suffering servant in Isaiah (Is 53). Jesus did not whine. Although the prophet Micah, speaking for God, does lament, "O my people, what have I done to you? In what have I wearied you? Answer me" (Mi 6:3). One of the most moving Good Friday services I ever attended was at a Trappistine women's monastery. At one point they alternated between verses of this sort and "Holy God, Holy Mighty One, Holy Immortal One have mercy on us" in Greek, thus juxtaposing God's power and majesty with the sorrowful complaint of the rejected lover.

Heart of Jesus, salvation of those who hope in you, have mercy on us.
Hope:

It is important to place our hope in Him so that He may work His salvation in us. Hope is called a theological virtue because it directs us to God. It is not something we can get just by will power or practice; we need to beg God to revive our souls with hope. When you find that hope comes hard, try reading through Psalms 42 and 43. For patient hope try: "I wait for the Lord, my soul waits, and in His word I hope... more than watchmen for the morning" (Ps 130:5-6). "Lord, let your mercy be upon us as we place our hope in you" (*Te Deum*). We want to be saved — delivered from evil — so that God will keep or hold us, redeemed from out of the darkness and corruption of the world, and cleansed from that darkness that has been infesting our souls also so we can be with Him at last. So we cry: "Help us, save us, have mercy on us, for you are good and a lover of mankind" (Ukrainian Rite prayer).

Heart of Jesus, hope of those who die in you, have mercy on us.

Our refuge in the hour of death:

Here we must reflect about something we often try not to think about — namely death. An old Bob Dylan song says: "Well, well, well, so I can die easy, Jesus gonna make my dying bed." A *Sacred Harp* song says, "Jesus can make a dying bed feel soft as downy pillows are; while on His breast I lean my head, and breathe my life out sweetly there" (*The Sacred Harp*, p. 30). We need to live with an awareness of our mortality and have some forethought for how we will face death when it comes. If we make the Sacred Heart of Jesus our refuge now amid the storms of life, we can hope to find shelter there in the hour of death.

Heart of Jesus, delight of all the saints, have mercy on us.

Eternal Delight:

"Thou spreadest a table in my sight, thy unction grace bestoweth, and oh what transport of delight, from thy pure chalice floweth" (a Kentucky folk hymn "Resignation" based on the 23rd Psalm, from the singing of Jean Ritchie). "Sweet fields arrayed in living green, and rivers of delight" (*The Sacred Harp* p. 439). "There is a land of pure delight, where saints immortal reign" (*The Sacred Harp*, p. 66). This verse adds a very important dimension to the things already said in this book about finding

delight in God, and one that makes it a fit ending to the Litany
— namely the communion of saints. Think of how we are united
in Christ with all who have gone before us. Yes, we each have
our own walk with the Lord, but our joy in the Lord has a social
dimension as well as an individual one. When Jesus tells the disciples at the Last Supper that "I am in my Father and you are in
me and I in you" (Jn 14:20), He is addressing them as a group.
We are one in Him — members of His body — and part of the
delight of Heaven will be the fact we will be united with each
other in our joy and praise of God.

*Lamb of God, you take away the sins of the world,
spare us O Lord.*

*Lamb of God, you take away the sins of the world,
graciously hear us O Lord.*

*Lamb of God, you take away the sins of the world,
have mercy on us.*

The term "Lamb of God" is of enormous theological sig-
nificance. It was used of Jesus by John the Baptist (Jn 1:35-36),
and indicated that Jesus had taken the place of the Passover lamb
that the Jews sacrificed each year. The blood of the lamb was
used to ritually mark the doorposts of their homes, remembering
how God passed over their houses (which were marked in this
way by the blood) and did not smite them with the plague that
struck the Egyptians.

"Spare us O Lord" is a bit of a jolt from the peaceful sense
of resting in Him that was conveyed in the last line of the Litany.
We are like the servant who owed his master more than he could
possibly repay (Mt 18:24-27), and could only plead with him to
be patient with him. His lord graciously heard him and forgave
him his debt out of mercy. Yes God is merciful, but we wait on
His mercy with fear and trembling — not presuming upon it
as though we had some claim to it. We are always in the position of the singer in the "Old Rugged Cross": "In my hands no

gifts I bring; simply to Thy cross I cling." "Graciously hear us, O Lord," goes along with the theme of crying out to Him from our darkness and need, and the "have mercy" brings us back to the recurring refrain that runs throughout this Litany.

Jesus meek and humble of heart, make our hearts like to yours.

Here we come upon a beautifully clear statement of the central theme of this book. For the purpose of the method of prayer we have been exploring here is the transformation of our hearts that God effects when we pray — a transformation that makes our hearts more and more like the heart of Jesus.

Almighty and Eternal God, look upon the heart of your beloved Son, our Lord Jesus Christ, and on the praises and satisfaction that He offers you in the name of sinners, and to those who implore your mercy, of your great goodness grant forgiveness through the same Christ our Lord.

Jesus Christ, through His perfect obedience to the Father, has become the channel of grace for us. In some moods I think of myself primarily when I say "those who implore your mercy," but it is also good to think of all those in desperate straits and pray that they will be given the grace to implore His mercy and receive it through the heart of Christ.

ST PAULS

This book was produced by ST PAULS/Alba House, the Society of St. Paul, an international religious congregation of priests and brothers dedicated to serving the Church through the communications media.

For information regarding this and associated ministries of the Pauline Family of Congregations, write to the Vocation Director, Society of St. Paul, 2187 Victory Blvd., Staten Island, New York 10314-6603. Phone (718) 982-5709; or E-mail: vocation@stpauls.us or check our internet site, www.vocationoffice.org